# Praise for RESTRICTED ACCESS

"At a lesbian event in the late 1970s, my first which provided a signer for hearing impaired audience members, a door opened inside me to another aspect of my world. It was more than twenty years later when I helped lead the March on Washington alongside Sharon Kowalski and Karen Thompson in 1993 that I felt the profound impact of that early move toward accessibility. *Restricted Access* is another urgent effort to give voice to lesbians who remain unheard and unacknowledged. Victoria Brownworth honorably fulfills her calling as a social activist and critic by using her own imperiled physical condition as a springboard into the world of lesbians—both ordinary and heroic—who live with disability."
—Jewelle Gomez, author of *The Gilda Stories*

"Two of our community's most astute anthologists, editors Victoria Brownworth and Susan Raffo have assembled an absolutely compelling collection of interviews, essays and artistry by and about lesbians living with disability. The stories contained here are not only well-written personal accounts; bound together as they are under one cover, they become a political action, raising the consciousness of those who are able-bodied, supporting and validating the experiences of those whose lives they reflect. I read it from cover to cover and could not put it down."
—Judith Katz, author of *Running Fiercely Toward a High Thin Sound* and *The Escape Artist*

"How wonderful that there is—at long last—this much-needed book about the struggles and joys of disabled lesbians! Read this ground-breaking anthology and savor the writings of women like Eli Clare, who writes with fierce honesty about her fear of, and connection to, other disabled women; and Patricia Nell Warren, writing in both personal and political terms about how the very definition of diseases, and creation of hierarchies about them, is fraught with political consequences—just two of the many women who illuminate aspects of the lives of lesbians with disabilities. This book is rich with sexiness, anger, humor and understanding."
—Anne Finger, author of *Past Due*

# RESTRICTED

# ACCESS

## LESBIANS
## ON
## DISABILITY

**Edited by Victoria A. Brownworth and Susan Raffo**

**SEAL PRESS**

Copyright © 1999 by Victoria A. Brownworth

All rights reserved. No portion of this book may be reproduced in any form, except for the quotation of brief passages in reviews, without prior written permission from Seal Press, 3131 Western Avenue, Suite 410, Seattle, WA 98121, sealprss@scn.org.

"Two Communities: Lesbian and Deaf Cultures Meet." Transcript reprinted by permission of In the Life Media, Inc.

Nicola Griffith, "Writing from the Body" from *Women of Other Worlds: Excursions through Science Fiction and Feminism,* ed. Helen Merrick and Tess Williams, University of Western Australia Press, 1999.

Cover design by Joseph Kaftan
Cover photograph by Linda Kliewer/Out and Out Productions
Text design by Alison Rogalsky

*Library of Congress Cataloging-in-Publication Data*
Restricted access : lesbians on disability /
    edited by Victoria A. Brownworth and Susan Raffo.
1. Handicapped women—United States.   2. Handicapped Women—Civil rights—
United States.   3. Lesbians—United States.   4. Lesbianism—United States.
5. Sociology of disability—United States.
I. Brownworth, Victoria A.   II. Raffo, Susan
HV1569.3.W65R48   1999      362.4'086'6430973—dc21      99-38054
ISBN 1-58005-028-X

Printed in the United States of America

First printing, October 1999

10     9     8     7     6     5     4     3     2     1

Distributed to the trade by Publishers Group West
*In Canada:* Publishers Group West Canada, Toronto, Ontario
*In the U.K. and Europe:* Airlift Book Distributors, Middlesex, England
*In Australia:* Banyan Tree Book Distributors, Kent Town, South Australia

*For JMR, RR and RLH, the women who sustain me—*
*with boundless affection. —VAB*


*To Raquel. —SR*

# CONTENTS

# INTRODUCTION

Whenever a new collection of writing is published, the primary question to be answered is: *Why this book?* The answer in this case is remarkably succinct: *Because there wasn't one like it.* Though we hover on the cusp of a new millennium, to date there hasn't been an American anthology of writing by lesbians on disability. There have been anthologies of lesbian disability writing from other countries, but those books reflect the impact of socialized medicine or of vastly different (some might say more enlightened) political structures on the lives of disabled lesbians. There have also been American anthologies of disability writing by women, but living as a lesbian in a society predicated on heterosexual privilege presents many challenges in every aspect of daily life—challenges left unaddressed by these heterosexually defined writings.

*Why this book?* I have always sought solace and recourse in books. Therefore when degenerative neuromuscular disease began to overtake my life, I searched for a literature that would help me to cope—but found a disturbing lack of writing reflective of my own particular experience as a working-class lesbian, now disabled. The majority of writing by disabled women resonated with a kind of privilege I couldn't even imagine; the writing that seemed closer to my own experience in terms of socioeconomics and class invariably came from England or Canada where the State made tremendous efforts to provide access for the disabled. And so *Restricted Access* reflects a distinctly lesbian, and with only a few exceptions, American perspective on disability. The restrictive nature of social services and the geographical vastness of the United States often coalesce to make disabled lesbians feel terrifyingly isolated—separated from nondisabled society, from other disabled people and from other lesbians. *Restricted Access* attempts to bridge that chasm.

As a disabled lesbian, my desire to understand my role and that of other disabled lesbians in queer, feminist and mainstream society has been intense. As I talked to and corresponded with other disabled lesbians I discovered this need was pervasive among disabled lesbians of every race, class and age. The questions being asked by myself and other disabled lesbians were—are—as numerous as they are varied and would, of necessity, define the writing I culled for this book. Among the most significant and pressing questions: How does lesbianism impact disability and vice versa? Can disabled lesbians have a role in queer community now that assimilation and mainstreaming of queers predominates as the political focus in the lesbian and gay community—or do the combined oppressions of sexism, homophobia and disability isolate and ostracize disabled lesbians? How do women come to lesbian identity while also coping with disability? Does homophobia marginalize lesbians within the disabled community?

As what was then called gay liberation evolved in the late sixties and early seventies into today's queer civil rights movement, concurrent with the second wave of feminism, the concept of inclusivity was preeminent among lesbian community leaders and groups. Sensitivity to issues of race, ethnicity and ability was a given, despite political factionalism (and despite not always being achieved). But as mainstreaming and assimilation of queers into straight society became the predominate political foci of lesbian and gay political groups, inclusivity has taken on a different cast. As the millennium approaches, mainstream lesbian and gay politics emphasizes a different form of inclusivity— inclusivity of queers into straight society. The desire to present to straight society a community "deserving" of heterosexual privilege, a community that is comprised of straight-seeming, monied, middle-class and otherwise "normal" queers, looms large on the mainstream political agenda as a polemic that argues "We are no different from you" is emphasized.

Those of us who have been activists in one or another political movement know this: Inclusion often depends on the loudness of voice, the cohesion, solidarity and access of a particular minority within a collective minority. Disabled queers, who have always skirted the margins of queer community, have become virtually invisible. And as the backlash against so-called "special rights" intensifies, those who are queer and disabled find themselves not only less visible, but more marginalized than ever.

The issues posed by *Restricted Access* are personal as well as political. I have been a political activist since early childhood; I began my political education stuffing envelopes and doing other scut work for the black civil rights movement my parents were deeply involved in and committed to. In high school I graduated into my own politics: antiwar work, feminism and what was then called gay liberation. I spent several years in the domestic Peace Corps and a few more doing a range of community organizing. Activism has been the foundation of my adult life. And so just as reading seemed an appropriate approach to encroaching disability, so did activism. But disability rights was one political arena I had never entered. And like many newly disabled, I was unsure how to move from the nondisabled world where I had lived my entire (physically active) life into a territory that wasn't merely unknown to me, but to which I felt I had been exiled against my will. I didn't choose disability, it chose me.

As some contributors to *Restricted Access* note, when one becomes disabled, either suddenly through accident or gradually through chronic or progressive disease, the nondisabled tend to flee—in fear, in revulsion, in conflict. For most nondisabled people it is acutely disturbing to recognize how arbitrary disability can be—and how easily *they* could become disabled, too. Christopher Reeve has become the national poster boy for the terrible whimsy of disability; one wrong move and you can go from being Superman to life on a ventilator. But while sympathetic, most nondisabled people shun proximity to the disabled. One in six Americans is disabled; no one wants to find out they could be next. Not surprisingly, friends—the ones I had thrown parties for, gone to movies and dinner and dancing with, traveled with, led marches with—all began to disappear out of my now-disabled life. For some reason they couldn't understand that if their houses or the restaurants we used to go to or the movie theaters or the bookstores weren't accessible to me in my wheelchair, I couldn't go there. Some fled, some drifted, but the impact was the same: isolation tinged with just a little bitterness. I needed, like many other disabled lesbians before me, to assert my place in lesbian community—a community I had helped to build, but which was now, ironically, inaccessible to me.

*Restricted Access* was conceived in part, then, as a dialogue between disabled lesbians and their own communities. And as such, it asks many questions and demands forthright answers. I wanted answers myself, but although I *am* disabled—that incontrovertible fact constantly reinforced by a failing body—I couldn't quite accept *being* disabled. Just as coming to grips with one's lesbian identity takes time—more for some than for others—so too does acceptance of one's new disabled status. Learning to live with and accept the non-normative (by society's standards) within oneself can be tremendously difficult, a goal some never achieve. And how could I presume to leap into a political movement— disability rights—I didn't really want to be a part of, unless it was as adjunct, someone supportive of another minority group's quest for civil rights. I didn't want to be disabled; disability was an identity—unlike lesbianism—I found difficult, if not impossible, to accept. Thus *Restricted Access* has been a journey of self-discovery, an attempt to answer questions—not merely (and selfishly) for myself, but for other disabled lesbians as well.

One basic question is: *What is disability?*

Everyone answers this question differently. The 1990 Americans with Disabilities Act (ADA) offers a broad definition, which the courts continue to attempt to refine, most recently in several cases before the U.S. Supreme Court in the 1998–99 term. The ADA as written allows disability to be defined as nearly any obstacle or impediment to accessing public accommodations, the workplace or institutions of higher learning. Though originally instituted to allow the seriously disabled—particularly those in wheelchairs and the blind—access to jobs, the somewhat vague writing of the act has created its own problems. A series of court cases has been brought under the ADA claiming discrimination based on back pain, headaches, attention deficit disorder, obesity and a range of other physical differences that many would not consider "disabilities." In addition, Title VII, enacted in the 1960s to "mainstream" disabled students into the nondisabled population of public schools, has also incurred numerous court challenges over the past thirty years to make it more inclusive of variant levels of disability. As a consequence, a backlash against the ADA, and to a lesser extent Title VII, has fomented in the past few years, in particular from businesses in the private sector; the ADA requires changes in the physical plants of many businesses, public accommodations and schools that owners and taxpayers complain are unnecessary and costly.

For the purposes of this collection, I have defined disability as any condition—disease, illness or syndrome—that impedes or prevents a woman from living what our nondisabled society considers a "normal" life. In this context normalcy would be defined as being able to work and play much like nondisabled women, having access to everything from jobs to sexual relationships.

*What is access?*

Simply stated, access means inclusion—the main thrust of the ADA was to create an atmosphere of inclusion for all disabled Americans. Access means that I, in my wheelchair, can get into any public place that someone on two nondisabled legs can walk into. Access means that Vicky D'aoust, one of the Deaf contributors to this anthology, can go to any public function for the hearing—a theater production, a political forum, a lecture—and have it signed in American Sign Language so that she can participate. Access means that Marj Schneider, a contributor who is blind, can go to her local ATM or get into any elevator and find Braille instructions for how to use those facilities. Access means that Sharon Wachsler, a contributor with multiple chemical sensitivity (MCS), should be able to go to the local supermarket or her own doctor's office without suffering a serious relapse from the intensity of perfumes and other chemicals in those environments. However, access doesn't simply mean inclusion in the physical world of the nondisabled; it also implies inclusion in the community itself—acceptance, encouragement, an effort to involve the disabled woman in all aspects of "normal" society, despite the differences wrought by disability. Many of the women writing in this anthology lament the inaccessibility of community; many are able to work and even have thriving careers, but find themselves impeded in leading a full—and fulfilled—life by the limits placed on them by nondisabled society in general—and nondisabled lesbians in particular.

In compiling this collection I was forced to define disability and lesbianism; my initial call for submissions garnered numerous queries about my definition of both. For the purposes of this anthology I defined disability as something—congenital disease or deformity, accident or late-onset disease, specific syndromes—that impacted every aspect of a woman's life in a way that separated or isolated her from nondisabled society. Still, I found myself in the same position as the courts—determining disability on a case-by-case basis. My determinations may seem to some as whimsical as the courts', but assuredly they were not. Rather they were based quite definingly on "otherness"; just as lesbians are "other" from the straight community, so too is the disabled lesbian "other" than her nondisabled sisters. And within the context of disability certain diseases have received a level of attention others have not. There can be no question that HIV/AIDS has dominated the queer community for nearly two decades. More recently the impact of cancer—particularly breast cancer—has become a focus of lesbian attention. But disabilities outside these two diseases have been virtually ignored by the queer community, and thus I wanted to turn our collective focus to those disabilities that have yet to be acknowledged, let alone addressed. As a consequence, the inclusion of women with HIV/AIDS and cancer has been limited in this collection—not because these diseases are not disabling, but because as a community we recognize them. I want that same level of recognition for *all* disabled lesbians.

Then there was the sexuality question. Were women who self-identified as lesbian but had never actually had a female sexual partner lesbians? (Yes, disability often results in lack of access to sexual partners.) Were people in physical transition from male to female—transgendered women—lesbians? (They might well be, but for the purposes of this book, acculturation as a female from childhood to adulthood was a defining aspect of how women would experience disability.) Were bisexual women lesbians? (Women whose primary relationships are not exclusively with other women have access to heterosexual privilege, which lesbians are denied.)

Susan Raffo, my co-editor, and I had many—and heated—debates on these issues; she wanted a more expansive definition of lesbian identity. I acknowledge that the final determinations were mine; as the disabled editor of this book, as the person whose idea this collection was, I felt it was essential that I make the ultimate decisions about what—and even who—was included in the anthology. The elements of choice and decision-making are often taken away from disabled lesbians, myself included. I assure the reader that each choice was well considered. It was difficult for me to turn down any piece at all, because I believe access by disabled women, and most especially disabled lesbians (as well as other sexual minority women), to a public forum has been consistently stifled or denied by the straight, nondisabled society in which we live. But I also had the limitations of space to consider; there would be a finite number of pages available in the book—my choice was to fill those pages with as diverse a group of disabled lesbians as possible.

I also had one other criterion: I wanted essays that reflected toughness rather than timidity, determination rather than acquiescence. Susan and I received a plethora of what I would call "Good Cripple" pieces. I have written extensively in the mainstream and queer press about this Dickensian perspective on disability. The Good Cripple is, like Charles Dickens's Tiny Tim in *A Christmas Carol,* a role model for the nondisabled. Disability often acquires an oracular power in these tales (a modern version would be the best-selling *Tuesdays with Morrie).* Whatever platitudes the Good Cripple utters (Tiny Tim's "God bless us, every one") attain exaggerated importance because the nondisabled presume, since disability is so dreaded ("there but for the grace of God, go I"), that someone like Tiny Tim or Morrie Schwartz, happy in the role of cripple, *must* have some insight into life's mysteries. (Would thousands have bought *Tuesdays with Morrie* if Morrie were just an aging college professor pontificating to his former student, if Morrie had *not* been dying very slowly of the crippling disease of amyotrophic lateral sclerosis [ALS]?) The Good Cripple struggles against the restrictions of nondisabled society as well as disability, but is ever-cheerful and non-complaining, even (sometimes especially) in the face of nondisabled insensitivity and abuse. An invention of the nondisabled—a prototype as well as stereotype—of what nondisabled society would like disabled people to be, the Good Cripple is not unlike Uncle Tom, the slave utterly at peace with his enslavement and loathe to change that status quo. (The difference is we now view the literary Uncle Tom as a white, racist interpretation, not the truth. However, many blacks are still termed Uncle Toms if they appear to cater too readily to whites.) Like Uncle Tom, the Good Cripple is not a self-definition but a definition created by those in power—in this case the non-disabled—to restrict those not in power, the disabled.

No essays extolling the virtues of life as a Good Cripple appear in the pages of *Restricted Access*. It isn't that such essays don't have their role in disability literature; it is simply that they represent a cultural stereotype like Uncle Tom—one defined by those other than themselves. The experiences of the disabled are far broader than this one restrictive vantage point, which benefits the nondisabled by allowing them to laud the disabled for their "bravery" while alternatively denying them full citizenship.

Full citizenship means being able to have variant viewpoints, including perspectives others may find controversial or even offensive; this anthology offers full citizenship to disabled lesbians and many essays in *Restricted Access* challenge or contradict established rhetoric on lesbian and feminist politics. Perspectives rarely given a forum are explored—and some readers may find the substance and tone of those essays unsettling. Award-winning playwright Carolyn Gage and disability rights activist Mary Frances Platt challenge the nondisabled to adjust their attitudes—and take on lesbian and feminist lip service to disability in the process—in two very different essays. Veteran author Patricia Nell Warren presents a controversial view of autoimmune disease—including HIV and AIDS—and the dominant role it has played in the queer community over the past two decades and in her own life. Erin Lawrence details what it means to be a young lesbian with HIV in a community that disbelieves lesbians can even contract the disease. Carol Anne Douglas, editor of the landmark feminist newspaper *off our backs*, addresses the lesbian-feminist response to mental illness while rethinking some of her own long-held beliefs. Candace McCullough and Sharon Duchesneau challenge the very notion of what disability is as they candidly discuss their quest to have a child just like themselves—profoundly deaf. Huhanna details the horrifying intersections racism and homophobia can take and how these isms can result in disabling violence. I question the feminist lock step on abortion with its presumption that nondisabled life is more valuable than disabled life.

Although many of these essays address controversial issues, they also broaden the discourse on disability as well as on the parameters of lesbian community. One issue Susan and I both felt needed attention was mental illness. A significant percentage of the American population suffers from some kind of mental illness, yet more than any other disability, mental illness carries a social stigma that can be eradicated only through public discourse. However, within a lesbian-feminist context, broaching the subject of mental illness raises a plethora of conflicting concerns. The labels of mental illness—from hysteria to neurasthenia to depression to insanity—have been attached for centuries to women who challenged male authority or woman's place in society. Lesbianism itself was labeled a mental illness by the American Psychiatric Association until very recently. And many lesbians have found themselves medicalized by psychiatrists and psychologists because of their sexual orientation; incarceration of young lesbians in mental health facilities by families who reject their coming out remains common. As a consequence of this complicated and often brutal history, lesbians have frequently refused to seek help for mental illness—and have found wellsprings of support for that refusal within the lesbian community. Fear of the medicalizations of the past—which continue in some communities—has led to other problems for lesbians with mental illness; there remains far more support within our community for rejecting therapeutic care, particularly medications, than for utilizing those often quite necessary therapies. Susan and I both recognized the importance of signaling that mental illness is just another form of disability. Though mental illness has long been perceived as something people do to themselves, something they can just talk themselves out of if they really want, medical research over the past two decades has proven that mental illness results directly from changes in the brain's chemistry. Just as diabetes is a result of the pancreas's inability to process sugars, each type of mental illness, from extremes like schizophrenia to the mildest forms of depression, is symptomatic of chemical imbalances in the brain. Nevertheless, acknowledging mental illness remains stigmatizing for both the individual with the disease and those close to them. Each of the mental illness essays in *Restricted Access* works to break down these artificial barriers and to open dialogue on mental illness in the lesbian community.

Other essays cover groundbreaking territory as well. D.A. Watters was completing a second graduate degree in astrophysics when she was ejected from the car in which she was riding—onto her head. She survived—a miracle according to all concerned—but her life was altered irrevocably. It took her five years to regain enough short-term memory to be able to live on her own. Her contribution to *Restricted Access* presents insights into life with irreversible brain damage; this is a profoundly moving piece, but also writing that takes us into an area of disability rarely viewed from the vantage point of the brain-damaged person.

Wide-ranging as I feel the essays in *Restricted Access* are, and diverse as the complement of writers appears to be, it is important to point out that even working together from our very different communities, Susan's in Minneapolis and mine in Philadelphia, as well as from the extraordinarily vast realm of the Internet, we would have liked to have had an even broader representation, particularly from women of color. In the past, I have chastised other editors in reviews for lack of representation of people of color; I believe it is incumbent on white editors to make anthologies as inclusive as possible. In my other anthologies I have striven for racial balance and have managed to achieve it. This anthology, for reasons neither Susan nor I understand, and despite our best efforts, was far more difficult. Though Susan posted our call for submissions on every conceivable Internet site, the responses were, throughout the process, predominantly from white women. I do not make this point to excuse having fewer women of color—especially black women—than either Susan or I would have preferred in this anthology, but to signal what I believe is a concern for both the disabled community and the lesbian community. Access to the Internet by women of color seems far more restricted than it is for white women even when they are of limited income. And although Susan's and my attention to class, race and socioeconomics makes this anthology far different from the white, middle-class endeavors lesbian anthologies can often be, there are other issues involved in this question of representation. Nearly every woman writing in *Restricted Access,* regardless of her particular disability, geographical location or class status, speaks of a certain level of isolation. Not surprisingly to me, women of color and women who are not middle class felt this more acutely. If the writers in *Restricted Access* represent a cross-section, as we hope they do, of disabled lesbians in America, then women of color and poor and working-class women are even more isolated from lesbian community than their white, middle-class sisters. Perhaps an anthology of writing *by* disabled women of color *compiled by* disabled women of color would help bridge that gap.

A question some—particularly disabled lesbians—may have about *Restricted Access* is why I chose to do this book with my friend Susan Raffo, a nondisabled lesbian. The genesis of that choice was both simple and practical. Susan was the only friend I had who talked to me about disability; she didn't pretend my disease wasn't happening, she didn't compare the nondisabled Victoria to the disabled Victoria and find the latter wanting. She also never judged my discomfort with my own disabled status. Susan also consistently urged me to write about these conflicts, eliciting in the course of our many conversations the ideas that I would later turn into essays of my own. Because Susan and I share an activist agenda, our discussions inevitably led us back to the political. Much of the evolution of my disability politics is due to the ongoing dialogue we have had over the past three years.

I have co-edited several anthologies with my longtime partner, Judith M. Redding, with whom I have also written a book and collaborated on several film projects. She would have been my natural choice for co-editor. Judith contributed a great deal of work to this book throughout the process, including the massive job of inputting all the editing changes. But although she contributed more work than she, or I, ever intended, she chose not to be co-editor at the outset of the project. She felt this project, unlike others we had worked on together, was my idea, and to a certain extent, my identity, and that those factors would make me determined to control the project rather than have it be co-edited and co-designed. Disabled by the criteria of this anthology herself, she chose to put her limited energy into her own creative projects while I worked on this anthology.

Conversely, Susan had offered her services to help me with the anthology when I first discussed it with her, as adjunct, as not-very-glorified scut worker and without thought to being actual co-editor. In short, she offered to do everything I didn't want to do because she knew how important this project was to me and how poor my health had become. In fact, because she *is* nondisabled (and because she has a strong political consciousness), she had deep concerns about how her role in the book would be perceived. Would she be viewed as a nondisabled interloper in disabled territory, as someone who was condescending to the disabled or worst of all, as a kind of Dickensian character who took the crippled Victoria under her nondisabled wing out of pity? Needless to say, none of these images was flattering—nor would they be true. But Judith had been correct in presuming that I would want full control over this book while also wanting the help and occasional input of a co-editor; while I would consider my co-editor's opinion, I wanted to make all the decisions, no matter how seemingly insignificant. Susan accepted those conditions and more from the outset; I felt that level of work necessitated co-editor status. And although many may argue that I should have chosen a disabled lesbian as co-editor, Susan's history with a disabled mother gave her a unique perspective on this work. In addition, unlike the majority of nondisabled lesbians I know, Susan understands, perhaps in part from the experiences described quite provocatively in her essay "Against the Body of My Mother," that one can move from the world of the nondisabled to that of the disabled in the blink of an eye—or the time it takes for a traffic light to change from green to red.

Finally, this anthology presented unique—and often disturbing—problems. Communication with the contributors—some of whom are brain-damaged, Deaf, blind or suffering from cognition problems related to certain diseases—presented ongoing challenges. Several potential contributors died, several others were hospitalized and had to withdraw from the project and many of the final contributors—including myself—battled serious health setbacks and even hospitalizations during the course of this project. All of which tinges the final result with poignancy as well as triumph.

*Victoria A. Brownworth*
*Philadelphia, Pennsylvania*
*July 1999*

# RESTRICTED ACCESS

# TEARS

## Victoria A. Brownworth

You remember: the first bad diagnosis
lying on the exam table
so flat   you can hardly breathe
sun streams indecorously
from the window
behind you   yet blindingly bright
the gown is white—or is it blue?
you lie   flat
minutes—or is it seconds?
after the doctor leaves
tears running hot from the edges
of your eyes   into your ears
disappearing   into your hair
saline eroding small patches
of waxy exam paper
on either side of your head
like gram stains signaling infection on a laboratory slide

you remember: the first trip
to the surgeon
the manila envelope

so large and unwieldy in your lap
suspiciously light
inside
the secret of x-rays
the shadow areas
you still cannot feel


you remember: the operating room
the smell of betadine and ozone
sharp enough to taste
the blue-green drape a tent positioned over you
separating you
from the surgeon's cut   the silver trays   the blood
your blood
that will run down your side
            onto the table   onto the floor



you remember: the mask on the face
the cloying sweetness at the back of your throat
then nothing


you remember: all the other times
after that
each vial of blood drawn
each culture swabbed
each IV drip
each needle push
each tray of instruments
each white-swathed gurney
each consent form
each procedure
each wad of bandages

each hospital room
each cacophony of machines
each bevy of nurses
each bad diagnosis

you remember: all the bits and pieces
of skin and tissue   tumor and cell
once you    cut away
you remember: doctors  surgeons  specialists
you remember: diagnosis after diagnosis
you remember: pain
you remember: fear

what you do not remember:
what you do not remember:
what you cannot remember:

tears

# HOME AMONG THE TREES

## A Visit with Karen Thompson, Sharon Kowalski and Patty Bresser

### Marj Schneider

Their house is easy to find, even without knowing the address. The prominently displayed rainbow flag and the ramp sloping up to the front door are sure signs, as are the elm and blue spruce trees that surround the house and partially obstruct the view of the river. It is the Mississippi River, about sixty yards wide here, and the wildlife refuge on the opposite bank that fill the living room picture window.

Sharon Kowalski has never wanted to live in the city. This home among the trees is where she chooses to live, but her freedom to make that choice came only after an eight-and-a-half-year, hard-fought court battle that became an activist cause in the lesbian and gay communities in the 1980s.

My friend, Elissa Raffa, and I have made the one-hour trip from Minneapolis to Clearwater, Minnesota, to interview Sharon, Karen Thompson and Patty Bresser on a humid Friday in early September. I have wanted to interview them for a long time, to learn more about what their lives are like, now that the Sharon Kowalski–Karen Thompson case is no longer the subject of publicity, now that it's no longer a hot issue in the lesbian and disability communities. I wanted to know how they live their lives as a "family of affinity," as a sensible judge finally recognized in an appellate court ruling in December 1991.

This case, along with the AIDS epidemic, jolted lesbians and gay men into talking about and preparing the documents they hoped would ensure their legal rights to remain involved with partners or close friends in the event of accident, illness or death: wills, powers of attorney, health care proxies and living wills. As Karen Thompson was propelled out of the closet by the necessity to speak out publicly about what was happening to her and to Sharon, many advocacy groups and individuals became involved in raising money to help her with attorney fees. Those efforts revealed the significance of this case for the lesbian and gay communities.

Many of Karen's responses to my questions are well practiced; yet condensing nearly fourteen years of her and Sharon's lives into the "highlights" is no easy task. Patty Bresser has had fewer opportunities to talk about her life with Karen and Sharon, but she is almost as familiar with the case, having read through boxes of court documents for the book she and Karen are co-authoring about events since the publication of *Why Can't Sharon Kowalski Come Home?* by Karen and Julie Andrzejewski in 1988.

Sharon's participation in our interview is quite different. Sharon has short-term memory loss from the accident that disabled her in 1983. She understands what goes on in the present moment and may choose to participate, to answer questions, to laugh or to show initiative in other ways. She doesn't remember meeting me before nor will she remember me in the future, or that she was part of this interview. Sharon seems most aware of events and people from before her accident—topics that are in her long-term memory. She may know something of Karen today, but most of her "picture" of Karen is from before the accident. Other people and experiences in her life since the accident seem to sink in over time, but it's difficult to know what she retains and thinks about. Yet Sharon is vibrant, full of life, loving and playful, qualities evident once I spent time with her. She communicates generally in nonverbal ways that have to be interpreted for me, since I can't see her nods, head shakes or lip movements. Sharon also uses a "speech pack" that can display or speak what she types, a device vital for her to communicate with people other than Karen and Patty.

In November 1983, Sharon and Karen had been living together for four years. They were both teachers. Sharon had recently completed a two-year assignment teaching high school physical education and health; Karen taught similar subjects at St. Cloud State University. Karen says, "It's hard to even think back to that time because I'm a completely different person now. I was in total denial of who I was—I didn't want to admit that loving Sharon made me anything. I just happened to fall in love with someone who was a woman. I hadn't even told Sharon I was gay. Sharon was ready to come out, but I just wasn't there at all."

Sharon was driving her niece and nephew home following a weekend they had spent with her and Karen when their car was struck head-on by a drunk driver. All three were injured and taken to different hospitals. Sharon's niece Melissa later died. Karen got a call from Sharon's father, Donald Kowalski, telling her that Sharon was at St. Cloud Hospital. When Karen went to the hospital, it took her hours even to find out that Sharon was alive. No one would give her information because she "wasn't family." Overhearing the situation, a priest helped Karen learn that Sharon was in a coma in critical condition.

Sharon's parents arrived, and with Karen waited days for Sharon to come out of the coma. A month after the accident, when Sharon was moved from the intensive care unit to the rehabilitation floor, the Kowalskis returned home. They came back to St. Cloud for a few days every couple of weeks, staying at Karen and Sharon's home during these visits. Karen believes they must have found something during this time that made them begin to suspect Karen and Sharon's actual relationship. Their cordial attitude toward Karen changed. "I was taken out of Sharon's room and told by Donald Kowalski that no one could love Sharon like family loved Sharon, that family could meet all of Sharon's needs, and that if I didn't stop visiting so often they'd see to it I couldn't visit at all."

But Karen continued her visits. Sharon was in various stages of the coma for some six months and, at times, responded and communicated with Karen, who spent hours stretching Sharon's arms and fingers, legs and toes, hoping Sharon would be able to use some parts of her body as she came out of the coma. During this time the effects of Sharon's traumatic brain injury were being assessed.

Karen sought the advice of a psychologist, who helped her decide to give Sharon's parents more time before talking to them about her relationship with Sharon. But then the Kowalskis started making plans to move Sharon out of the St. Cloud area to a nursing home in Hibbing, Minnesota, closer to their home.

The psychologist advised Karen to come out to them, to tell them Sharon's home was in the St. Cloud area with her, that Sharon wouldn't want to leave. Karen wrote the Kowalskis a letter, hoping they'd be able to work through their feelings in private and then meet with her to talk over what was best for Sharon. Instead, they phoned, called Karen a "sick, crazy person" and said they never wanted to see her again.

The Kowalskis' reaction prompted Karen's first contact with an attorney. She asked if she and Sharon had any rights as a couple, what rights Sharon had as an adult—to medical care, to rehabilitation, to staying in the area where she had chosen to live. She learned that the only recourse she had was to enter into a guardianship fight against Sharon's parents. Karen filed a petition for guardianship because she felt she would otherwise be "barred from Sharon's life." The Kowalskis counterfiled, and that began a process of filing motions, with months passing before each succeeding motion was heard in court.

In the spring of 1984, Karen and the Kowalskis reached an out-of-court settlement in which Karen agreed that Donald Kowalski would be appointed Sharon's guardian, with Karen's rights to visit and her right to have input into Sharon's medical care protected. Under the agreement, Sharon couldn't be moved out of the St. Cloud area except by court order.

Karen hadn't realized what legal rights guardianship gave to Donald Kowalski. It allowed him to hire the lawyer in the personal injury suit against the drunk driver, and it meant he could hire the medical personnel who would say what he wanted them to say. The Kowalskis and Karen returned to court several times on motions to limit Karen's visitation rights and to move Sharon from the St. Cloud area. In the fall of 1984, Sharon was moved to a nursing home in Hibbing, which meant Karen had to drive three hours to see her.

In July 1985, the court gave Donald Kowalski guardianship with unlimited powers. Within twenty-four hours, Karen was banned from visiting Sharon, as were Sharon's friends, the Minnesota Civil Liberties Union and disability rights groups, which had become involved with the case. Sharon was essentially held prisoner, prevented from seeing anyone who wasn't on a list from her father.

Donald Kowalski was always the one to speak publicly about the case, but to this day, it is Della Kowalski who openly expresses her hostility and animosity toward Karen. Sharon's father didn't see his actions in the court case as denying Sharon's or Karen's rights. In his view, he was "taking care of his own," protecting Sharon, who "can no longer protect herself," as he said in a CBS News broadcast about the case. Karen believes that the Kowalskis felt hopeless and inadequate about Sharon's condition, that they believe Sharon can have no quality of life as a disabled person. Although her parents visit her regularly today, Donald Kowalski has said in more than one interview that he believes Sharon would be better off dead.

Karen filed an appeal to the 1985 guardianship decision, but every motion in the process took months before it was heard in court. While the case was being appealed, Karen should have had visitation rights under the earlier guardianship ruling, but she was not allowed to visit Sharon. During the visit that proved to be their last for three and a half years, Sharon looked at Karen and typed, "Take me home with you."

Karen's attorneys used various laws to file motions during the appeals process, including the Patient's Bill of Rights and the Vulnerable Adults Protection Act, but neither of these statutes helped Sharon. The court ruled that the Patient's Bill of Rights imposed duties on institutions, not on guardians. But the institution also has to follow the wishes of the guardian, and in Sharon's case her guardian didn't abide by these rights. The nursing home followed what Donald Kowalski wanted. Karen's attorneys cited violations of the Vulnerable Adults Protection Act. The court, however, ruled that Sharon was receiving the level of care directed by the physician in charge of the case. This physician had denied Sharon occupational therapy because she would never have an occupation, although such therapy goes far beyond helping people regain skills to enable them to return to work.

Karen points out how critical the rulings in this case regarding the Patient's Bill of Rights are for others who wind up in institutions following accidents. "I don't think anyone understands the implications of saying that the Patient's Bill of Rights doesn't impose duties on the guardian. That means the guardian can lock up a person in an institution, not allow them to see the people they want to see, not give them proper care, and there's nothing anybody can do about it. It's just frightening that that can happen."

After the accident, Sharon was considered incompetent. The label "incompetent" meant that Sharon was never allowed to choose counsel to represent her in court. While at the nursing home, Sharon had clearly typed out that she wanted the Minnesota Civil Liberties Union to represent her, after they had spent a day talking with her. She said she didn't think her rights were being protected. The court responded that Sharon didn't have the right to choose her own counsel because she was incompetent; and, no, she hadn't been tested for competency, but yes, she was incompetent and couldn't hire her own counsel.

More than twenty times, when this case went to the appellate court of the state of Minnesota, the court upheld the guardian's wishes, ignoring Sharon's rights. This prolonged, systematic violation of the requirement that Sharon be tested for competency, and the denial that the Patient's Bill of Rights should apply to guardians, have far-reaching implications for others in similar situations. These decisions serve as a guide for attorneys arguing in other cases and can become the justification for practices that violate people's rights.

It wasn't until September 1988 that Sharon was tested for competency, testing required annually under Minnesota law. Even though she had not been in a coma for over four years, it took a court order to have this testing done for the first time.

Sharon was moved to Miller-Dwan Polinsky Institute in Duluth for testing, which showed she hadn't received proper rehabilitation. Institute staff determined she was capable of making many basic life choices. This was followed by a court ruling in January 1989, ordering that Sharon receive additional rehabilitation at the institute. The next month, Sharon's medical team at Miller-Dwan said Sharon should be allowed to see anyone she wanted to see. Karen finally got to see Sharon in February of 1989.

Once the medical team saw how well Sharon responded when Karen was around, they said Sharon should be allowed to move home. The judge, contemplating the question of where home for Sharon might be, decided Sharon should go to Trevilla of Robbinsdale, one of the few nursing homes in Minnesota with a young adult rehabilitation ward. He saw this as neutral ground where Karen, other friends and Sharon's family could all visit. While Sharon was at Trevilla, another ruling said that she could be allowed out on passes from Trevilla, but the judge, fearing sexual abuse, required that a staff person accompany her on outings with Karen, a requirement that was in place for nearly a year before it was removed in February 1990. The judge's fear was based on groundless homophobic allegations that the Kowalskis' lawyer had made early on in the case to try to prevent Karen from visiting Sharon.

The summer of 1989, Karen and her attorneys once again filed a petition for guardianship, which wasn't heard in court until November 1990. During that time, Donald Kowalski asked to be removed as guardian because he didn't like Sharon's transfer to Trevilla of Robbinsdale, or that she was receiving visitors and going out on passes. That meant Sharon had no guardian during this time, so the judge acted in that role. Although Karen was the only party of record asking for guardianship and no one counterfiled, Karen could not win guardianship. In April 1991, the judge appointed a woman as guardian who hadn't petitioned for guardianship or gone through a hearing to determine her qualifications. She was a friend of the Kowalskis who had known Sharon in high school, but had visited her infrequently since the accident.

Karen appealed again, and in December 1991 an appellate court overturned the lower court's decision, saying that the judge had "abused" his discretion in appointing someone else as guardian. The appellate court ordered that Karen be appointed guardian with no restrictions. It also stated that Sharon had the right to be heard, to see whomever she wanted to see, to go wherever she wanted to go, to live in the least restrictive environment and to have the best possible medical care. Karen says, "Those were rights I thought we already had, but it took us over eight years to get a court decision to protect those rights." The actual implementation of guardianship had to go back to a lower court, where the judge stalled on the process, and it wasn't until August 1992 that Karen had the documents allowing her to act as guardian.

Then the fight shifted from the legal system to the health care system, where funding and programs are biased toward keeping people in institutions rather than finding viable options for them to live in the community. Karen searched for an affordable program that would enable Sharon to live at home. Finally they found the CADI (Community Alternative for Disabled Individuals) Waiver Program, a Minnesota program that says the state must spend as much money to enable an individual to live in a less restrictive environment as it spends to keep someone institutionalized. It was important to find a program that was flexible about how funds could be spent, so that, for example, Sharon could attend an adult day care program instead of having personal care attendants at home for so many hours. The CADI Program has made it possible for Sharon to live at home for the past five and a half years. Once Karen found this program, it was only a few months before Sharon came home in April 1993.

Now there was a home for Sharon to live in. Karen had searched throughout the St. Cloud area for an accessible home, but could find nothing that would meet Sharon's needs. She was able to have such a home built in 1990 when it seemed a real possibility that Sharon would eventually live there.

During our visit, Karen talks about all the things she has learned from Sharon, both prior to and since the accident: about being more emotionally open, about not being a workaholic. Speaking to Sharon directly, she says, "After I got separated from you, I almost lost that. I went back to being a workaholic. I was on the road, speaking and fundraising, and between that and my teaching job, I literally lost who I was. I was wishing my life away from one court hearing to the next. I finally realized that, to survive, something had to change. I had to give myself permission to move on with my life. I didn't know if I was ever going to be able to see Sharon again, and if I didn't, was this the way I was going to live the rest of my life? I made the decision that I would start dating and be open to another relationship, but that I would never walk away from Sharon. Whoever came into my life would have to understand that my commitment to Sharon was a lifetime commitment. Sharon and I would always be a package deal. If anyone could learn to love me, they would have to love us both."

Patty Bresser had taught in the physical education department and been an assistant coach at St. Cloud State from 1979 through 1981, and had known Sharon and Karen. She was living in Connecticut when the accident occurred and had followed the case. On one of Karen's trips out east for a speaking engagement in 1989, she and Patty spent time together. Over the next couple of years, Karen made frequent trips to the northeast, and Patty says she was always "only two hours away." She managed to rearrange her work and graduate school schedule to make time for Karen, and their relationship gradually developed, but was totally unexpected for both of them. They talked about what might be possible, and finally Karen asked Patty if she would move to Minnesota. Patty agreed to give it a try, knowing she could go back to Connecticut if things didn't work out.

Patty moved in May 1992. At first she wondered what she had gotten into: "I didn't know a soul. Like, where am I? I was kind of a city girl, and here I am out in the country, with so many trees and no sidewalks." Patty also had to get to know Sharon again over the next year, to build a relationship with her before Sharon came to her new home. In that time, the women concluded that their relationships could work. Because she knew Patty before the accident, Sharon remembers Patty and knows who she is. Karen reminds Sharon that Patty is the only one Sharon ever let ride her motorcycle. When Karen asks Sharon if they should "send Patty back to Connecticut," Sharon always says, "no."

This interview is not my first visit with Sharon, Patty and Karen. Each time I've been with them, I've felt their caring and pleasure in one another's company. Patty and Sharon are the playful, fun-loving members of this trio, giving balance to Karen's more serious personality. Karen talks about the teasing relationship that has evolved between Sharon and Patty, with Sharon playing mental games with Patty involving thought processes that would seem to be beyond Sharon's abilities. Sharon is clearly happy living with both of them.

"Our family's full of love, full of caring and full of unselfishness," Karen says. Each gives to the other. "We all get what we need when we need it." Patty says, "We work together on things, and tasks that somebody might think would be work, like giving Sharon a bath, or getting her standing up, we all do together. It takes just a few minutes and makes things so much easier." "The difference is," Karen says, "it can be fun. None of us is the martyr type. We've incorporated taking care of Sharon's needs into our routines."

Sharon can live successfully at home partly because she has the equipment she needs. That includes a Hoyer lift for making transfers, an adjustable hospital bed, a wheelchair that gives her support to sit up, a whirlpool bath and a standing frame so she can be on her feet for some time each day. Sharon also uses boots that allow for movement when she has spasms, but that return her feet to a ninety-degree angle. All this equipment is expensive; but Sharon has undergone surgeries and physical therapy that could have been avoided had some of these devices been supplied earlier. Having such equipment makes caring for Sharon far easier and is more cost-effective over time. But insurance and health care programs don't see it that way. "They never give people what they need unless they fight for it," Karen notes.

Patty and Karen don't provide all of Sharon's care. A personal care attendant (PCA) comes in the mornings to get Sharon ready for the Day Break Program, which she attends five days a week. The St. Benedict's Center program is more affordable than having PCAs with Sharon at home all day and allows Sharon to participate in activities like visiting public gardens and shopping. Sharon recognizes some of the program's staff and other participants and has developed relationships with them. PCAs also provide respite care for Sharon when Karen and Patty need a break for a day or a short vacation. Such breaks are critical for their living situation to work. "I can feel when I'm getting tired," Karen says, "when I need a break from getting up every night to turn Sharon."

Sharon also loves to travel and do things, but the lack of adequate access to so many public accommodations makes traveling hard on Sharon and exhausting for Karen and Patty. Sharon's wheelchair doesn't fit on aircraft, and access in hotels is often inadequate. Day trips to area lakes for fishing and other activities closer to home are easier to manage.

In some respects, Sharon's having a disability means they all have a disability, in terms of where they get invited and what they do. Potlucks and other activities in the lesbian community are often held in inaccessible locations. "People have to really want to get to know a person with a disability," Karen says, "especially with Sharon because each time someone sees her, it's the first time all over again for Sharon. It's difficult at times to honor friendships." Patty adds, "I think there're a lot of things we don't get invitations to. I don't think it's because people don't want us there, but they don't want to invite us knowing it's not accessible. . . . Sometimes I think it would be nice if they'd just say they're having an event, even if it's not accessible, and let us make the decision." "When the potlucks are here," Karen points out, "the house is packed. They like to come here, but it's difficult for us to go to some of the other places, especially in the winter."

Because Sharon was denied proper rehabilitation during the first few years following the accident—the most crucial time for retraining motor and cognitive skills—she will never regain some abilities. As a result, there are things Sharon could do when she came out of the coma in 1984 that she cannot do now. But though Sharon has to work harder now to make gains, she is making them and can do some things no one would have thought possible following the accident.

Karen points out that it took years to reduce the large number of medications Sharon had been on, medications with side effects that dampened her personality. She is certainly a far different woman now from who she was before the accident. She has survived many surgeries and physical hardships, the years of isolation and inadequate care in the nursing home and countless experiences that must have been frightening and damaging to her spirit. Yet she has come through all of this with amazing resilience and with her sense of humor intact. Sharon has begun to write a little, to speak and to show her pleasure by laughing out loud.


Driving back to Minneapolis, Elissa and I talk about our visit with the three women: how remarkable it is that Karen could sustain the legal fight for so many years, that she could devote herself so completely to attaining the medical treatment and opportunities Sharon deserved. Karen never gave up. We recall some of the publicity around the case and how poorly the mainstream press addressed the gay and disability issues at work in the court proceedings. In the lesbian community, some painted Karen as the strong, valiant lesbian doing battle for her defenseless lover. Sharon was too often cast as a victim—of a tragic accident, of her parents' prejudices, of an unresponsive legal system.

Sharon had no voice, but both she and Karen became larger-than-life figures doing battle against homophobia. I speculate with Elissa that the romanticizing of Karen and Sharon that went on among lesbians was a way to cope with some terribly hard, scary issues. I do believe that the variety of support the lesbian community gave Karen was vital to her surviving the legal struggle. Those of us around during the years when the case was a topic of community discussion or who heard Karen speak learned just how prejudicial the court system could be and how few guarantees we have that our wishes will be honored if we cannot speak for ourselves.

I recall that the disability community was less visibly involved with the case. Most of the participation on that front was by professionals who worked with disabled people. When Karen contacted one national disability rights organization, "they agreed that Sharon's rights were being violated, but they couldn't get involved because it was a gay issue." Individual disabled activists were involved, both in Minnesota and nationally. Sharon's situation gradually became more widely known among disability advocates, and she was invited to participate in the signing ceremony for the Americans with Disabilities Act in 1990. I believe today that the disability movement might be more prominently involved in a case such as Sharon's. There are more civil rights–oriented organizations and a stronger disability community, at least in some parts of the country.

Elissa and I talk about how well the Thompson-Kowalski-Bresser household functions. But there were moments when I caught myself wondering if how the women talked about their daily lives was too good to be true. In commenting on the PCAs who have worked with Sharon, Karen quoted one of them: "You know, there's more love in this home, in this family, than I have ever seen in any family."

How many disabled people have the help of a dedicated life partner and another devoted companion? How many of us could make such a three-person relationship work? Yet Elissa responds that what these three are doing "is still a model for how disabled people can live in the community." I want to agree and remember Karen's saying that one person can't meet all of the needs of somebody with a disability. It takes openness and willingness to be innovative in relationships to develop the kind of long-term living arrangements that will keep disabled people out of institutions. It takes advocacy for, and with, the disabled person: for adequate medical care, equipment and services. It takes government funding of flexible programs like the CADI Waiver Program. It takes other quality programs like adult day care and options for respite care. Thinking about the necessary pieces, and all the people involved in Sharon's life, I know there must be other versions of this model of how disabled people can live interdependently. Knowing that Sharon, Karen and Patty have been successful makes me want to hear other people's stories, makes me believe it is possible.

# STEPS AND CLIMBING
## An Interview with Joyce Peltzer

*This piece was compiled from an interview conducted by Susan Raffo.*

I was twenty when I contracted polio in 1951. I was on a trip to Mexico as a part of my education at Macalester College in St. Paul, Minnesota, and picked up the polio virus there. The incubation period is one to three weeks so I didn't begin to get sick until after I had returned home. The big polio epidemics were already past when I got sick, but the vaccine hadn't yet been created. I got sick about a day and a half after I got back home. I diagnosed myself because I knew some of the symptoms from watching the warnings broadcast during the polio epidemic, like not being able to get your chin down to your chest and having aches in your legs and your back. In the morning I went to the old Ancker Hospital in St. Paul, where I had a spinal tap and was immediately taken to a contagion ward. About an hour later I got up to go to the bathroom and my legs gave out on me. It was that fast. I was in the contagion ward for a couple of weeks.

My mother called around to tell my friends that I had polio and to warn them and the other people from the Mexican trip that they should watch for symptoms. There was another woman, Marian, who had been to Mexico and who lived in the dorm who also came down with polio. Marian was in an iron lung in the room next to me. One day I noticed I couldn't hear the iron lung anymore. I knew something had happened so I asked the nurse about it. The nurse I asked was a student and didn't know the rules. She wasn't supposed to

18

tell me anything, but I pressed her and she told me that Marian had died. That was hard. It brought up all of those feelings—"why her and not me?"

My polio had progressed to the point where my legs weren't working. Next, I couldn't turn over in bed, and then I couldn't raise my left arm. I was praying like crazy, please Lord, leave me my arms, I can take everything else but please, leave me my arms. That was the end of the progression. There's now only a minor weakness in my left arm.

There are three different kinds of polio viruses: spinal, spinal bulbar and bulbar. The bulbar virus affects your lungs and breathing. People with that form of polio had to use the iron lungs. I had some weakness in my breathing and a tiny little cough so there might have been some mild effect on my respiratory system, but not much. Mostly my spinal system was attacked. During this trip in Mexico, I had a number of long discussions with a pastor who was with our tour group. I was always a religious kid. I remember that the night before I came down with polio, I had a spiritual experience in which I made the commitment to live my life for God and to be the best person I could be. This experience felt very profound and important, so I wasn't really frightened when I first got sick. I wasn't afraid until I couldn't raise my arms. I mean, I figured with my legs that I would someday be up walking again, but when my arms got weak, I got very scared. I didn't anticipate that I would always have to use a brace and crutches. I thought I would walk like I had before.

I didn't realize how much my body was affected by the polio until after I had been transferred to the Sheltering Arms Rehabilitation Center and was involved in my physical therapy. It was a shock when I first got up at the bars and tried to walk. I realized I had only one muscle in my right leg and could only move the lower part of my left leg. I didn't have the muscles that would work from the knee up. I learned then that I would have to use a brace and crutches to walk. I must have been upset, but what I remember is just seeing this as the next obstacle to overcome. There was another woman at the rehab center also learning to use a brace and crutches. We used to race around the rehab center's open square to see who would finish first and to practice our walking. It was hard and exhausting but we knew we had to build up our strength.

I also used hot packs, developed by Sister Kenney. She came to Minnesota from Australia as a nurse and believed that exercise and very intensely heated hot packs, cloths heated up in a steamer and then placed steaming hot on your limbs, would positively affect your recovery from polio. I was in a room with about eight women, kind of like a ward, and we did a lot of crazy things. After we were all in bed for the night, when the night nurse had come by, we would turn the lights back on and have a party even though we were supposed to be sleeping. The women were all in their twenties and thirties and all had polio. Some were married and had children, some were unmarried.

Polio doesn't exist anymore, at least in the United States, thank God. The trouble is it still exists in other countries. The vaccine was developed about four years after I had polio, but they still haven't vaccinated people in many countries, although that's slowly changing. We need to spread the vaccine so that polio can be completely eradicated, like we eradicated smallpox. While I was in rehabilitation, I was still taking classes at Macalester College. They let me take some sociology courses and conversational Spanish, which was a riot, because there was no one at Sheltering Arms to practice with. After I was released, I went to summer school and then back again in the fall for a full year.

I was not aware how much I was a victim of handicappism, especially my own attitudes toward people with disabilities, until many years later. Much much later, I realized how I had overcompensated to make sure I could do as well as everyone else. I was given tests by the Division of Vocational Rehabilitation, and because I'm pretty organized, I scored high on clerical skills, so they wanted me to take shorthand, typing and business machines. That meant climbing up to the third floor of one building and then getting down to ground level in ten minutes and going across campus on ice and snow and up to the second floor of another building so I could take my social work classes. I had to negotiate with them to take my social work classes. They were tracking me into a clerical career, but I wanted to be a social worker, so I talked them into letting me take social work classes also. A Ramsey County Division Director told me that I wouldn't be able to practice social work with my disability. And, in part, she was right, because the job included a lot of going out and visiting homes and climbing stairs. But I was fortunate and stubborn and social work was what I wanted to do.

When my mother suggested I go to a group she had heard about for people with disabilities, I didn't want to go, although I finally went. This was the first thing I did that was organized around disability. There were a number of people I couldn't relate to, but there were also people I really liked. I felt more connected to those who had become disabled later in life and I also felt more connected to people with an education. In those days, kids with disabilities were segregated into special schools. It's sad to say that a lot of the schools for kids with disabilities didn't provide good educations, so when it was time for the kids to enter the work world, they not only had to deal with the discrimination aimed at people with disabilities, but they also weren't adequately prepared for the work world.

I had a different experience. Ever since I was thirteen or fourteen, I wanted to be a social worker. My mother used to take child development courses as an adult and bring her school books home. I would read the books and then counteract her. This gave me the idea of being a social worker. Plus we had a neighbor girl who was a social worker and my mother encouraged me to look into it.

I talked the administration at Macalester into letting me go through the graduation ceremony with my class even though I hadn't completed my degree. I finished seven elective credits in night school after I got a job. When I first started working for the American Red Cross, sometime around 1953, and before I started graduate school, I was going into some of the poorest parts of St. Paul and going up and down staircases, outdoor staircases, that were covered with ice. It was just what you had to do. I was frightened a lot with the ice, because ice is the scariest thing when you're on crutches. Sometimes during the winter, rather than driving myself and needing to find parking, I would ask the American Red Cross vehicles to drop me off and then come back and get me. That was one adaptation, but I didn't use it very often.

When I say I went up all of these flights of stairs, I was using crutches and the brace. I was younger then and had more energy, but it still took a lot. I was exhausted by the time I got to the top and I would stop and rest for a second. Everything for moving my body and getting around was related to my shoulders. When I was at the Red Cross, I walked up three flights of stairs every morning. They had a freight elevator but I don't recall ever asking to use it. I don't think it ever occurred to me. I didn't think about it. It was just what you did to get the job done.

When I started graduate school, I had my first-year field placement at Jewish Family Services in St. Paul. Again, I had to climb stairs to get to work and I had to find parking. I had a handicapped parking permit, but in those days that just meant you could park at a meter without paying. You still had to get from whatever meter you found to the front door and, in the winter, that meant climbing over big mounds of snow and ice. Everything was about steps and climbing, steps and climbing. You had to do it, and I had to do it if I wanted to become a social worker, and I really wanted to become a social worker. It was the same with my living situation. I moved into a house with a friend of mine from Macalester. This was an old house with outside stairs and no railing. It shocks me when I think about it. There were lots of scary situations when I could have fallen and really hurt myself. I was lucky because I had a car by then and that made me more mobile than lots of other people with disabilities were. But still, I'm amazed I didn't break any bones.

During the last six months of college, I saved $25 a month to have spending money to go to Europe. In those days it cost $1,500 for ten weeks in Europe. That was a lot of money. I got a loan from my parents for that. But you should have seen how far that money stretched. I bought so much stuff! Silver spoons, Belgian laces, Irish linens, Swedish crystal, woolens from England, and still traveled for ten weeks. Our meals were provided as part of the $1,500. We traveled across the Atlantic on a ship and my room was down two or three flights below the main deck. My traveling companion also had a disability and used two braces and crutches. I first met her during that disability group my mother had suggested. We had a wonderful time. Of course, there were a lot of things we couldn't do. I couldn't kiss the Blarney Stone because I couldn't climb all the stairs with no railing and then lie on my back and reach way underneath, but the bus driver told me it was just as good to kiss him, so I did. Sometimes we couldn't go on all the tours. They didn't think to stop at the Roman Forum and let everyone else out but then drive us to the top where there was a parking area. No, they stopped at the bottom for everyone. They didn't pay any attention to how things would have been made easier for us, but then I don't think they pay much more attention these days. We still managed to see a lot. Of course, every place we stayed was on the third and fourth floor. If we were lucky, it was on the second floor, but that was rare. In those days I could get on and off buses with a lot of hard work. I could do it but it was hard. That's why after forty-two years of doing that, my shoulders wore out and I had to have a left shoulder replacement.

About nine years after I had polio, I realized that I could sort of stand on my right leg with my ankle bent and it would hold me. So I went to the University of Minnesota rehab department and the doctors said they could do a triple arthrodesis to stabilize my ankle, and then they did a right hip flexor release. Because of my weak abdominal muscles, they wanted to do an operation that would attach fascial sheath muscles to my hip bones and then criss-cross and attach them to my ribs. That was supposed to give me more support. I called it my built-in girdle. Because I could hold my left leg back—I had a hamstring but I didn't have the quadricep—they disconnected the hamstring, pulled it under my knee cap, and that was supposed to give some stability for that leg. After that, I walked around for nine years without a brace. It was like going through polio all over again, because I had to learn to walk again. I needed to learn a different gait, but I figured it out. After nine years, I again had to use a brace on my left leg because the left leg was starting to hyperextend and was painful. That was after my second trip to Europe where I did a lot of walking. It was a choice of having further surgery to take a piece of bone out of my left leg or use a brace. I said no more surgery, I was starting to feel like a piece of bread always being cut up. I decided I would just go back to a brace again. With a different balance system, now I needed to use a railing when I went up and down stairs.

My relationship with my first partner, Annalee, started in graduate school. Annalee was a year behind me. I met her when a few second-year students, who were the friendly sort, served on a welcoming committee for new students. When I came back from Europe I knew I wanted to find a place to live and didn't want to live at home. Someone told me Annalee needed someone to move in with her, so I did. We were just friends at first, but that changed pretty quickly. I was twenty-five and Annalee was twenty-eight, almost twenty-nine. She was crazy about me, and I liked the fact that she was crazy about me. That was the subtle kind of seduction, having all of this wonderful adulation about how great I was. I mean, she's a physically affectionate person so it just sort of developed into a relationship. The fact that we were using the same bed because there wasn't space for another bed, well, that certainly helped. The first time we got involved, I remember getting up afterward and both of us were talking. I was saying things like, this is going to destroy us. I only knew about gays and lesbians from reading social-work books. Much later I learned that Annalee had attractions in grade school and an experience in college, but we didn't talk about that when we were together. For each of us, this was the first big relationship. She was in field placement at Jewish Family Services and I was working there. After that early hot passion, it was awfully wearing to go to work the next day. We were both worn out for quite a while.

I never thought about having a disability as a problem in this relationship. Annalee was amazing, kept telling me how wonderful I was, how beautiful. If there was any problem, it was with me having to accept my body. I still had all of those "perfect body" messages inside of me and I would struggle with those, even if Annalee was okay with it. Most of my discomfort was more around the usual woman stuff, and not as much around the specifics of my disability. Like I had a tummy that stuck out and I had to deal with that.

Annalee learned, from being with me, about all the obstacles in the environment which made it difficult to function independently. She gradually became more of an advocate. Living with a disability means you have to allow more time to accomplish tasks or spend time finding out whether or not a building, a restaurant, a friend's home is accessible before you can go somewhere. A friend of mine with cerebral palsy says, "Able-bodied people have the luxury of haste."

We had some friends, another couple who were social workers, who we assumed were lesbians as well, but we never talked about it. We socialized, did things, but never acknowledged what was going on. I mean, I was in a lesbian relationship, but told myself, "I am, but I'm not." In those days, "lesbian" was a psychiatric label and the discrimination was unbelievable. There wasn't any acceptance there, so I had a certain amount of shame and fear. It's ridiculous when

I look back on it. For example, we wanted to buy a house but, as two women, we developed a cover story about being two friends who wanted to invest their money rather than paying out so much rent. It was pretty new for women to buy houses anyway, but to buy a house together, that was even stranger. We got the house by assuming the mortgage and Annalee's dad took out a loan on his insurance to help us pay the balance. Everyone just thought we were best friends buying a house together. We didn't spend much time talking about being lesbian. We knew we were in a lesbian relationship, but we didn't acknowledge it to other people until we split up after twenty years together.

The closest we ever came to being out or being outed was when Annalee was running for county commissioner in about 1970. We were interviewed by a woman reporter for a local newspaper because we were talking about adopting two boys. I think people put two and two together and realized we were lesbians. We were spending the evening with the treasurer of Annalee's campaign, and he said that rumors were going around that we were lesbians. I just remember looking at the rug and saying nothing, keeping a straight face. I don't remember what Annalee said, but that was my reaction. We just didn't acknowledge it. There was already a small but very visible gay rights movement, but we didn't participate in it. We had friends, other friends who lived together but, to this day, they haven't acknowledged that they are lesbians. We all knew, and you could say it was obvious, but they didn't talk about it. That's just the way it was and, for some people, still is.

At one point in my career, I developed transracial parenting groups for white parents of black children. I was working with unwed white mothers, some of whom had children by black men. Many of them didn't really understand what discrimination was all about. I wondered how they could help their kids develop a healthy self-concept as black people. Since I was white and had never lived inside a brown skin, I sought out a black coworker. I learned a lot from that experience.

For one all-day parent's workshop on racism, I got in touch with the national American Lutheran Church to speak with a black woman who was working there on sexism and racism issues. We asked her to come do an all-day workshop with the parents on racism. At one point, she asked me if I would apply for a position at the American Lutheran Church to develop a ministry for people with disabilities. I accepted. I sort of got thrown into the whole thing; it was a brand new position and needed lots of development. This was in 1978. Through reading, I found out about various conferences around the country and different political and advocacy groups working to integrate kids with disabilities into public school classrooms. Up until this point, the American Lutheran Church had worked on disability issues by developing ministries with people who were deaf or blind or developmentally disabled, but there was much more to be done. I was involved in developing what I called "the prepositional ministry," a ministry to, with, of, for and by people with disabilities. We worked to eliminate obstacles, environmentally and attitudinally, that prevented people with disabilities from participating in the life of the congregation. I was also involved with looking at the difficulties disabled seminarians had in getting a call to a congregation after completing their theological training. For example, there was a woman who had cerebral palsy and couldn't get a call from a congregation. She did have her internship placement, but after her training was completed, the Church didn't know what to do with her. Most congregations were unwilling to call someone with cerebral palsy. She finally got a call to a church in Detroit.

It was during this job that I really began to learn. I realized how much I had been overcompensating over the years and learned more about disability communities and the amount of handicappist attitudes both by people without disabilities and by people with disabilities directed toward themselves and toward other people with disabilities.

I planned a national conference. Ours was the first church body to have a nationwide conference for people with disabilities to both come together and talk about their needs within the Church and also to get leadership training to go back and work within their synods. In that process I discovered how many disabled people had feelings of discomfort about people with disabilities that were different from their own. The most satisfying part of my job was watching people who had held themselves back due to their disabilities and had carried all kinds of negative feelings about what they could or couldn't do, and had then blossomed and become involved in the world.

I remember a young woman with cerebral palsy who wanted to get a degree in theology. She had suffered severe depression during her undergraduate course work. She was brought to see me by a church official who wanted me to help her find a field experience to complete an unfinished undergraduate requirement. He said that maybe I could find her a placement in a residential facility or other program for handicapped people. I turned to her and asked, "Do you want to work with people with disabilities?" Her response: "Not particularly." He assumed that because she had a disability that she would want to work with other people with disabilities. He failed to see her as someone who could be an "ordinary" minister.

The Church was at the point of saying they weren't going to accept anyone into seminary with disabilities anymore. So I had a consultation with ministers with disabilities of various kinds who had been working in the field and developed two different approaches, one for disabled seminarians looking for a "call" and one for pastors who became disabled later in their careers. My theory was that there was a difference between those people who had become disabled after they had become pastors and those people who were disabled beforehand. The ones who developed disabilities after they were pastors needed help in dealing with their congregation and their congregation's feelings about this new disability, as well as their own feelings about their change in abilities. Both the congregations and the pastors needed to be taught that you could still accomplish the ministry by working in a different way. When you're working with someone who was disabled before attending seminary, then you need to encourage congregations to consider applicants with disabilities. A congregation must be willing to go through a process of education, learning how it is possible to make a number of adaptations that will allow a minister to function in a pastoral role.

My program was focused on helping congregations take more of a role in making their buildings accessible, as well as in creating more programs for people with disabilities. People with disabilities also need to be able to participate in ministering to others as a full congregational member. We taught that disability is a physical, social, mental or emotional condition which may or may not be handicapping. For example, a truck driver who loses a finger has a disability but not necessarily a handicap, but a violinist who loses a finger has a distinct handicap. We also taught about discrimination and access and the internal feelings of handicappism that all of us carry.

It took me longer to deal with my feelings about being a lesbian than about having a disability. I was totally threatened when Annalee and I split up and she began getting politically involved as an out lesbian. I thought, oh my God, people will see her and then, by implication, everyone will know about me. This was all during the process of us splitting up. She said, well, we can tell people I just came to this recognition about myself and it doesn't have to include you. I knew that wouldn't work and I knew that I had to figure out all of this on my own. I went to therapy to decide for sure whether or not I was a lesbian and finally decided that I am.

Some time later, Annalee asked me to talk with a woman who was also questioning whether or not she was a lesbian. That led to a relationship that lasted about eight years, although we didn't live together. She had a young child and was fearful that, in the process of divorcing her husband, she would lose custody of her child, a real fear in those days. I therefore remained in the closet out of respect for her situation. Only in the latter part of a deteriorating relationship did I begin to attend community events and begin to come out more.

I had also feared losing my job. I worked for a church-based organization. I had always been an advocate and many times had rubbed people the wrong way, so I feared they could use past disagreements as an excuse for firing me if they knew about my lesbianism. Little by little, I came out to "safe" people at work.

I was already retired when I met Sandy. A mutual friend invited us to attend a winter solstice event. I had been to one before and wasn't much into it but decided, what the hell, I'll go along. Afterward we went to a bar and were talking and I asked her to kiss me. She did and I thought, wow, that was nice! Let's do that again. Immediately she told me she didn't want to start a relationship because she had a daughter and had just started a new job. She said she wanted to date a lot of different people. Two weeks later she called to again tell me why she couldn't be involved and we made a date for a movie. We dated for three or four months and finally she just said, I really love you and I want us to build a life together. It's been wonderful ever since.

We had a ceremony in my church. This was important to both of us. Even after I retired, I continued to be involved in the Church on various boards. I got myself appointed to the Joint Synod Task Force. By this point, I was a very out lesbian and when I was appointed, they knew what they were getting. I wanted to work for changes within the Church for gays and lesbians.

One day Sandy and I asked our pastor to come over and told him we wanted a ceremony. We said, we don't want a "wedding" because we already consider ourselves married, but we want a worship service of thanksgiving to God for our relationship. He said fine but there are three things: First, you need to invite the congregation; second, I will inform the Church Council that this is happening but they won't have a vote on it; and third, I will inform the bishop. I had already tangled with the bishop around some gay and lesbian issues and, in the process, had done a lot of education. The bishop was great and supported the "pastoral role" of the pastor, acknowledging there was no church edict against this role in relation to two women. At the same time, a local lesbian couple was having a "blessing" ceremony. Some conservatives in the Church heard about it and began making waves, trying to get the national Church to rule against having same-sex ceremonies. When our local bishop supported the pastor in his role, they went to the National Council of Bishops to ask them to prohibit "blessings" and "unions." They were unsuccessful.

This year, 1998, our congregation voted to become a Reconciling in Christ Congregation, which means it is open to the complete inclusion of gay and lesbian persons. The vote was sixty-two to three. I don't think most people in the congregation knew that it was Gay Pride Sunday when they voted. It was a long process to get here but, during the process, other gays and lesbians in the congregation have come out. It's been a very wonderful and powerful process.

I also worked with our congregation to become more accessible for people with disabilities. I had made one congregation accessible before this, but then I changed congregations, and now this one needed to become accessible, too. The congregation explored it for years and said, yes of course the church needed to be more accessible, but it took a while for anything to happen. Finally, they knew they needed a bigger space for a growing congregation and making the space more accessible kind of got folded into the expansion of the building. It's a good thing, too, because since my shoulder surgery, I wouldn't have been able to get in and out of the old space.

Originally when I heard about this anthology, I didn't want to participate because it seemed like the editors were saying that there is something different about being a lesbian who is disabled. I don't think there is anything different. Lesbians have just as many prejudices and stereotypes as everyone else and, as a lesbian, I have to struggle just as much as any other disabled person. All "isms" are alike and you have to struggle with the internal attitudes developed by living in our culture. You have to know the attitudes and barriers that exist in society. To be an integrated person, you have to accept your wholeness. We cannot be compartmentalized people. I had to integrate everything. I am a person who happens to be a lesbian, who happens to have a disability, but most importantly, I am a whole person.

# SEEING IS BE(LIEV)ING

## Deborah Peifer

Gaydar: the almost mystical way we have of spotting our sisters and brothers. It is gaydar that turns the phrase "we are everywhere" from wishful thinking to a living, breathing reality. We all believe in it, we lesbians; we're certain that, merely by looking, we can say that she is and she isn't and she will be. Ask any dyke if she can pick out the queers in a crowd, and she'll snap to and start identifying.

When I first came out, more than thirty years ago, part of the excitement of knowing myself as a lesbian was realizing that I was now appearing on other lesbians' gaydar. My blip had changed from straight to gay, despite nothing *external* having changed. I wore men's jeans and T-shirts, but I always had. I didn't wear makeup, but I'd stopped doing that years before. My hair was just as short as ever. The plain fact was that long before I came out to myself, my appearance had embodied every Sapphic stereotype. Despite that, I had not been seen as a dyke by other dykes until I came out to myself. Something changed with my own coming out, and that something let other lesbians see me as a lesbian, and let me see other dykes as a part of my new identity.

I was now a part of a couple—a couple of women. It made sense to me that when I appeared with my lover, we would be seen, especially by other dykes, as more than just friends. The body language of two people who have an intimate relationship is different from the body language of even very close friends. We touched each other with ease and comfort; we anticipated the other's moves. Added to the physical connectedness was a tendency to finish each other's

31

sentences. The word "we" was omnipresent in our vocabularies, as in "We loved that book" or "We're busy this week." I understood that my couple status gave obvious clues, especially to people who were looking for them, that I was a proud member of the Sapphic sisterhood, but what about when I was by myself? Why was I still "reading" as lesbian to the lesbians who saw me in a store or on the street, and why was I able to see them when I never had before?

When I first came out as a lesbian, one of the things that confirmed my dykeness was the way other lesbians looked at me. I also defined other women as lesbians, not by how they looked, but by how they *looked*. To clarify: How they appeared wasn't the clue to sexual identity, but how they *gazed* was an absolute indicator. When I saw a woman look at another woman with real plea-sure in her eyes, with a grin that said, "Oh, yes," with an obvious interest in getting closer, I knew I was seeing a lesbian. And when she saw me looking with the same interest, she saw a lesbian, too, and the lesbian was me.

In the shared glance, perhaps in appreciation of a third woman, perhaps in connecting, with a wink and a nod, to our being sisters, we created commu-nity. We never had to feel isolated, because even if we didn't know each other's names, we knew we were not the only lesbians in the world. Over the years, the regular manifestation of the presence of lesbians, everywhere, has been a con-tinuing joy for me, a positive affirmation.

I've lived in New York, Chicago, Los Angeles and San Francisco since I came out, all cities with large and visible gay populations. It was in Arizona, however, that I learned the vital importance of gaydar. Arizona in 1990 didn't have any of the advantages of a large city for a newly transplanted lesbian. My lover at the time and I made a remarkably obvious pair of dykes in the cities, but in Tempe, we looked just like all the straight women out shopping with their straight friends. The first lesbian group we discovered had monthly meetings at members' houses, but when we called for directions, we were told not to look or act too dykey because that could threaten the safety of the woman hosting the meet-ing. In these isolating circumstances, gaydar was literally the only safe way to make a lesbian connection with women you didn't know. "Looking lesbian" at other women was suddenly dangerous in ways it had never been in larger cities.

To feel connected but at the same time feel (relatively) safe, I had to focus on those secret signs that read obviously to other dykes, but were less obvious, and therefore less threatening, to the apparently straight people I kept running into. My focus was on the pleasure I saw when I saw a lesbian looking at a woman. The glow, the grin, the languorous look were all obvious visual signs that lesbian looking was going on and that I was welcome to enjoy and to join in the looking.

I was out at work and where I lived, but the everyday interactions in which I looked like a lesbian were far fewer, far more fraught with anxiety than when I'd lived in a large city. Being able to see other lesbians and to be identified as a lesbian by them made me feel less afraid, more free, but the occasional ocular proof was not enough to sustain me. After a year in the wilderness, I moved to San Francisco and gloried at the sight of all those queers.

That delight changed, drastically, when my vision, which had never been good, crossed over into the uncharted and frightening territory of legal blindness. My visual acuity is 20/400-negative, the negative meaning that if they had all day they could figure out just exactly how bad my eyes are, but because anything worse than 20/400 counts as legally blind, it isn't really worth the time and effort to nail down a precise number. In addition, I have bilateral functional diplopia, which means that at the worst times I see four of everything and they are all blurry.

Although my life changed in every way when my eyes stopped being useful, I want to talk here about the differences in my life as a lesbian since my eyes gave out. I realize, as I begin to think about this topic, that since my eyes deserted me, I feel less like a lesbian than I have in all the years I've been out. Don't get me wrong—I am a dyke and I love being a dyke, but my sense of community membership has significantly lessened because I don't get that daily reminder, that regular validation of my status through visual interaction with other dykes. I can't see faces anymore. Because I can't see the wink or smile a lesbian, thinking she has spotted another dyke, sends my way, I can't respond. This has the effect, I suspect, of making those unseen dykes wonder if their own gaydar is out of order. The interaction that was to me a vital part of what being gay meant has dropped out of my daily life. I no longer see myself as others (dykes) see me, and the result is a sense of isolation that is sometimes overwhelming. I freelance for a gay and lesbian weekly newspaper, and I live at the center of the gay universe; those circumstances ought to provide plenty of community, but they don't. I don't *see* lesbians seeing me as a lesbian, and that makes it much more difficult to see myself as one. I don't see other lesbians as lesbians because my visual gaydar is permanently broken.

I can see a little, which means I have neither the white cane nor the guide dog that would mark me as blind to my lesbian sisters. I don't look blind, so strangers, sisters, don't realize that I'm not seeing them. After so many years of being defiantly out of the closet as a lesbian, I am, in some ways, passing as sighted. Other than wearing a "Yes, I am legally blind" sign, I don't know of any way to provide that information to strangers, and as a result I may appear uninterested in the dyke gazes that, in fact, have always filled me with such delight. As I am not able to use my visual gaydar to play spot-the-dyke, I find myself using a verbal equivalent of gaydar. I make a much greater effort to come out wherever I am. Not that I've ever really been closeted, but they now know at the grocery store ("As a lesbian, I wish to buy these peaches") and the drug store ("As a lesbian, I wish to explain that the yeast infection for which I am purchasing this ointment was the result of taking antibiotics, not heterosexual intercourse") that I am a lesbian. My hope is always that the clerk, the woman in line behind me, the pharmacist will come out as well, but so far that hasn't happened. Of course, maybe some of them are coming out with supportive glances that I can't see, but their efforts to connect are lost on me, much to the detriment of all.

Poets and philosophers have written profoundly about blindness. I am not profound. My experience has not been profound. Instead it has been a series of small difficulties. Reading has become something I must plan for; never again will I know the simple pleasure of just picking up a book and reading it. But most of all, I miss the delight of seeing faces and, especially, the joy of seeing myself being seen by lesbian faces that I must encounter, whether I know it or not, because surely the lesbians have not disappeared simply because I can no longer confirm their presence in my world by sight. I miss letting other women know that we are not just everywhere, but right here, right now. My contribution to the community of sisters and strangers who are lesbians has been diminished because I can't see them. And they can't see me seeing them.

# BACKWARD BY THREES

## Faith Reidenbach

In the neighborhood lesbian bar where I came of age, it was not unusual for Rachel Fransen* to step onto her chair, then clamber atop one of the little round tables, kicking the ashtrays aside, and belt out lyrics along with the jukebox, waving her arms as if to conduct the other patrons.

Even we teenagers soon learned not to sing along, learned to look away so as not to encourage her. When Rachel got like that, she might keep singing, or she might start screaming at one of us, pointing, stomping her foot, cussing us for imaginary slights. She might jump down, grab a stranger and try to dance her around the room. Once, rebuffed, she ripped her shirt off and ran outside into the street. It was best not to catch her eye. It was best just to shrug and say "There goes Crazy Rachel."

I don't know whether anyone called me Crazy Faith in December 1979, when I was a sophomore at a women's college in Massachusetts, pulling all-nighters to prepare for final exams. It suddenly occurred to me, one day after lunch, that all four subjects I was studying—the English novel, symbolic logic, geology and South African politics—were parts of One Large Truth. I decided that, instead of taking multiple exams, I would write an integrating essay and submit it to each professor.

To my roommate, Katie, this plan was the last straw. For weeks she'd

---

* All names used in this essay, except the author's and her partner's, are aliases.

35

watched me skip classes and stay up most of the night, writing stories. Now, the three clocks in our room showed three different times. I was talking too much and too fast, and I was unable to concentrate on anything for very long. Irritable and hostile, I'd broken up with my lover in a very public shouting match and had screamed at other dormmates over petty problems.

That was Katie's perspective. Mine was that I felt euphoric and omniscient. I could think incredibly fast, and my writing seemed brilliant to me. I was getting a lot done, because instead of wasting time sleeping I worked all night and took daytime naps. Lacking much appetite, I had lost fifteen pounds and thought I looked great. I was bewildered when, one afternoon at about three o'clock, Katie and a cluster of other friends woke me to insist that I go with them to the college health clinic.

The college psychiatrist asked me a few questions and then told me that if I would stay at the clinic overnight, I could go back to my dorm the next day. That was a lie. Without my knowledge, the health staff called my parents in Columbus, Ohio, who arrived the next day, frantic.

The psychiatrist told my parents that I might be having an episode of mania—the opposite of depression. He was placing me on medical leave, he said. In order to return to the college I'd have to see a psychologist or psychiatrist and get that doctor's written permission.

My parents drove me back to my dorm and started packing my stuff into the suitcases they had brought. I stood in the hallway in a daze. My clearest memory is of my lesbian friend Angela coming by.

"I locked myself in my room yesterday," Angela said quietly so that my parents wouldn't hear. "Katie asked me to help, but I wouldn't." I gave her a big hug and thanked her. I learned later that she and two other friends had met several times to plot how to keep me away from the clinic.

"You know, they're going to send you to a *psychiatrist*," Angela whispered.

"What?!" I laughed. I hadn't yet heard about the "possible episode of mania."

Angela's dark eyes were filling with tears. "Just be careful," she said. "Be careful what you say." She hugged me again and hurried away.

Angela was at our elite college on full scholarship; she had grown up in inner-city Detroit. Her father was an alcoholic and depressive who would later commit suicide; a lover of hers had been raped by a male therapist when she came out to him. (He called it "treatment.") What Angela knew about "mental health care" made her scared for me.

My parents were scared for themselves. Apparently believing that psychiatric disorders do not affect white, upper-middle-class, churchgoing families, they would not hear of me seeing a psychotherapist. I was quite literally instructed not to tell the neighbors that such a thing had been suggested.

Fortunately, as is typical, my first manic episode was like a first menstrual period—light. I was able to recover fairly quickly without medication. As soon as I could concentrate well enough to drive, a friend directed me to a gay-friendly psychologist. (I didn't understand yet how psychiatrists differ from psychologists, but I had discovered that psychologists were cheaper.) The psychologist told me that I needed to learn active-listening skills in order to deal with my parents, which I was happy to try to do. After five sessions I got my permission slip.

Permission from a doctor was the easy part; next I needed permission and financial support from my parents. Unfortunately, my parents had decided that my "problems at school" must have been due to my lesbianism. Never mind that I had come out to them two years before my manic episode; they mentally wrapped one stigmatizing condition inside the other. Without fully realizing why I was doing it, I gradually became more straight-acting. I acquiesced to my father's long-held desire to send me to modeling school, I started wearing makeup and artificial fingernails, and I found a man I could stand to have sex with and paraded him in front of my parents.

The deceptions worked. My parents agreed to pay for another semester at college, and I returned a year after I'd left. But within six weeks, I had developed mania again, apparently triggered by the stress of moving and reintegrating into college life. This time, the mania progressed to psychosis—the inability to assess reality accurately.

Two common psychoses are delusions and hallucinations. For example, after I was shipped home again, I decided that a newly installed phone jack in my bedroom was a link to my favorite radio station. Twice daily, whatever music

I played on my turntable was simultaneously played on the radio, I was sure. Then I'd speak into the jack for ten or fifteen minutes, giving my listeners news, political commentary and jokes. I didn't listen to the radio while my shows were being broadcast because I didn't want to create feedback. I knew my messages were getting across because of the music and words the station broadcast in response.

Delusions related to radio, television and, now, the Internet are common among psychotic people, I've learned, but my new career got my parents' attention. Unable to convince me that I wasn't a disc jockey, they changed their views about the stigma of having their daughter treated by a shrink and I became the patient of Dr. Paul Porter, a Columbus psychiatrist who was "the best around," according to the friends my parents consulted. He seemed indifferent to my lesbianism, which I found as insulting as prejudice, but he did sit my parents down to explain that lesbianism had nothing to do with my new diagnosis: manic-depressive illness (commonly known as manic depression).

A manic-depressive's moods cycle between two "poles," mania and depression. For this reason it is also known as bipolar disorder. Manic depression is not a mental or emotional illness; it's a chronic disease of the brain. The most recent theory is that it's caused by an excess of glutamate, a chemical that transmits messages between the brain cells that play a role in emotions and behavior. Lithium carbonate, the drug most frequently prescribed for manic depression, is thought to work by restoring glutamate levels to normal. Lithium helps a person "come down" from mania to a normal state and helps prevent further episodes of mania and depression.

Thus, manic depression, a disease of the brain, is controlled with lithium (and/or other drugs) in much the same way that diabetes, a disease of the pancreas, is controlled with insulin. Unless the mood swings are minor or widely separated in time, manic-depressive people need long-term drug therapy in order to live stable, productive lives.

That's what I know and believe now. The 1980s were a different story. At the invincible age of twenty-one, it was difficult for me to accept that I had *any* chronic disease, not to mention a psychiatric disorder. Once I recovered from my second manic episode, I felt completely normal. Then as now, lithium didn't make me feel sedated or drugged, and it didn't change my personality or affect my range of emotions. At that point lithium wasn't doing anything for me except preventing another episode of mania.

I'm what's known as a "slow cycler." Whereas some people have depressive and/or manic episodes weeks or even days apart, my manic episodes come a year or more apart. So it was easy to settle into a classic state of denial: "Why should I take lithium every day? I don't feel any different when I don't." I'd routinely miss doses, then take extra pills to compensate. Although Dr. Porter had cautioned me not to mix lithium with alcohol, I continued to drink regularly and heavily.

Because of taking lithium improperly, I lived in a near-constant state of hypomania, a mild degree of mania. I felt more creative than usual, more energetic, more sexual and more intelligent. When I watched TV or read a magazine article in a hypomanic state, the simplest image or phrase could trigger a cascade of ideas.

I was also chronically sleepless, anxious, irritable and unable to concentrate well. I finished my bachelor's degree at Ohio State without making a single friend there and without participating in any campus activities or living anywhere but my parents' home. After I graduated, I got a job as a sales clerk and rented an apartment with a lover who drank even more than I did. She encouraged me to take my pills more regularly, saying that they seemed to help me. However, she tolerated my highs and lows because she was unemployed and had nowhere else to go. I tolerated her physical abuse because I felt lucky to have a lover at all. During our eighteen months together, we went to two lesbian therapists, but neither one discussed my manic depression as a factor in our problems, even though I reported it during the intake interviews.

When my lover and I broke up, I landed in a lesbian Alcoholics Anonymous group. Now I developed a new rationalization for not taking lithium: I wasn't manic-depressive at all! I was an alcoholic who had been misdiagnosed! When I had a year's sobriety, I visited a lesbian psychologist, Dr. Cheryl Gillian, and told her my story. She agreed that I had been misdiagnosed but explained that withdrawal from lithium needs to be supervised by a physician. With my permission, she called Dr. Porter to ask for his help.

No experienced psychiatrist is ever surprised to hear that a manic-depressive patient wants to stop taking medication. Dr. Porter called me that week with a calm but firm prediction: If I went off lithium, I'd have a major manic episode within three or four years. Inwardly I scoffed, and outwardly I politely said that my mind was made up.

At my next session Cheryl told me, rolling her eyes, that she had called two other psychiatrists, both women, who declined to get involved once they heard that I was Dr. Porter's patient. Cheryl offered to supervise my withdrawal herself. "It's probably malpractice," she warned me, grinning. I grinned back, relieved.

At this point, in mid-1988, I had been living with a new lover, Bev Caley, for about two years. Bev was leery of my plan to taper off lithium, because she thought it helped me and too much of her life had already been affected by psychiatric illness (when Bev was young, her mother had experienced depression and was hospitalized for electroshock therapy). Despite her concerns, Bev supported my decision to withdraw from treatment and helped me all she could. She cooked for me, she gave me backrubs or sang me songs when I had trouble sleeping, and she let me know when I seemed "wound up." I got along so well that within a few years we both virtually forgot that I had ever been manic-depressive. Looking back, I see that I continued to have regular bouts of hypomania, but I was able to manage them—until the summer of 1992.

After twenty years of working at low-paying jobs, Bev had gone back to college and then to law school. That summer she landed her first lawyering job, in Cleveland, Ohio, two hundred miles from where we were living. Her new employer asked her to start work three days after she took the bar exam in July. I was no support to Bev, I'm ashamed to say, as we prepared to move to a new city at the same time that she was studying for the three-day exam. In fact, I was a terrible hindrance.

Under the stress I stopped sleeping well, and that made it hard for me to concentrate on my job as a copy editor. If I hadn't already given notice, I probably would have been fired. I gradually stopped doing chores or seeing friends, preferring to sit alone for hours, writing. It didn't occur to me that I was hypomanic, which is typical for someone in the throes of the illness. Bev didn't think of it either; my original diagnosis of manic depression seemed far behind us. But Bev did realize that I was unwell, so in the midst of studying for the bar exam, she started trying to get me some help. By that time I couldn't concentrate well enough to drive a car, so the first thing she did was drive me to my therapist's office.

Two years before, I had started seeing a new therapist, Pat Lewiston, to deal with issues that surfaced while I was attending Adult Children of Alcoholics meetings. Pat had taught me to recognize my history of emotional incest and had shown me how that history was affecting my spirituality, my creativity and my relationship with Bev. I felt grateful to Pat, and Bev knew I would do whatever she suggested.

"I don't believe in psychiatrists," Pat reminded me. She'd said the same thing at my first visit, after I told her that I'd once been misdiagnosed as manic-depressive. Her tone had been bitter, emphatic, and that's what it was now. "Don't worry, I'll keep you away from Them."

"What you need is REM sleep," Pat continued, in the understatement of the year. "Dreaming sleep. If you can't get some, you should see your family doctor." I had no ongoing relationship with a doctor, but I had seen a family physician up the street a couple of times. Bev drove me to the doctor's office the next day, where I squirmed and fidgeted and paced for what seemed like hours. Finally a nurse came in, chided me for wanting sleeping pills, and told me that I was years overdue for a Pap test. I got mad and left.

A few days later, I'd still had no sleep longer than a fitful nap. I had stopped going to work because I couldn't concentrate well enough to read anymore. My speech was incoherent, and I wandered the apartment at night, muttering to the people I was seeing in my hallucinations. Bev drove me back to Pat's office.

First, Pat read me a guided meditation.

Pat then made sure we understood that she was leaving for a vacation the next day. She did not give us the name of any backup therapist who might have felt an obligation to see me. Instead, she gave us the phone number of a lesbian physician whose office was thirty-five miles away. Bev scheduled an appointment for the next day, but I didn't last that long. That night, feeling out of my wits from the continued insomnia, I sat on the side of our bed, held my head in my hands and started screaming.

At 5:30 A.M., Bev called the doctor. She said she would meet us at the hospital where she practiced and gave Bev directions. But when we got there and the emergency department staff called her, she denied that I was her patient.

One of my delusions at that time was that I was self-employed and had no health insurance, so that's what I told the hospital staff. (I was under the impression that I was at a bridal shop, anyway, and I thought it was a strange question for them to ask.) Bev protested that I did have insurance, but because I had no card with me, the staff referred us to a nearby psychiatric hospital for low-income people.

At the second hospital, I became convinced that I had discovered the cure for AIDS. I ran around telling everyone: the clerks at the reception desk; the woman in the waiting area who was lacing and unlacing her fingers; another woman in the waiting area, who kept silent and continued staring at nothing; and a long line of leather- and denim-clad outpatients who inched forward from somewhere far down a hall, waiting to be administered their daily meds.

After hours of waiting, a woman summoned me to her office, talked to me for five minutes, then handed me a paper cup full of pills. She said she was going to admit me, which was fine with me, since I had more to tell the other patients. Bev argued with the woman, repeating her claim that I had health insurance, but the woman just smirked. Fortunately, it turned out that the hospital was full.

In the evening rush hour Bev drove me back across town to our apartment, got my insurance card and our durable powers of attorney for health care, and took me to our community hospital. Both of us had been out for years, and Bev had no qualms about presenting us as a couple. The durable powers of attorney helped establish Bev as the person the hospital should keep informed, and the social workers were good about doing that.

That first night I slept for eighteen hours, heavily drugged. It takes a week or more for lithium to start working, so hospitals typically also give tranquilizers and antipsychotic drugs to manic patients. I was so fuzzy the next day that it took me three hours to take a shower, the nurses told me later. Who knows what I did all that time. I remember only a minute of it—trying to figure out which way to turn the faucets.

Once I was well enough to get dressed, I was allowed to do whatever I wanted. I sat in the sunroom, played solitaire and swam in the hospital pool. What I remember best, though, is talking on the phone. One hallway of the ward was lined with pay phones, and by the phones were lines of manic patients, chattering with each other, waiting their turn to chatter with friends. My telephone manner was to spew forth a few rapid-fire sentences, then say, "Okay, bye," which was puzzling and upsetting to my friends. It was impossible for me to convey what was on my mind because my thoughts raced too fast.

We manic patients were never invited to group therapy!

In that private, suburban hospital I was not restrained, interrogated, scolded, humiliated, felt up, harassed by another patient or, as far as I can tell, overmedicated. I was simply given time for the antipsychotic drugs to work. Time by myself—no occupational therapy or long sessions with a psychiatrist. Just time. Enough time for it to dawn on me what Bev was going through.

I spent a week at the hospital and came home just before Bev started the three-day bar exam. I've never been stoned and on speed at the same time, but I think that would approximate how I felt. Everything seemed overstimulating. I couldn't watch TV or ride in a car sitting up because the rapid changes of screen or scene felt physically painful. I couldn't read because I couldn't keep my place or remember what words I had just seen. Yet I was too restless to sit still.

Bev arranged for friends and family to stay with me while she took her exam. They walked me around the neighborhood, told me to take naps and helped me pack for the move. But Bev was the one who had to wake up at intervals all night to see if I was wandering around the apartment. At the test center, she told her fellow law students, "This is the *easy* part of my day!" And she did pass the exam easily.

I learned some important lessons that summer. Hypomania can be fun. Mania and psychosis are not. When I'm hypomanic, friends and lovers can help me through. When I'm manic or psychotic, my behavior is often hurtful to others. Hypomania can be about creative productivity. Mania and psychosis are about loss.

Because of mania, I lost friends and lovers by scaring them off with weird or hostile behavior. After college I won a fellowship to one of the top graduate schools in my field, but I turned it down during a hypomanic episode. Instead, I took one low-paying job after another. I stopped reading and writing fiction, scared of the creative ideas it sparked in me.

By the grace of the gods, I did not lose Bev. I moved with her to Cleveland, where I spent my days alone in our new apartment, deep in rebound depression, a biochemical side effect of recovery from mania. By the time Bev got home from work each day, tired and wanting to relate her new experiences, I'd be sobbing. She started giving me assignments before she left in the morning: "Write two pages of affirmations." "You need to be around people; find an Alcoholics Anonymous meeting you can walk to." Feeling desperate, I followed her suggestions.

In the years since, after I've had a series of restless nights, for example, Bev has occasionally asked me to call my psychiatrist or to take my lithium in front of her, and I don't argue. I realize that when I become hypomanic she can recognize the signs more quickly than I can. Because we've been together a long time (twelve years, at this writing), I know she's not on a power trip or trying to humiliate me. I trust her judgment, and I do what she suggests, grateful for her loving help. I never again want to put her through an awful time like the one we had that summer.

Once I was well enough to work, I took another low-paying editing job, not sure that I could handle even that. It was months before I regained my confidence and mental stability, which is typical. Most manic-depressive people find that each psychotic episode is progressively more severe and more difficult to recover from. But after three years I felt able to quit my job and become a freelance writer. That led to my current position, a high-paying, high-pressure job I never thought I could handle, working in daily journalism for an international wire service. I also write fiction again, do volunteer work and sing in a community ensemble.

I doubt that new acquaintances know I'm manic-depressive, but I'm pretty open about saying so. As with being a lesbian, I consider it important to let myself be known to people I care about. And, as with being a lesbian, I want others to understand that a person's appearance and behavior don't tell the whole story.

Manic depression is a hidden disability. Most days I don't feel disabled, partly because I'm lucky: I'm lithium-responsive, I'm a slow cycler and I have an incredibly supportive partner. However, I also work hard to keep myself in balance. I have a strict bedtime, I swim laps and I avoid mood-altering drugs, including nicotine, alcohol, sugar and caffeine. If my thoughts run wild at night, I count backward from one thousand by threes to put myself to sleep. I'm much like someone with chronic pain who manages it with both medication and self-care. Even so, I still have occasional episodes of hypomania, mild depression and anxiety.

Psychiatric treatment is not a big deal for me. At my first visit with my current psychiatrist, she gave me a choice: Did I want her to provide talk therapy as well as manage my medication, or did I want medication management alone? Since I'd already had nine years of talk therapy, I chose the latter. My psychiatrist had me come in fairly often for a while, but now I see her only once a year for half an hour. We chat about my work and Bev and the rest of my life so that she can evaluate my mood, and then she gives me a prescription.

I'm not saying that I'll never again need talk therapy or that no one with manic depression needs talk therapy. Neither am I saying that lithium is a wonder drug. Not everyone is helped by lithium or by the other drugs that are prescribed for manic depression, and some people develop troublesome side effects. I myself have a memory disorder that my psychiatrist attributes to long-term lithium therapy, and I have early signs of kidney damage.

Correct diagnosis can be problematic, too. Doctors sometimes mistake manic depression for depression or another psychiatric disease. Many people with hypomanic or manic symptoms avoid doctors in the first place, not wanting to relinquish the exhilaration of hypomania. In addition, of course, some people, including many lesbians, are unable to afford health care.

My socioeconomic class shaped many aspects of my experience of manic depression. It is only because I attended a small, private college, where the administration took its *in loco parentis* duty seriously, that I was diagnosed at a young age. I was able to do my denial and rebellion against psychiatry while I was still young and had few obligations. Even though many of my jobs have been dull and low-paying, I've always had flexible hours and sick leave, which

I've used freely during periods of hypomania to avoid making serious mistakes or getting fired. And the three times that I had to be hospitalized, I was cared for gently, not institutionalized in a harsh, loud or dangerous state hospital or jail.

As an outpatient, I had excellent care from nonpsychiatrists about issues such as codependency, alcoholism and emotional incest. But all five non-psychiatrists I've seen for therapy (the first psychologist who taught me active listening, Cheryl, Pat and the two therapists I saw when I was in the battering relationship) treated me inappropriately regarding manic depression.

I understand that many lesbians have had traumatic experiences with psychiatrists, not just because of individual bad-apple doctors but because of systematic homophobia and other forms of violence. I understand that many therapists, particularly lesbian therapists, have witnessed homophobic psychiatric treatment or have heard horror stories. But I want therapists to stop trying to "protect" or "rescue" lesbians from the drug treatment that is now known to be necessary for brain diseases. Unless a health-care professional is licensed to prescribe a drug, she is not qualified to judge whether it's needed.

I want other lesbians to educate themselves, too, and become more alert to the signs of manic depression. Substance abuse is the norm in too many lesbian circles, so we often fail to notice when a lesbian is using alcohol or other drugs to self-medicate symptoms of manic depression. And because we lesbians are "deviants" in the first place, we tend to tolerate craziness or even violence from each other, not wanting to restrict anyone in the way we've been restricted or to judge others as we've been judged.

In trying to keep me away from the college health clinic, Angela, my former dormmate, did what she thought was best for me, especially considering her own experiences. I love and respect her for that, but I no longer consider her my heroine. I never again want to be the last to know that I'm acting nutzoid. If I someday run around berserk at a bar or women's concert, as I've been known to do, I don't want other lesbians to pretend that nothing's wrong. I want them to offer me a ride home, or a meal, or a quiet place to sleep. I want them to ask me, not in a joking or sneering way, whether I've been taking my medication. If I seem very ill, I want them to take me to a psychiatrist instead of plotting how to keep me away from one. I don't want them to shrug and say, "There goes Crazy Faith."

※

Seven years ago, I ran into Crazy Rachel at an AA meeting. I hardly recognized her calm face and long shiny hair, brushed out of her eyes now. She didn't seem to remember me, so I introduced myself and we chatted. Then, as recovering alcoholics often do, we decided to exchange phone numbers.

I noticed her hands shake as she wrote, and that's when it clicked for me. I thought fast, decided to take a chance. "Darn lithium can make it hard to write, can't it?" I said.

She shot a look at me. "Yeah," she said, and ducked her head.

I stood stock still until she looked up again. This time, I wasn't afraid of her. I wanted to catch her eye, and smile.

# FROM EACH . . . TO EACH

### Lizard Jones

$M$y girlfriend does my dishes. She does a lot of things for me. It's not always an even trade, and I can't always say it's because she loves me. It's just the way the relationship is. I depend on her for money, and I also depend on her for things that I could do with some effort, but that she can do easily. She depends on me for things I can do, like writing letters and making telephone calls.

As a person with a disability—multiple sclerosis—one of the most difficult aspects of coming to terms with my health has been learning to ask for help. This is a fairly common and well-documented hurdle, but each of us has to overcome it for ourselves anyway. As a lesbian, and a lesbian with some history of social activism, I think this hurdle has a particular shape. The shape might be a crossroads, or a vibrating unarticulated border state, between the trajectory of disability activism on the one hand and the canon of lesbian identity and politics on the other.

Much of the writing about and for people with disabilities—activist writing that I find inspiring—is about the struggle for independence. Many people with disabilities have been trapped in a snare of dependence by their parents or institutions or both. These are people who want their own apartments, their own money, their own lives. Their demands are for an accessible world that they can afford, and for acknowledgment of their right to be autonomous human beings. That shouldn't be a tall order, but it seems to be.

As I try to position myself within the activist disability movement, I run into a particular conundrum. As a lesbian feminist, I have spent my adult life steadfastly asserting and fighting for my economic and social independence. It hasn't always been easy, but I have my own apartment, my own work, my own responsibilities. Frankly, what I want now is some dependence. I don't want my own apartment anymore. I want to just say "Help me." But I feel that lesbians don't say that. Maybe the struggle for lesbians with disabilities is categorically different from many other disability struggles because we have to convince our chosen families not to let us out, but to take us in.

I like to think that there is a place where these roads meet, merge, rather than collide head-on. I guess such a place would be called not independence, not dependence, but interdependence. Right now, though, I think I am sitting more at an intersection than anywhere else. And I am sitting here dissatisfied with both roads.

> *It's spring. I am bicycling with my girlfriend. This was a long time ago. This is my first girlfriend, the one who is busy teaching me everything there is to know about being a lesbian: You wear cotton underwear. You carry a Swiss Army knife. You fix your own motorbike. In case you get the wrong idea, let me say that cycling is not a regular activity for us. But we are having a good time, toodling merrily along, until my chain comes off. I stop and call to her, look stupidly at the chain, and then fiddle with it. Before she gets back to me, a guy stops and asks me if I need help. Yes, I say, I need to put my chain back on. He smiles genially and puts the chain on and cracks a few jokes and we both laugh and he cycles away. It's then that I realize that my girlfriend is fuming. You didn't need a guy to fix your chain, she says, you could have done it yourself. Maybe, I say, but not as fast. Or I could have, she says. Yes, but he was there and he fixed it, I say. We don't need guys to fix our bikes for us, she says, you're not helpless. Yes, I know, I say, but I feel fine about it. And the day is over, and we go home to our separate apartments.*

Here are some of the ideals I have learned as a lesbian in this culture. Historically, we are the women who stand independent, who buck the system of dependence on a male provider. It was not long ago that women living on their own and supporting themselves were *de facto* on the margins of society, but we did it anyway. We have spoken out against the tyranny of Relationship as Salvation and limited views of the family. We fix our own cars and bicycles. We question the simplification of gender and its attendant essentialism. Many of us have left our biological families behind.

I have found boundless joy and excitement and love. I have overworked and scraped and made do and sat in endless meetings. So here I am, sort of scrappy, sort of principled, but above all making my own way as best I can. I am thirtysomething. I have learned a lot from books and magazines, and I think that is fine. When I discovered feminism, when I came out, when I learned history, when social change became more than a concept—these are among the moments that live with passion and excitement in my memory. Inserting my puzzle piece into larger struggles, and seeing the whole puzzle reflect me—I can't explain it. The giddy balance between experience and theory, on the smallest and strongest point of intersection.

Lots of people have done a much better job than I ever could describing this. What I want to say is that I am personally moved and sustained by ideas. That is the kind of person I am.

Living with multiple sclerosis has been a bit of a rude awakening for me. Things I thought were possible aren't. I had thought everything was possible, right down to nonviolent revolution. In moments of enthusiasm, I thought that I could start the revolution myself. Now I think: can't do that by myself, can't do this by myself. Certainly can't start the revolution by myself.

I have a friend who refers to the "cult of self-sufficiency" in our community. Obviously self-sufficiency is not a bad thing, and of course all those things about lesbians and independence are positive. However, the fact remains that I somehow feel that I am letting the Lesbian Nation down if I am not going it alone. I have happily let achievement define me, and self-sufficiency has long been the substance of the important things I say about myself—never lived with a lover; never had a joint bank account; always supported myself; always did my own housework, taxes, holidays, writing.

Not being able to support myself now strikes right at the core of my self-image as a dyke. Now I live off the government, which I have to remind myself every day is a right, not a privilege. I do my best not to be ashamed that I take handouts, but I often am—ashamed, that is. And then I'm ashamed of being ashamed. And my girlfriend pays for a lot of things. Not that she has money particularly, but more than I do. I am dependent on her. There, it's out. I have no illusions about the fact that I am lucky to be closely associated with someone who will let me live off her. But it is very hard to get away from the idea that a) I am lazy, and b) a good lesbian doesn't rely on her girlfriend for anything.

Who are our lesbian heroes? Are they the women who buy pants for your kids when back-to-school is coming up? Are they the women who ask you to buy pants for their kids because they can't? No. Neither one. One woman I know says, "It's not enough to survive a breakdown in the middle of poverty. No one cares unless you write a book about it." As a society we still value individual achievement—the books, the videos, the performances, the jobs—much more than the individuals themselves. We value ourselves—okay, *I* value myself, but I know I am not alone—according to how much we stand out.

Do I really believe that I am all right even when I have no gainful employment? Religiously splitting things evenly, right down the middle, every time, is sometimes unfair. I believe this. Well, I believe this in a larger political context. On a personal level, it gets wrapped up in who I am. I pull my own weight. That is very important. I guess the question is—what is that weight? And why is it my job to pull it all by myself?

This is personal for me, but I do not think it is politically unimportant. As long as dependence is seen as a personality flaw in the lesbian community, our ability to be a truly diverse and inclusive force to be reckoned with is nonexistent.

Remember Marx? Remember "From each according to his ability, to each according to his need"? Remember anarchism and mutual aid? Remember the principles of union organizing, that a better situation overall is more lasting than periodic improvements for a few individuals? I am sometimes a fount of rhetoric, and it is usually of the "let's-all-work-together" variety. I really believe that none of us *do* go it alone. As long as we think that some of us are going it alone and others aren't, we are ignoring the very real facts of social structure. The possibility of going it alone is just an illusion that distracts us from organizing.

You are either successful on someone else's back, or arm in arm with her. Your choice.

> *Here is a story about a lesbian couple I know: two women committed in hearts and minds to radical social and cultural action. One of them has a job, and the other one doesn't. They live in a housing co-op, where the rules are that the residents of each unit pay twenty-five percent of their income for their rent. The salary of the employed member of this couple drives the rent way up. But when it comes to paying the rent, the two women split it down the middle, because lesbians always pay half. Even though they both understand why someone making $300 a month might pay less than someone making $2000, even though they agree completely with the concept of twenty-five percent, within their relationship these principles disappear. I know only one lesbian couple who pro-rates their expenditures according to their relative incomes.*

I think this story is a kind of parable for a disjuncture between political theories and lesbian life as we live it. I do not think this disjuncture is trivial, even though I experience it mostly on a personal level. First, it is not trivial because the people most consistently getting the short end of the disjuncture stick are the people who can afford it the least. Second, social change has to start everywhere, including at home. Third, my community is not nearly as reliable as I have always hoped it would turn out to be, given all our ideas.

I've been looking at the perpetuation of this blind spot. First, I have to admit my own role in it. I mean, I put these expectations on myself. When I talk to various people I know about dependence/independence/interdependence, part of the flood of response is from the lesbians who have already had to affirm the joining of self-worth with interdependence.

I know there are woman reading this and saying to themselves, "Well, no shit, Sherlock." There are many lesbians in my community who have spoken out for a long time, saying that the whole is greater than the sum of its parts. Closest to home, my girlfriend is a mother, absolutely dependent on a web of support, and responsible for two human beings who depend on her. Complete self-sufficiency is part of what society thrusts on mothers, and she refuses to shoulder it. Poverty is not something anyone can lick on their own. And on and on. Generosity of spirit and material well-being are part of the glue that holds us together. And even when it is not explicit or conscious, no one is doing this by themselves, no matter how appealing that notion is.

Among the stories of the women I know who berate their friends for not changing their own oil, or for relying on their girlfriends to balance the checkbook, are the friends who offer childcare without asking and drop me off at the theatre before parking the car farther away. We're not a community of assholes.

Sounds good, doesn't it? It is good. But what I want to articulate is a place in me, and in a lot of women around me, where this rhetoric breaks down. This rhetoric conflicts profoundly with the language that governs my picture of who I might be as a lesbian. Good lesbians don't need anybody. We can't expect much, and we've learned to take this as a strength. When there are things that could hold me back, and I cling to an ideal of myself doing it all alone, I end up in a crisis of self-*in*sufficiency. When I can no longer do five jobs and fix people's personal problems on the side, I feel worthless. What happened to thinking we all have a contribution to make? Why can't I remember that interdependence is not charity, but unity? Why can't I remember that?

Enter multiple sclerosis. Every person's experience with disability is different, and every person's experience with MS is different. My MS is, so far, not a huge hindrance to my life. I can walk short distances, and read, and stay up late within reason. I cannot, however, do the work I used to do—freelance graphic design and writing—because my memory for detail is sketchy, my eyesight can be terrible, and my waking hours are sometimes limited. Maintaining my apartment is difficult at best, and some of the things I used to do, like strolling on the beach, are gone.

Imagine someone, me, steeped in lesbian culture, finding out she has MS. What is the first thing I do? I try to find things to read. This is my new movement! I am looking for the MS version of *Rubyfruit Jungle*. Instead I find endless homilies and aphorisms, profiles that say things like, "with Jane Doe, nothing is impossible." MS magazines are full of this.

Is it just that I am too jaded to be swept away by another bunch of inspiring truisms?

The magazines and newsletters that I get about MS speak out against helplessness as though being against helplessness were a new idea. There is always an inspirational story about someone with MS who has just taken up ballroom dancing or two full-time jobs. There are aphorisms about believing you can do anything. I find all of this frustrating. I have had two full-time jobs before. I don't want to do it again. I have already read a lot of feminist literature, which is full of very inspirational stories about a lot of women who do a lot of amazing things. I know we can do it. I can do it by myself.

But is it okay if I don't want to? Not all the time?

And where did I get this "by myself" idea, anyway? I think I got this idea from all that reading. First from a wider mainstream—parents, teachers, newspapers—that told me to pull myself up by my own bootstraps, and to admire people who do. Help those who help themselves. Then from powerful, inspiring stories of lesbians that say, "with Jane Doe, nothing is impossible." I bought it. I was going to be Jane Doe.

So when Ms. I-don't-need-anybody gets a diagnosis and she needs people, she is terrified to ask. She/I thinks that that is not the way Jane Doe behaves. She/I is looking for a way to say that asking for help is all right. There are no inspiring lesbian books about this, and the disability stuff she comes across is a) het, and b) going in the other direction.

Stuck. I feel like I am swinging from "yeah, but" to "what about" to "on the other hand" to "of course," and trying desperately to make a direction out of them. There has to be a way out here.

I take those "yeah, buts" and I read those disability pieces again, looking differently. I see that though the overt thrust of them continues to run contrary to this lesbian's yearning for more dependence, the end place is familiar. It's just a question of emphasis. Coming from a situation where they have been told repeatedly that life is over, women with MS are saying, "No, it's not." They are not, however, saying that they are doing everything for themselves now. That might well be impossible. What those articles are saying is that autonomy and dependence can be achieved at the same time, though the stress in the writing is on diminishing dependence to make the balance.

On the other hand, lesbians are coming at that balance from a scale already tipped the other way. There is massive resistance in many of us to the idea of dependence of any kind. There is fear that we will not be able to extricate ourselves from it, that it will run rampant. There is the worry that dependence only diminishes both parties. There is a fundamental agreement to pretend that we don't need each other for anything. It's patently ridiculous, but there you are. I've certainly held up my share of the illusion, so I know it's possible to do.

Hence my stuckness. But there are possibilities here. We have common ground. This is the place where my lesbianism and my possible disability activism meet or collide, and I think, I hope, that if we open up this stuck place, what we might see is that the whole is really greater than the sum of its parts and that a better situation for everyone is possible if we see our interdependence.

This means a lot of value shifts for lots of us. We in North America are immersed in a culture that valorizes get-up-and-go and devalues assistance, and this attitude leaks right down to the bottom of the heap where the lesbians are. But we can do it. Not by ourselves, but we can do it. We do each other's dishes, and we listen to each other's dreams.

*I have MS and my balance is terrible. This summer when I went on holiday, on the first day of the holiday I tripped and fell and broke my foot. I couldn't walk at all. I was in the country, on an island. I could have been hiking and swimming and picking berries, but instead I had to stay in one spot and read books, or be wheeled in a makeshift chair to the outhouse. I loved it. After years of visiting this friend and feigning enthusiasms, and her making every effort to help me overcome my restrictions, I could ignore the issues altogether. I like a walk as much as the next gal, but when it is something I only do because I can, and there is work before, during and after, the walk is just a chore. I have no interest. Maybe I don't like a walk as much as the next gal after all. Maybe I just want to rest.*

*Postscript*

I meant to avoid the topic of that "codependence" buzzword, but I have to say something about it. I hope that all this does is date this essay irrevocably. I hope that the bandying about of this word has already passed by the time you read this.

"Codependence" is a concept that comes from a very specific analysis of addiction and relationship dynamics. I don't even know what it means, exactly. I do, however, know that the word is used freely as an insult. It can mean anything from "I resent how much she wants from me," to "How come she gets so much from her relationship?" to "They should break up." The spectre of being labelled "codependent" is standing in the way of us really supporting each other. I suggest modestly that we make our lives free of "codependence" shorthand, and call behaviors what they are. More words when the arguments happen, but healthier in the long run.

# THE LAWS OF PHYSICS
## A Conversation with D.A. Watters

*This piece was compiled from e-mail written by D.A. Watters to Victoria A. Brownworth over a year's time.*

I live alone in Springfield, Missouri, with my cat, Murphy. I am very happy being able to live without supervision as it shows the mental improvements I have made. Why?

On the day of September 13, 1992, I was a business manager and a college student. That evening I was comatose from a freeway accident where I was thrown eighty feet and landed on my head. When I awoke and spoke five weeks later, I was an unemployed dropout, my plans for pursuing a Ph.D. in astronomy as scrambled as my brains. My left side was paralyzed from right brain hemorrhages; I couldn't propel my wheelchair properly, but moved it backward with my right foot.

My short-term memory was good for maybe two minutes when I was released on December 18. I needed constant supervision. By 1995, I became a loner, living by myself, my short-term having improved so much.

I've collected disability and walked with a quad cane since February 1993. My thinking skills remain poor. By playing video games and watching TV (learning to follow the plots on sitcoms and sci-fi), my memory is almost normal. I do have problems noting small but important details.

I spend most of my time with the TV: cable, VCR, video games and the

Internet on WebTV.

In January 1998, I contacted an old physics professor who had visited me in the hospital five years before. I wanted to let him know I was fine. He followed my home page links and, well, thought they were great. The college was looking for someone to maintain their "teachers" Web site. My professor showed my letter to the dean, who looked at my Web pages and offered me the job. WebTV cannot use the college's FrontPage program, so my dad bought me a computer. I was petrified, but thrilled. As it turns out, I am learning! And remembering!

I still collect disability, as I don't make very much money. But I'm *doing something.* Yes, I have gone from a "vegetable" prognosis to a productive member of society.


I am D.A. Partying used to be my life. I had a good life of going to college and being a business manager. Everything changed with a car wreck. I stopped partying completely because I can't do it anymore. I can't walk without a quad cane and have only one hand that works. But one thing I can do is tell it like it is for me.

I pretend to want to go out in the world. I don't. "No Smoking" signs went up everywhere while I was in a coma. I say it's my disability (left hemiplegia) keeping me home. Well, it is, but I'm also okay with that—there aren't any smoking restrictions in my living room!


The party was over—for me, forever. We broke up into buddy groups with designated drivers for each car. I had come alone, so one car followed us as my designated driver headed down the freeway to my home.

He mistook my rack and pinion steering for manual, and oversteered when we slid on gravel. We drove directly into the median ditch, hitting nose first and flipping the car. No seat belts meant we were thrown through my sun roof as the car landed upside down. He broke his leg and went home from the hospital in a month. I broke my left arm and my right brain. I went home in three months.

The car wreck was fatal. D.A. was dead (no blood pressure) when paramedics arrived on the freeway median. One pounded my chest so hard he broke my sternum and my heart started beating. D.A. was still dead. D.A.2 was alive in D.A.1's body.

I was flown by helicopter to the ER where D.A.2 was not expected to stay alive very long. I did. But I wouldn't come to. I had multiple hemorrhages of my right brain. While I was in a deep coma, my father learned I might not wake up, but if I did wake up, there was a good chance I would be a paralyzed idiot.

I went directly from the ER to the intensive care unit (ICU). My father was out of town when he was notified. He was at a church, preaching, and told to remain there and request prayer. My doctors held little hope for me being alive by morning. They wheeled my comatose body into the ICU after attaching a device to drain the brain fluid that was seeping out of my right ear.

I remained comatose for five weeks. During most of this time, I am told, my eyes were sealed shut by the massive swelling of my face. After three weeks of lying totally motionless and quiet, one day I made a grunt when the nurse took my blood pressure in my left arm, squeezing it with the pressure band. Friends were visiting and told her my left arm had a metal plate with six screws in it. It had been broken twice before and the pain was why I grunted. A note was put on my chart to only use my right arm.

The next week, a new nurse didn't see the note on my chart and used the left arm. This time, I batted her with my right arm, opened my eyes and said, "Ouch!" The corpse had swatted her!

I woke up from the five-week coma and was able to talk. I talked in quotes from TV shows. My memory was only able to find reruns, shows I'd seen many times, like *Andy Griffith*. I alluded to characters from shows, used their phrases and even alluded to plots.

My left side was paralyzed, but I was not a total idiot. I just seemed like one to strangers. Friends who knew what I was talking about understood me. The hospital personnel thought I was out of what was left of my mind. They'd ask a question and I'd respond in a seemingly nonsensical manner. If friends were there who had watched TV with me, they'd know instantly what I meant and that I was making a joke.

That's all I did my first month after awakening—make jokes that alluded to TV shows. This was the only way I could communicate. Most people use TV or movies to elucidate a point—"She loves her home like Scarlet loved Tara." I used TV as my only source of description or meaning—the words would not come, only pictures in my head from TV sitcoms.

I went from ICU to stroke rehab. I was in a daze. I was D.A.2. For a month, I thought I had had a stroke. At that time, whatever was at the end of the tunnel got my attention. I had no "mental peripheral vision." A lot of coma survivors stay in that tunnel. Any excess input confuses them, and they can only do one thing at a time. And it better be only one thing. Don't even think about baseball: Stand, look at the pitcher, hold your bat up, practice swing, watch his arm, follow the ball as it comes toward you, swing the bat to hit it, run to the white square up there before that man gets the ball. Aaaargh. We're still watching his arm.

At one point, I was taken into a room, still not grasping my new situation. The lady had a computer—hooray! I loved computers. I don't exactly remember how the exercise went, but I had to match written words with either spoken words or pictures. I did well and the lady was pleased. So much so that she gave me an IQ test after only three weeks of rehab. She had to read and write for me as I could not see—no thought was given to my needing glasses. No thought was given, also, to discovering my preinjury IQ—it was in my chart. My father told them that my IQ was 212. The new IQ test was given and the lady was thrilled.

"You have a normal IQ! See here on the bell curve, you're near the top—120!!" I was shocked, dismayed and angry at her cheerfulness. She was smiling as she told me I was not a genius anymore.

Two changes that should be made in speech therapy—if someone can't see, get them glasses. And find out a person's IQ before giving them an IQ test.

Occupational therapy (OT) is poorly named. In my frazzled, scrambled brain-state, I thought they were going to make me get a job while still living in the hospital. They should change the name to game therapy.

It was the best therapy I got. My short-term memory got better because I really cared about the time spent playing games. It taught me a good way to wake up my brain cells. The only problem is that OT stopped too soon. The day I understood who my OT worker was and what game we would play, I was "cured." If she had kept coming, I think I would have had enough brains to later not get ripped off in New Mexico (more on that coming up). But I had to leave. I moved back to Springfield and got a Phillips CD-I video game. It has remote control joysticks so there are no wires to trip over. I started playing Jeopardy, moved on to chess, and now have a memory game where I can repeat thirty-three things in order.

Occupational therapy was good—it just didn't know how good it was and stopped too soon. It was like being fifty pounds overweight, going on a diet, losing five pounds quickly, saying, "Wow! Five whole pounds!" and quitting. I needed continued therapy. I have progressed greatly on my own, both mentally and physically, but OT would have helped even more.

When I got out of the hospital, I was thirty-nine and unmarried. My only immediate family was my traveling evangelist father—he could not afford to stay home with me. We shared a duplex: He was on one side and I was on the other. None of my relatives close by were single. What to do with me?

My father looked into a nursing home. Friends who knew me well said, "Ack! She'll never get better unless she's home." Two offered to stay with me. One worked days, the other worked nights, so I would never be left alone.

They took me to physical therapy (PT) at the hospital. I was learning how to walk with a quad cane. I had completed speech and occupational therapy while still in the hospital. I graduated PT when insurance ran out. Good. I hated it. I did more at home with my friends.

I received $110,000 in liability settlements and we moved from Springfield, Missouri, to Belem (near Albuquerque), New Mexico. The move was their way of alleviating my depression. Before the accident, I had been attending school to obtain a second degree in physics, with plans to move to Soccorro, New Mexico. There I had planned to attend the state university and get a Ph.D. in astrophysics, hoping eventually to get to work at the very large array (VLA) telescope there. Now, having virtually no short-term memory, I was extremely depressed—suicidal.

In an effort to help my emotional state, my friends, Tammy and Sue, suggested we move to Soccorro anyway, as I'd always loved the desert. They thought moving cheered me up. I didn't want to be seen by my friends in Springfield in my new condition. Tammy was my lover when I had the wreck. She stayed by me until she moved to Albuquerque and got a new, better job. Turns out, she had just wanted to move. Sue was a gay friend who was a bum. She'd just moved uninvited into my house before the wreck. But it turned out she also treated me the best. She cooked, cleaned, shopped and made me exercise.

Tammy dumped me for her ex from Springfield, and she moved the ex out on our land. I had two rental trailers on my five acres of desert. Tammy moved into one of the trailers with her girlfriend and paid me rent. Then Tammy got a job in the big city and a new girlfriend, and dumped both of us, leaving Kelly (her ex) to live with me and be my caregiver.

Kelly got a new drug-addicted girlfriend and moved her into my four-bedroom trailer. Linda (the druggie) moved in her friend, Dallas, a straight guy. I was going insane. I saw them being "normal" (walking and going out partying) and wanted to be "normal," too. They shot up drugs. That was the only "normal" thing I could do, too, so I started getting stoned. They had to shoot me up because my paralyzed left arm was no use. Then they started in on "Your money isn't getting any interest in the bank. We'd give you more." So I ended up lending them and others $60,000. The rest of the $130,000 (I sold a house and got another settlement for breaking my leg in a hazardous place) was spent in hotels.

Friends from Springfield visited me on January 1, 1995. They found hypodermic syringes in the bathroom I didn't use. They also found the dregs of white powder in spoons. They whisked me away. I spent a month in an Albuquerque hotel on my credit cards. I had spotless credit prior to my car wreck. My future was being pondered by relatives and friends. Nursing home again, thought my father.

I was flown home in February 1995. None of my relatives would take me in as they are all nonsmokers. I had no Medicare insurance for the first two years after I was disabled. I fell and broke my wrist and leg. Hospital, doctor and ER bills combined with three months' hotels, room service and pay-per-view combined with the loans to "friends" led to me paying for credit cards with credit cards.

Back home, my cousin located an apartment with managers there all day. It had a pool, a dishwasher and air conditioning. She arranged for Meals on Wheels and a home health care facility to provide grooming, housecleaning, laundry and physical therapy. I would be well taken care of—the kindness of strangers was much better than that of "friends."

But I didn't like the idea of being alone. Except for the times the bad caregivers had left me alone with no food (I had lost twenty pounds), I had not been alone for almost three years. So I got one of those "Help, I've fallen and I can't get up!" devices for, well, when I fell and couldn't get up. It gave me the confidence to live alone. I did fine. I would fall, but figured out a way to stand again using a sturdy chair. After three months I had never used the "Help!" button, so I gave it up.

I have lived here for over two years. Living alone has been the best mental therapy I have had. I *have* to think, and think correctly, so I do. And it's given me confidence that I never had when I was living with "normal" people. I see their "normalcy" as just a reminder of my inadequacies.

My cousin came for me at one o'clock for my two-thirty bankruptcy court appearance. We were both nervous. She brought skirts and blouses for me to wear.

(Skirts, blouses, money, have I none.) I squawked at the skirt but wore it anyhow to be nice. Lily looked at the brown skirt with black blouse and also squawked. Then I wore my shorts.

At one-fifty we left for the courthouse. Lily always has my handicapped parking tag, but not today. I had a rented wheelchair, as the day entailed a lot of walking and standing. She let me out at the front door and then parked somewhere way out in Egypt. I beeped on the metal detectors and asked, "Will I have to miss my plane?"

We were in front of the bankruptcy room at two-twenty; the lawyer was not. The two-thirty group was set back to three-thirty. I started to turn purple, which Lily knows will soon turn the air blue, so we "stepped" outside for a smoke. Lily is my relative, so you know she doesn't smoke, but she is always ready to go out of her way so I can have a cigarette.

The lawyer walked into us sitting in the sun and said we should go up at three-thirty.

Lily pushed my chair into this huge room with folding chairs everywhere. It was inaccessible until enough chairs were shoved aside. Feet were run over, and then we were in our spot. Most of the women wore pants. In my wheelchair, my shorts were fine and that long skirt would have been, well, run over.

It was like this group citizenship ceremony. The clerk said their names, they stood up with their right hand raised and said "here" and then said "yes" to the "promise to tell the truth" spiel. Everybody stood and said "here" and "yes." It was a conformist group until the clerk said "Anne Watters." I sat and said "yes" and "yes." It was okay. Let the disabled person be . . . she's probably brain damaged.

Then the bankruptor sat at a table and answered some questions. I had expected to be grilled (Perry Mason style) on how I had come to this point. I was all ready with "hospital bills, unscrupulous caregivers, hotel bills, pay-per-view," but that wasn't asked. I was afraid the creditors would want my TV and WebTV. No creditors ever came. I now know firsthand the meaning of "small potatoes." In the business world, I'm not even a french fry.

It was done! I could go home, debt free, to my TV and WebTV. To my recliner, cup of coffee and a smoke. Good riddance. No more credit, no more bills. I am happy. I get enough from SSDI. I am confident in my ability to survive—I am a severe traumatic brain injury survivor and thriver.


A while ago, I went out to dinner with four women who were starting a head injury group. I met one on the Internet, so she invited me along. I went out with total strangers for the first time in five years. I thought I'd be scared but I wasn't. But I was the only one there diagnosed with a severe brain injury. I was the only one leaning on a cane. I was the only one who didn't drive. I was the only one who didn't complain of being treated unfairly at work or school. I can't walk, I can't drive, I can't go to school or work. I was the only one who had nothing to complain about, so I didn't complain. I did, however, decline to join their group. They plan to meet once weekly to complain about the 3D world. Having few dealings with the 3D world, and having no complaints about virtual reality, once again, I didn't belong. Nope, my 3D world starts with Meals on Wheels and stops at my pool!


I'm going to make this a public diary. I plan to write in it whenever anything happens. Yes, I said anything. Many days, nothing happens. My birthday is August 31, and I'm sure I'll want to say something about making it to forty-four. Ask anybody who knows me. I've already lived longer than anyone thought I would.

For my birthday, Lily threw a party with her brother and sister and their families. It was great fun. As usual, a "smoking lounge" was set up outside for me. I leaned on the plastic chair in my smoking lounge to sit down and fell over. As I was lying on the ground looking up into their worried faces (I was unhurt), I said, "I've heard smoking will be the death of me. Who knew?" They all laughed and we had a great time.


As I thought would be the case, not a lot has happened. It is now near Christmas and I have finally done something. I went to my uncle's for Thanksgiving. He doesn't smoke so I had to sit outside where they had set up a fine little smoking lounge. He lives in the country so it was quite pleasant sitting on his back porch in the woods.

I would shut my eyes and remember what I was seeing. That way, I knew I could do the same thing here in my living room. I just shut my eyes in my recliner and I'm out here in the woods!

I also went Christmas shopping the day before. Wal-Mart has those little go-carts, so that's where I go. It was great fun, scooting around and seeing all the new stuff. I go 3D shopping just once a year, for Christmas.

Dad gave me his credit card and unlimited credit. I finally stocked up on things I use every day—soaps, shampoo, toothpaste, etc. I spent over $500. He said, "No way on just toiletries." Well, "Yes way!"

I also bought presents for relatives. And wrapped them all myself. Just one hand and a foot and they look great. I sat them around my tiny artificial tree with the lights and tiny garland. It's Christmas here! I'd like a bigger tree, but it would pose an impossibility if I needed assistance after Murphy (my cat) attacked. She's knocked my little tree over three times now and I've set it right by myself.

It is now December 30. What a Christmas. I went to my cousin Lily's with my dad on Christmas day for dinner. We opened presents. I got purple scrubs, a bathrobe for swimming, three video games, a Rolling Stones T-shirt and CDs, and assorted cakes and candies.

Dad bought Lily's ten-year-old girl a keyboard with keys that lit up to tell you what to play. I played piano before I "lost" my left hand (it's still here, it's just useless). At least, I thought it was useless. That piano (keyboard) has built-in songs and a setting where all you need is to hit a lower key and it will play a bit of song in that key. Change keys, it changes. So I was able to play boogie woogie with my left hand and right thumb. Dad was excited that my brain injury hadn't completely destroyed my musical ability. He asked if I'd like one. I chirped, "Sure." He said he'd look into it. We ate dinner and no more was said about it. That was Thursday.

On Friday, I was brushing my teeth when I heard him use his key to come in. I finished and walked into the hall to say "Hi." He was holding a huge Yamaha keyboard. I got so excited I almost fell down. He also bought a desk to sit it on and a typing chair for me. Two Christmases!

I have my new "piano" in the bedroom. It doesn't have keys to light up. I really don't need that. It does have songs and the "play with my thumb" aspect. I plan to go in and practice scales and stuff when I get offline here. That's why I sent you this. I want all my friends on the Internet to know I have *something else to do now!* So, I won't be online all day. I plan to be here mornings and late nights. I am setting several lists to "no mail" for a while. So if you want to talk to me, write directly to me. I will probably go back to e-mail when all is settled in a few months.

My bedroom has a bed, a therapy bed, a heart circulator (trampoline) and a grand piano (sounds like). It's stuffed. But I may be getting my space problem solved soon . . . more on that in January.


I am moving! I'm just changing my apartment number, same complex, bigger place. I'll have two bedrooms, one to sleep in and one will be my sanctuary. Everything's bigger! And it's only $20 more a month. I'm getting up at 6 A.M. in preparation for moving day, unlike the 10 A.M. I've been getting up, for *The Price Is Right.* I'm ridiculously excited!

I will write more in February. I'm moving January 27th into number twenty-seven. Good luck, eh? And I hope to have yet more good news on the business front next month. Things are really going forward for me. They've just been sitting still—like me—for five years. I'm alive again!!


My life sounds miserable to others. But they're wrong. Before the accident, sitting in my chair and playing on my computer was my favorite thing to do and now it is the only thing I can do. I always hated going to work. Now I work at home and get a monthly check provided I don't go to work. If you ask me, it's a dream come true.

I recently took an online IQ test and scored 144, with 140 ranked as genius. So, I've still got it! And a job!

# A DIALOGUE ON DISABILITY
## To the Person Who "Helps" Me

### Maura Kelly

Recently I was asked if I had trouble "passing" since, other than being in a wheelchair, I don't seem disabled, and the questioner wondered if I had to expend energy correcting people when they expected me to be able to do things I cannot do. This question fascinated and perplexed me.

I've been told many times by friends that once they got to know me—even a little—they would sometimes "forget" that I had a disability. For instance, we'd get to a situation or place where I'd have to take a different route and, for a moment, they'd forget that any "special" (I hate that word) accommodations would have to be made. Even though I usually take a moment to tease my friends when that happens (depending on how close we are), ultimately it makes me smile with great satisfaction. I smile because I don't see their temporary lapse in memory as a sign that they are thoughtless or careless, but rather that they truly see me and not just someone in a wheelchair. They relate to me as Maura, with all of my humor, annoying habits, intelligence, obnoxious attitude, irksome behaviors and generosity; that I'm using a wheelchair to get around is basically irrelevant.

This is not denial on my part, though, since I am more than willing to open a discussion about my disability with my friends. In fact, I'd rather they ask me questions than either remain confused or make a wrong assumption. Usually the discussion takes the form of some simple questions at the beginning of the friendship and never really comes up again.

But I've never even thought of it as "passing" before. I guess I always associated that with race or sexual orientation. I've always used a wheelchair and so no one's ever assumed I was not disabled. Usually the trouble is in getting people *not* to make assumptions about how little I can do. I am the youngest of six kids. No one else in my family has a physical disability and I was mainstreamed in school from the beginning. I associated (and still do) more with them and the other (nondisabled) people around me. I grew up wanting to have mannerisms, style, rhythm, "coolness" and personal power like they did.

I certainly wanted to emulate them more than the pitiful examples I saw of disabled folks on the Jerry Lewis telethons or those sad cases I'd see in the state rehabilitation hosptial, when I went in for physical therapy or surgery, who were there for long stretches of time—and often without family around (nearly institutionalized)—and whom the nurses infantalized a great deal. (I remember being so angry as a child when I would witness a nurse saying something like, "And how nice you look today!" to someone whose clothes were totally out of style and all askew. To me, it was as if the nurses were saying, "Well it doesn't really matter what you look like, because nobody's looking anyway. So instead of helping you to look more stylish or together as we would for anyone else, we'll just patronize you.") In fact, because I hated being identified with these kinds of people, until I was a teenager I didn't even use the word "handicapped," which was the popular term back then. Instead, I'd simply say, "I can't walk."

This is actually ironic, because I now say, "I use a wheelchair" instead of "I'm disabled" most of the time—but for different reasons. When I was young and had little exposure to disabled people, I was basically prejudiced against "them." I mean, hey, we all got the same images—who would want to be associated with some pitiful creature who seemed to have no personal power or dignity—or, God forbid, a sense of humor? As I grew up and grew into myself, I didn't have such a narrow view. Besides, I was going to a college that had a wheelchair basketball team and other folks who had a life beyond their disabilities. So I got used to the word "disabled."

It eventually dawned on me, however, that with all the terms for disabilities—often silly ones and seemingly a new one every week—why not forget all that and deal with what people need to know? If I need to go into a building for an appointment, it's not important that I'm characterized as a "disabled person." It may be important for me, however, to ask about wheelchair accessibility. I don't see myself as a "disabled person," but as Maura, who happens to use a wheelchair to get around.

I believe those new and ever-changing terms—like "differently abled," "physically challenged" and "handi-capable" *(sheesh!)*—are really attempts to make what people see as a "horrible thing" sound nice. A disability shouldn't be thought of as a horrible thing in the first place! And how about that word "special." *I hate that one!* It would be different if people really saw disabled people as special, in a good way. But I think saying "special" is their attempt to make what they really feel—pity—seem palatable. What they need to do is stop seeing disability as an end-all tragedy.

Of course, I am not saying that I never have an issue with having a disability. I definitely do, but it's not all of me by far. It's one of my issues. It's on the large side, but it's only one of several I have, like all of us. For me it's always been, without a doubt, people's attitudes that are most disabling. For example, if I said rigid, consistent prejudice is bad, most people would probably agree with me. Of course, they'd assume that by "prejudice" I meant hateful attitudes toward those of a particular race, religion or sexual orientation. But what if I said I believed that prejudice expressed in subtle acts of misguided, uninformed "kindness" was not only equal to that mentioned above, but potentially more damaging and probably more difficult to change? How many would wonder how I could make such a statement? How many would cite instances where people have been discriminated against, shunned or even killed because of extreme prejudice?

Okay, maybe I wouldn't say subtle prejudice is worse than extreme prejudice exactly, but it is something that needs to be addressed, absolutely. If you shout epithets at someone from your car as you drive by because you don't like the person's skin color, or you beat up someone because of who they love, it will be universally considered a negative act. (Even those who say the victim "deserved it," or in some other way validate the act, probably won't characterize the act itself as a kind gesture.) But, hold the door for someone or let them cut in line at the bank, and who could argue with you that either was an unkind thing to do?

Well, it's not the isolated act I'm speaking of here. I, too, will hold the door for someone who has her hands full, let's say, or let a father cut in line if I'm not in a terrible hurry and he has a cranky infant on his hands. I enjoy performing acts of kindness and—it's important for me to mention this here—appreciate kind acts bestowed upon me.

The difference between a kind gesture and consistent prejudice, from my perspective anyway, is that when I cut someone some slack, I'm doing it based on what I'm seeing in that moment. In other words, if I see someone struggling with the door, I'll offer a hand. If someone has dropped something and her hands are full, I'll offer a hand. If I'm on my way to throw away my fast food tray and my companion has trash, too, I may offer a hand. However, what's so incredibly frustrating to me is when people see me sitting in my wheelchair and immediately make the leap in their mind that I could use some help—regardless of what I'm doing and how easily I'm doing it.

I cannot tell you how many times I've come to a set of doors, for example, at a mall or store and I am easily opening it and about to fly right through, when someone a few doors down practically climbs over me to get the door for me—taking three times the amount of time it would have taken me to go through the door in the first place. I politely assure the person I've got it, but he's already holding the door. Now, in this millisecond, do I stop him and try to explain the underlying insult of infantilizing me? Most likely, the response would be, "But I was just opening the door for you. I was trying to be polite." Now, how do you argue with that? Or should I say, how do you argue with that and not sound like a petty, bitter, disabled little cripple?

People can be so focused on my being in a wheelchair that they don't even hear me saying I don't need any assistance. This is the part that is so demoralizing, that continues to astound and sometimes enrage me. How do I explain this in the thirty seconds I might have before we both rush off in separate directions? How do I tell someone that what she thought was a helpful gesture was comparable to someone locking their car doors for no reason other than a young black man was walking by? That just because a prejudice led to a *kind* act doesn't mean it's not still prejudice? Do I take the time to explain that when they thought they were being generous, the message that really came through was that *I* am helpless and—even worse—not even capable of deducing when I need help and when I don't?

People who hold the door open for me don't know this happens to me seven out of ten times I go to this mall. They can't see the look in their own eyes, a look that tells me that the sight of me triggers some old lesson they've learned that it's nice to help people in need—and that people in wheelchairs *need*, period. They don't know that my frustration or even anger is a cumulative response to the other people who have underestimated me that week, or even that day. And last, they have no idea that what they've done, while certainly with the best of intentions, has actually insulted me on a very basic level.

Now, don't get me wrong. I'm not some bitter, jaded wheelchair-user who turns down on principle alone any assistance offered. If someone is just ahead of me in a doorway and pauses briefly so that the door doesn't slam in my face, that's fine. Hey, I do the same for those behind me. No, I resent the people who feel the need to help me so much—though I am clearly not struggling—that I must wait and allow them to assist me, just to make them feel better.

One could argue that having someone open the door for you isn't such a high price to pay for kindness. And it's not. What is a high price is the fact that it happens fairly frequently. Many of the people I come into brief contact with—it is clearly written on their faces—put me in an altogether different category than they do other people. It's a little offer for help here, an extra hand there. Each is not bad in and of itself—but they add up.

I get those "helping hand" reactions a lot, so while they can be exasperating, they are familiar. When I get a more extreme reaction from a passerby, I am often more stunned than offended. On two separate occasions (so far) complete strangers have told me they feel sorry for me. And that's not even the ironic part: They said it while I was doing something very independently—in one case while I was getting into my van alone and once when I was food shopping alone.

These comments were so uncalled for, so wrongheaded, and reflected so badly on them that I couldn't even get angry. I mean how much more independent could I be? I was alone getting into my van *to drive it*. I was quickly and easily going about my business, but all they saw was the wheelchair. It was such an extremely ignorant reaction, I hardly knew how to respond. If I had had more time, I might have tried to engage these people in conversation—mainly to ask them what they felt so sorry about. And I'm not trying to be funny here. I'm genuinely curious as to what they see of my life in that brief moment that made them pity me.

The obvious answer, of course, is that they saw the chair and figured my life must be pretty empty because I can't walk. I still wish I'd talked to them, though. Asking why they felt the way they did might have gotten them to think a bit differently—even if only for a moment—about what makes a life good and full and what makes it empty.

# HANG-GLIDING
## An Interview with Maura Kelly

### Victoria A. Brownworth

I interviewed Maura Kelly on a sultry night in mid-May. Like most Saturday nights, people were out and about, thronging South Street in Olde City—Philadelphia's version of Greenwich Village. Maura called me on her cell phone from a tattoo parlor. Over dinner with friends, after a long afternoon of organizing the upcoming lesbian and gay pride month Dyke March, one member of her group had decided the long contemplation of a tattoo had ended: It was time. The sound of laughter filtered through our conversation as Maura waited for her friend's body art to be completed.

Nothing in this scene signals anything out of the ordinary for a group of twentysomething dykes out on the town Saturday night. And this ordinariness is defining, because Maura has been disabled from birth by arthrogryposis. Relatively rare, arthrogryposis is a maldevelopment of the joints and muscles that affects the body's joints, muscles (sometimes including the heart), limbs and extremities. A syndrome rather than a disease, arthrogryposis is not progressive, but *is* severely disabling; some whose hearts are impacted die in childhood. Maura has no heart involvement, but her joints, muscles and extremities are all affected. She also has scoliosis, a curvature of the spine quite common in girls and women, both disabled and nondisabled. Because arthrogryposis isn't neurologically based, she has no spasticity. Maura has extensive movement in her arms, less in her legs, though she notes, "If you look closely you can see my toes move." Although limited in her fine-motor skills, she explains, "I can lift things. I could probably arm-wrestle someone—and lose—but give them a run for their money." And she has full sensation throughout her body. But her disability makes her legs too weak to bear weight. Unable to stand or walk, Maura has lived her life from a wheelchair. However, as the raucus call from the tattoo parlor elucidates, any limitations on Maura are external, not internal. "I pretty much do what I want, if logistics allow," she asserted. "I have to consider if I can get into a place because of my wheelchair, if there are stairs, that sort of thing. But my friends don't think 'Maura's disabled'—they just think about whether or not a particular place might be difficult because of access."

Involved in Philadelphia queer politics for several years, Maura has been one of the organizers of the Dyke March for the past two years. A fundraising event was held recently on the second floor of the local lesbian bar, Sisters. "This meant my friends had to carry me upstairs," she noted. "But once up there, I was very involved in what was going on. That isn't my preferred way of getting where I need to go, but it's okay when I'm with friends."

Unlike many disabled from birth, Maura has always led her life from the center of nondisabled society, in part because that was where her family placed her. Though hospitalized for a series of essential surgeries on one knee and both ankles to release pressure on her joints and allow her limbs to straighten more, these surgeries when she was five and seven years old only slightly delayed her entrance into public school. "It was a small school," she said, "but that was because we lived in a small town. I can't really say how it was different than if I had gone to a 'special school,' but when I visited Widener [a school for the disabled in Philadelphia] recently, it freaked me out to think of being there. I thought about writing a letter to complain. It isn't that the treatment of these children is bad, and it *is* important to point out people's strengths, but I think there's a *tone* that goes with telling someone [disabled] how *well* they've done something. It's very infantilizing. I guess what I want to say to people sometimes is, 'Sit down for a second. Do you feel any less intelligent?' But that is the way people talk to [those of] us [in wheelchairs]. At Widener there was no sense of being in the real world. There's this separation between how the disabled get treated and how everyone else gets treated."

The youngest in a Catholic family of six children, Maura said there might have been subtle ways in which her family treated her differently than her siblings, but because she is the baby of the family "it's hard to differentiate why I was treated differently—because of the disability or because I was the youngest." In a family where everyone has his or her own strong and declarative personality, Maura was expected to lead her own life and be independent, regardless of her disability.

Maura was born in a small community hospital where the doctors were unfamiliar with arthrogryposis; there had been no indicators prior to Maura's actual birth of any problems in development. As a consequence, Maura's parents were informed after her birth that she might be seriously brain damaged in addition to her physical maldevelopment. But early on Maura's mother realized her daughter appeared to have suffered none of the brain damage of which the doctors had warned. "Two days after I was born," Maura explained, "my mom said she was crying while she was holding me and her tears were landing on my face. She says I looked up at her then and it was as if I was saying, 'Don't bail on me now, we're in this together.' There's a certain amount of metaphysical thinking there, I realize, but my mom explains it as really intense, with me actually looking into her eyes. She says I was staring her down. And so she says she always knew I'd do what I wanted, that I'd be independent." And Maura's mother fostered that independence in her youngest child. "Her friends would ask, 'Will she be on her own?' She would say, 'I'm not going to be around forever. Of course she'll be on her own.'"

When Maura contemplates disability issues, she often feels enraged by the extent to which the disabled are infantilized. She explains, "Many [disabled] people have no mental involvement—no mental disability—but you can hardly tell because of how they behave. Infantilized behavior has been imprinted on them—no sophistication, a kind of humor without awareness—just like a small child. My mind and words are the strongest thing about me. It's what attracts me to other people, that elusive thing, that spark. It's a real turn-off to me when people don't strive for that in themselves."

An avid sportswoman, Maura goes hang-gliding with a group of disabled and nondisabled friends with whom she also rows weekly. At one such event someone exhibited the kind of infantilized behavior she most abhors in other disabled people. "This guy was chatting in this annoying way to people, like a little kid who just keeps making demands even after his mom has said no," she said. "It was so obvious no one had ever said 'no' to him. He wasn't raised to be responsible for himself, to understand your actions *mean* something. I was disgusted. People need boundaries—it makes them less by not giving them boundaries. By *not* doing this [parents of disabled children] say disabled people don't count enough—they're just like some annoying little insect flitting around that doesn't matter enough to pay real attention to, give real boundaries to. You can't be a real adult, be really part of any group—disabled, nondisabled, whatever— unless you understand how to act with other people, how to *inter*act with other people, how to respect who they are and have them respect who you are."

Disability has never created *artificial* boundaries for Maura, however; she has never separated herself from any activity—work, rowing, hang-gliding or sex—because of being disabled. But her coming out as a lesbian held the same complexities and sense of isolation as it has for many nondisabled lesbians struggling with their sexual identity. "I was barely aware of the concept of homosexuality growing up," Maura asserted. "I'm from a Catholic family. We just didn't talk about sex. Not in a bad way, but we just didn't talk about it. In seventh grade I had a best friend—we'll call her Lisa—who was a year younger than me. We said we were more like sisters, because we tried to describe ourselves as more than friends. She'd spend weekends at my house, vacations. I'd daydream of kissing her, but it wasn't part of our friendship. Then I started to allow myself to think about this. I started to feel so strongly for her that telling her I loved her wasn't enough. The sad thing was she didn't feel the same—we would have had unlimited access to each other, could have had a really involved relationship. We would lay in bed together talking about sex with boys. The most graphic my fantasies got about her, however, was just laying there in bed with her, very close to her."

There were moments of intense sexual and emotional tension between the two teenagers. "I went baby-sitting with her," she explained. "She lifted me [out of my chair] and my face was against her neck. I wanted to just put my mouth on her neck. In a way it was really good that I was in a chair because we wouldn't have had that closeness otherwise." The intensity of her feelings led

Maura to talk to her mother. "I told my mom how I felt about Lisa. She told me my older sister, who's straight, had an affair with *her* best friend—so my mom wasn't too upset. But after that experience I began to wonder if I was gay. In high school I looked around and didn't find anyone else who made me feel like Lisa did. Through the rest of high school I had crushes on guys."

But when Maura went to college, her latent lesbianism came to the fore once again. She always wondered if feelings like those she'd had for Lisa would resurface. "I got involved with a group of sexually ambiguous youths," she said. "I had missed going to this party and heard later that two girls were all over each other. I realized that I really wished I had been there. I wanted to have seen this, to have watched this."

A summer internship at a major corporation brought Maura close to another young woman. "Our friendship was based on discussions of sex," she asserted. "Though the discussions were all about heterosexual sex, they were very charged. We became really good friends and then she came out to me. I had had a crush on this guy all summer and when she told me this I realized I had been concentrating on the wrong person. We had a big group of friends we'd go places with. I'd joke about being her date, but I liked thinking about her being my date. Then she spent the night. I ended up asking her if she had ever thought about it—with me. We didn't go to sleep that night. It was really sweet. We kind of had a fling." And once again, Maura's disability added a bit of *frisson* to the sexual equation. "We had been with a group of friends and we were spending the night together. This friend of ours, this very *macho* guy, carried me upstairs. And I'm looking over his shoulder at her. She later said, 'I felt like he was delivering you to me.' It was fun."

Whether they are sexual partners or friends, Maura finds it "more natural to be involved with nondisabled people because that's how I grew up. Disability isn't my focus. I don't wake up every day and wonder what am I going to tackle today. I don't think about it. I run into obstacles. I was born into this world the way I am and so I am often surprised when places *are* accessible, like the local lesbian bar, Sisters. I can actually pee on the premises! But a lot of places aren't accessible and so there are a lot of obstacles. I guess I just don't focus on them. My family—we're all pretty powerful individuals, we all like control—and so when I was younger and needed to be lifted, it was always very subtle, people were careful and I learned a lot from that. Reducing the humiliation factor by control, surveying the situation. I take responsibility for myself and the situations I'm in, make a decision about whether it's worth it. My father might be a little freaked out by the situations I put my chair and my van in. But since I grew up around nondisabled people, I identified more with them."

Living independently since she graduated from college, Maura works as a technical writer. She shares an apartment with a roommate, but not because she needs help with anything other than splitting the rent—and maybe washing the floors. "I can do everything she does, though some things might take me a lot longer," Maura asserted. "I do the bills, she does the floors. She helps me with the laundry because of how the laundry room is set up, but she isn't actually doing it. I transfer to go to the bathroom and to a shower bench. I feed myself. I don't do a lot of cooking. If there are vegetables involved or chopping it would take a long time. It *is* a factor. I eat take-out a lot—more than I should."

But while she may not spend much time cutting up veggies for dinners in, Maura spends many evenings out. One regular activity she's engaged in is rowing. A Philadelphia tradition for two centuries, rowing has been an integral part of the city's cultural—as well as sports—heritage. Boathouses from various rowing clubs line the Schuylkill River, providing one of the city's most picturesque sights; Thomas Eakins was celebrated for his exquisite renderings of scullers along that river. National regattas are held annually, bringing rowers from around the world to Philadelphia. Maura became involved with the Philadelphia Rowing Program for the Disabled when a disabled friend suggested she come along. "I thought, rowing for the disabled—is this glorified physical therapy? But it isn't, it's the real thing. I love the actual rowing because you're out on the river and if you're watching, unless you know what you're looking for, you wouldn't know we're disabled—it's so smooth." The group has a mix of disabled and nondisabled volunteers, which streamlines some of the work of getting the boats into the water. "I couldn't be a part of it if it wasn't this mix, disabled and nondisabled, rowers and volunteers. I love it, the collective attitude. The people with disabilities are ones like me that have a life. We're not all angry at the world and we're not all defenseless. These are the kinds of friends that I make. We have all sorts of disabilities in the group. For people with spasticity issues, because rowing is a very smooth motion, it can be very therapeutic. We have some amputees. Occasionally there will be a leg with a pair of jeans laying in the back of the boat and it can be a little creepy. We have people who can only use one oar—but there's adaptation for each person. We have people who really compete, some who just like it. For the last three years I've rowed in the singles. You come back sweaty, it feels good. There's no condescending, no pity. Our coach has coached rowing all his life. It's very real. We always have our refrigerator stocked with beer, we throw something on the grill and just sit around together by the river and talk. It's good. It gives me a lot."

Rowing, gliding, political action, sexual expression and work are all aspects of Maura's multifaceted life. Independence has been the defining element of her life as a disabled woman and lesbian. She wishes that were the case for more disabled people; she remains disturbed by how often she sees disabled people infantilized and accepting it. "I live my life pretty much like everyone else does," she asserts. "But I was taught to live that way, it was expected of me. I did it and I like it. If there were one thing I would say to parents of disabled children it's that—don't treat them so differently that you take away their independence. There's a point where everyone has to be on their own. You should be able to enjoy it, not fear it. I like my life—my friends, my work, all of it. Disability just isn't all I am. It never will be."

# AUTOIMMUNE DISEASE
## A Personal Perspective

### Patricia Nell Warren

I had always been iron-clad healthy—ranch-bred from pioneer and Native American stock, a horsewoman and distance runner.

In 1973 I had a watershed year. At age thirty-seven, after sixteen years of closet marriage, I wrote *The Front Runner*, got divorced and came out. That year I ran a hundred miles a week and competed in 10K runs and marathons. The following year I settled in rural Westchester County in New York State, where white-tailed deer grazed in my yard. I added raising show horses to my vigorous life, and two years later, purebred fancy cats. Throughout this time, I worked as a book editor at *Reader's Digest*.

I also spent happy times on Fire Island, partying up a storm. Until around 1978, I was more or less bisexual, dating both men and women. Between dates I watched whitetails roaming the sunny dunes. I had no health problems bigger than bruises from falls off a horse and the occasional tick bite or two. Things couldn't have been better.

Then, quietly, the first shadow of a cloud moved across the landscape of my new life. My immune system was slowly going haywire. I was familiar with autoimmune disease, but only in animals. I was surprised to be battling something I'd seen only in horses and cats.

It wouldn't be until years later that I'd learn of the more than eighty congenital and infectious diseases that can affect the immune system and that seventy-five percent of autoimmune disease occurs in women. In autoimmune illnesses, the immune system starts to attack the body's own cells, tissues or organs. Possibly women's ability to tolerate foreign tissue in our bodies (a fetus during pregnancy) can, if it goes awry, make us vulnerable in a way that men are not. No one knows for certain.

Today an estimated thirty million American women have autoimmune disease—compared to thirty-four million people who live with HIV/AIDS worldwide. According to Dr. Susan Blumenthal, U.S. Assistant Surgeon General, autoimmune disease is the fourth leading cause of disability among women. Yet because of its complexity, and because of lingering prejudice toward female medical needs, women's autoimmune disease has been called by Blumenthal and others, "understudied, misunderstood, often misdiagnosed."

In 1977 I began experiencing recurrent flu, fatigue and joint pain so crippling I could hardly get on a horse. Since I don't enjoy being sick, I soldiered on. With chronic bronchitis and wheezy lungs, I piled up so many sick days that the *Digest* insisted my doctor at Mt. Kisco Medical Group verify my condition. Dr. Russell did, but told me he didn't know the cause. I blamed overwork—my job, my writing, caring for and showing my animals—and a post-closet rush to burn the candle at both ends. If I didn't cut back, Russell said, he would hospitalize me for what bordered on bacterial pneumonia. So I accepted treatment at home.

By 1980, I was also experiencing premature menopause. Running and riding were history. In the cat fancy department, it was exciting to have a national all-breed winner, but I couldn't keep up the pace there either. Then Random House contracted me to write a historical novel, *One Is the Sun,* that celebrated my Native-American roots. That fall, I met a tribal cousin who was a medicine man. He listened to my graveyard cough and said, "You need a healing." Disgusted with white men's medical science, I was open to any suggestions. The ceremony was done by a mixed-blood woman, a renowned crystal healer in the Native world. Crystals, having piezoelectric properties, transmit and store energies, which is why the electronics industry uses them. Crystal healing is thought to correct severe imbalances in the body's "energy centers." Amazingly, after the healing, my lungs cleared rapidly, the joint pain vanished, and my menstrual problems stabilized.

In 1981, I gave up my New York life, moving to rural northern California, where black-tailed deer now drifted past my window. I had been determined to keep stress at bay, but by the late 1980s, stresses had piled up again: I was finishing *One Is the Sun,* working in an artists' co-op in Mendocino County and—to make ends meet—raising one thousand free-range chickens, turkeys, pheasants and ducks. Meanwhile, back in the studio, we twenty-five professionals were constantly (despite hygiene efforts) trading colds and flu. The old shadow of joint pain and fatigue was falling across me again, but this time it also brought sleep disorder, relentless weight gain, profound depression and an irregular heartbeat. More frightening were the "acquired dyslexia" and problems with short-term memory. My brain was now at stake—the seat of learning, memory and, most important for me as a writer, imagination.

Gay men I knew were dying of an immune-deficiency disease called AIDS. I wondered if good times in the 1970s, the men and women I'd dated, had exposed me to the beginnings of the epidemic. Since I'd committed to the politically correct thing of going to women doctors, there were trips to the Women's Clinic in Redwood, California. But my HIV test was negative, and the doctors were stumped.

With *One Is the Sun* published in 1991, I bailed out of both studio and poultry farm. I moved to southern California, settling in rural Malibu, another spot graced by my old friends the deer. Symptoms worsening, I decided the hell with political correctness and went to a male doctor friend, Victor Burner, a Pasadena general practitioner known as a good diagnostician. Pondering my medical history, Vic asked, "Have you ever been tested for Lyme disease?"

I'd heard of Lyme disease, but never suspected it—it causes distinctive skin rashes that I'd never had. My test showed a high titer. Being a research-oriented writer, I learned that Lyme disease is another autoimmune disease. First identified in the 1970s, Lyme disease was recently put on the list of emerging world epidemics. It is caused by a spirochete, *Borrelia burgdorferi,* related to the one that causes syphilis. Ticks are infected as they feed on deer and other mammals that host the spirochete. When the ticks bite humans, they inject *Borrelia*. With time, the spirochete destroys both the immune and central nervous systems. If not treated, Lyme disease can be fatal. Today it is so prevalent that testing is recommended for anyone who lives or vacations in tick country.

By a quirk of fate, I had lived in several Lyme disease hotspots and was probably at risk from my friends the deer! Westchester County is near the original zone around Lyme, Connecticut, where the disease was first discovered. Fire Island was another hot zone; so were Mendocino and Malibu. I probably got reinfected several times. While living in Malibu, I met Lyme activist Barbara Barsocchini, who was convinced that Lyme was epidemic in the area, spreading to domestic pets and creating a new reservoir of animal hosts. The Malibu media and Los Angeles County health authorities ignored her. Finally, the *Los Angeles Times* broke Barsocchini's story.

Millions of tiny spirochetes were corkscrewing into my joints and central nervous system. Fortunately, Lyme disease can be treated successfully with antibiotics, but this treatment is controversial because resistant organisms can mutate (a similar controversy involves AIDS drugs). I couldn't tolerate tetracycline, but a new antibiotic—doxycycline—worked well for me. Barbara told me about Dr. Shun Ling, a Lyme specialist in Tarzana, California. After several months of treatment, my titer fell to the not-detectable range.

Amazingly, over time, the sleep disorder and memory problems disappeared. The brain evidently has an incredible power to heal itself—good news for a writer who treasures her gray matter! But Lyme spirochetes can go dormant, encysting themselves deep in one's tendons. At any time, stress can wake them up. Although I felt much better, the nagging fatigue remained—another shadow was about to reveal itself.

Exactly what triggers the immune system downhill is not always known. Some diseases are triggered by infectious agents. Recent cadaver studies suggest that multiple sclerosis may be activated by human herpesvirus 6 (HHV-6), whereas Epstein-Barr virus (EBV) might be a cofactor in lupus. Other factors might be environmental, including exposure to toxins and pollutants, PCBs, asbestos and pesticides.

Dr. Ling noted I had a high EBV titer. EBV, a herpesvirus, attacks B cells;

its best-known manifestation is mononucleosis ("mono") in stressed-out college students. Less well-known is its broader threat as a possible cofactor in AIDS and other autoimmune diseases. Like Lyme, EBV lies dormant in the body, but stress or illness can waken the sleeping demon. Some experts consider it a cofactor in chronic fatigue and immune dysfunction syndrome (CFIDS)—many people with CFIDS have a high level of EBV antibodies. For me, treatment with Zovirax (acyclovir, an antiviral medication)—and rest—got EBV under control.

For the first time, however, I ran into the fierce politics of disease. While being interviewed by the *New York Native,* I mentioned my health challenges. The *Native* had angered some community AIDS leaders by running articles by Neenyah Ostrom, who was investigating pesky unanswered questions about AIDS, like why some people with AIDS symptoms test HIV-negative. *Native* editor Chuck Ortleb called my attention to a best-selling book, *Osler's Web,* by Hillary Johnson, another medical reporter. With mounting interest, I read Johnson's chronicle of efforts to raise awareness of CFIDS and explore its possible relationships with HIV, EBV and HHV-6. The first clusters of CFIDS cases appeared in the early 1980s, and over seventy percent were female.

I had been diagnosed with EBV, not CFIDS. Yet much of my health history matched what Johnson described. Some researchers consider EBV infection to be a marker of CFIDS, perhaps its cause. Unlike AIDS, CFIDS seldom kills, but the long-term disability and suffering can be devastating. My immune system is naturally strong, and is now repairing itself, so I escaped the progressive disability that puts some women in wheelchairs. Evidently CFIDS doesn't require sexual transmission to spread. Judging by the clusters—whole families, organizations—it may spread, like flu, through simple socializing. Had I caught CFIDS (or EBV) while working in the co-op studio?

CFIDS is still dismissed by some in the medical establishment—the way Lyme was. A decade after the spirochete responsible for Lyme disease was determined, some doctors and researchers were still writing off Lyme-sick women as hypochondriacs. Now CFIDS has been similarly dismissed as a "female psychiatric problem."

Paradoxically, the CFIDS patient movement is uncomfortable about possible links between CFIDS and AIDS. The stigma of HIV/AIDS—the risk of losing housing, jobs, health care, insurance, social acceptance—represents a barrier to gaining national attention for the CFIDS epidemic. On the Internet, some women's autoimmune-disease sites mention CFIDS but not AIDS—a heartless omission when thirty percent of the new AIDS cases reported in the United States are women. Right-wing government officials, the Centers for Disease Control (CDC) and other entities might be equally reluctant to admit that AIDS and CFIDS may be linked, because this link might jeopardize classification of HIV/AIDS as a sexually transmitted disease. What would the fundamentalist Right do if they couldn't point to AIDS as the retribution for promiscuous sex?

Nationally, the reality facing women with HIV/AIDS is finally getting more attention. Yet women who suffer from other autoimmune disorders are still almost "invisible." Barbara Spivack, a Detroit clinical social worker who does workshops for women with autoimmune disorders, notes: "They often look healthy, so people don't understand that they are suffering greatly." It's like trying to wipe a cobweb off your face—you know it's there, but it's hard to see. In the gay community, women with autoimmune diseases are made to feel "less important" than those living with HIV/AIDS.

The statistics are disturbing. If there are an estimated thirty million U.S. women with autoimmune disorders (including 98,468 women with AIDS), and ten percent of these women are not heterosexual, where are the three million lesbians, bisexual women and female transgenders who have CFIDS, multiple sclerosis, lupus, Lyme disease, myasthenia gravis and so forth? Where are their community support groups, patient groups, organizations, book lists, newsletters and Web sites? What is the cost to the gay community of their pain and depression?

Though CFIDS has the largest, most vociferous patient movement in the mainstream, there is no national CFIDS organization in the gay community, though a few local support groups do exist. Internet searches for "lesbians + autoimmune disease" turn up only links for HIV/AIDS.

We already know that lesbians, bisexual women and female transgendered people are ignored by the U.S. health care system. But why do we face this lack of care in our own community?

The article "Invisible Women: Building a Lesbian Health Agenda,"[1] suggests that some of us don't pursue health care aggressively because of poor self-esteem or fear that the health care system will invade our privacy. This article says that, "Unlike heterosexual women who access the health system more frequently due to more pregnancies and the need for contraception, lesbians often skip Pap smears, breast exams and mammograms. . . . One out of twenty lesbians over fifty-five years of age has never had a Pap smear. One out of six has never done a breast self-exam."

Beyond our personal hangups, there are political reasons for this avoidance of the health care system. First, fierce competition for money and grants: Community resistance to new health causes may be motivated by a "protect your funding" mentality. In our small world, money is in short supply; donations to AIDS organizations are down. New diseases such as CFIDS might siphon dollars and volunteers away from AIDS efforts, which still control the power structure of gay community health care. Unfortunately, women in the gay community tend to be less monied than the men, and therefore are less able to fund their own health support.

Second, the gay media focuses on official AIDS policy as set by the CDC. The government has been forced to admit that AIDS affects women differently, that women's AIDS statistics are catching up with men's in the United States as they have worldwide. Yet our media, bookstores and Web links are piled high with conventional information. There is little room here for new information or diversity of views. Journalists who try to discuss unconventional new research or possible links between AIDS and other viral diseases are shrilly denounced as "AIDS heretics" or are greeted with chilly silence. This happened to me in 1996, when I published a *New York Native* piece about my experience with CFIDS. It is shocking to see gay people censoring one another, when we as a community have fought so hard to get First Amendment rights from straight America. There is much to think about as women with autoimmune disease face the millennium in the shadow of a health care system that is increasingly tyrannical, coercive and invasive.

We dare not underestimate that factor called "stress." Stress alone can undermine the immune system. Health management for animals is literally structured around minimizing stress. Again and again, I saw animals with borderline health who went into immune collapse after an episode of stress such as a fight, accident or move to a new home.

Stress permeates American society, and in the gay community, there are additional stresses. Closet cases live in fear of discovery. People who are out still worry about employment, family acceptance, relationships, domestic violence and basic civil rights. Many lesbian, gay, bisexual and transgendered students live with the horrible strains of gay-bashing, family rejection, social isolation at school and economic hardship. Activists live with the battlefield stresses of politics—we spend as much time fighting each other as we spend fighting straight homophobia. And women in the gay community experience economic wear and tear, especially single mothers with children, low-income women and women of color.

As medical cases, we women are individuals, and positive change can start with each of us. Through grassroots networking and Internet communities, we can work toward creating a national organization that provides information to and support for those with autoimmune disease, with an emphasis on women.[2] We need enlightened doctors and health care professionals. We need our national media to be more honest in medical reporting. Last but not least, we need more education about alternative medicine and laws that allow us to use it. In short, women with autoimmune disease are a major demographic in the gay community, challenging its ability to meet diverse needs in education and healing.

Information shared in this article is *not* offered as medical advice. Always consult your physician about your health.

[1] Aradia Women's Health Center. "Invisible Women: Building a Lesbian Health Agenda." *Aradia Advisor* newsletter. http://www.gynpages.com/aradia/Articles.html (April 1999).

[2] The Internet is a good place to find up-to-date information, book lists and support on autoimmune disease. Use a search engine to look for up-to-date links on "lesbian health," "women's health," "autoimmune disease" or specific autoimmune diseases.

Autoimmune disorders include achlorhydria autoimmune disease, Addison's disease, allergies, antiphospholipid syndrome, asthma, autoimmune atrophic gastritis, autoimmune hepatitis, autoimmune thyroiditis, celiac disease, congenital complete heart block, dermatomyositis, discoid lupus erythematosus, Eaton-Lambert syndrome, fibromyalgia, Goodpasture's syndrome, Grave's disease, Hashimoto's thyroiditis, idiopathic adrenal atrophy, idiopathic thrombocytopenia, lymphopenia (some cases), mixed connective tissue disease, multiple sclerosis, myasthenia gravis, myositis, pemphigus, pemphigus vulgaris, phacogenic uveitis, premature onset of menopause, primary biliary cirrhosis, primary sclerosing cholangitis, Raynaud's phenomenon, rheumatoid arthritis, sarcoidosis, scleroderma, Sjögren's syndrome, sympathetic ophthalmia, systemic lupus erythematosus, thyrotoxicosis, Type 1 (insulin-dependent) diabetes, Type B insulin resistance syndrome, ulcerative colitis, Wegener's granulomatosis.

# THE MADWOMAN OF
## *OFF OUR BACKS*

### Carol Anne Douglas

Although I know that many women suffer from depression, psychoses and other mental illnesses, I never expected it to happen to me. I thought that if I ever had a mental illness, it would be Alzheimer's disease, which my mother had for ten years before she died; I fear that I may have inherited a predisposition to that terrible illness. But when madness struck, it was not Alzheimer's.

As a lesbian feminist living a double life—twenty-four years at the newspaper *off our backs,* which pays no salary, and twelve years at my paying job for a liberal nonprofit publisher (let's call it News Pubs)—I felt that my life was somewhat schizophrenic, but I didn't expect literal madness.

Looking back, it's hard to tell when the madness began. News Pubs was changing for the worse. Many people had been fired, including my dearest friend there. There had been a nasty power struggle, in which I supported Tom, my boss, who also is my friend. He won the power struggle, but the place was still full of tension.

I had seen the actual plots accurately, but then I began to see too many plots.

Bill, an editor who had been rude to me, cutting me out of conversations, became more so, no matter how polite I was to him. I was having a difficult time coping with his fierce competitiveness with me and his temper. One day he started talking about a prominent member of our advisory board, who had just left me a message on my voice mail. I was certain that Bill had bugged my telephone.

Terrified, I called a detective agency and asked if they could determine whether someone was bugging my phone. A handsome man who looked as if he were straight out of a TV detective series came to check out my office on Sunday when no one else was there. He said the phone was not bugged.

Then, I thought my home phone was bugged. Then my home and work computers were bugged, and someone was reading everything I typed.

When I told Tom I was afraid my phone had been bugged, he responded gently that my fears sounded paranoid, and he advised me to ignore them. Instead, in a panic, I called other coworkers and asked for their help in stopping the bugging of my phone.

Tom requested that I see a therapist and urged me to stop worrying. I agreed to see a therapist, but only the lesbian therapist I had seen several times over the years, Lorraine.

I began looking for another job, certain I could never forgive Tom for calling me paranoid and not believing me. I went to Lorraine, who listened to me and appeared to believe me.

I told my lover (let's call her Jane) only a little because I didn't want to alarm her. When I had the locks changed and gave her the new key, I said only that someone had been coming into my apartment and stealing things. I became terrified that if enemies did come into my apartment they would take my cat.

Soon there seemed to be more police in the streets and I became convinced the police were after me. Perhaps someone from work had framed me for a crime. The FBI was after me. I wanted to tell them I was not guilty. Why wouldn't they just arrest me and give me a chance to tell my side? But no, they were playing cat-and-mouse games with me, waiting for me to slip and commit a crime. They wanted more evidence. Well, no matter how much they pressured me, I wouldn't commit a crime.

After having my locks changed twice, I stopped. If it was the FBI after me, I thought, they could get in no matter what I did. I believed they had taken over the adjoining apartments and were looking into my apartment, seeing everything I did.

This was not the first time I had considered the FBI an enemy. My first month at *off our backs* in 1973, the Weather Underground (a leftist political dissident group) left us a communiqué to publish. Not long afterwards, someone broke into our office; nothing was taken, but all of the papers were scattered. We were sure it was the government.

Political movements in the seventies were full of paranoia about the government. At *off our backs* we believed our phones were tapped. Once someone claimed that an out-of-town collective member was a government agent. We published an article charging that Gloria Steinem was an agent, and I got a phone tip accusing another famous radical feminist of being an agent (I didn't believe it). Some collective members even insisted we use pseudonyms. When I said that my code name would be "Coca-Cola," I was criticized for lack of revolutionary seriousness.

Of course our fears weren't without some basis: The government *did* question women in feminist communities about the whereabouts of underground activists, and some were jailed for refusing to cooperate. It was not uncommon then to know people who had committed illegal political acts (and I don't mean just sit-ins), and *off our backs* published articles advising women not to talk to the FBI.

I hadn't worried about the FBI in many years, but it was not impossible to imagine that they were out to get me. My straight employer, News Pubs, covered a lot of news about the Internal Revenue Service, and I thought that perhaps the government wanted to take over News Pubs secretly as well as take over the feminist movement via *off our backs.* I had been naive to imagine that I could hold both a straight editorial job and a position at *off our backs:* Now, the government would use me to get at both.

The news stories that came to my desk at News Pubs suddenly seemed so difficult that I found them impossible to edit. I went to Bill and another editor and demanded to know whether one story was fake; the next day my boss had the personnel manager tell me that I had to take medical leave and couldn't come back to News Pubs until a psychiatrist said I was fit to work. I was devastated.

I thought I had been framed and that what I really needed was a lawyer, not a psychiatrist. It seemed that my food and water were being drugged. If I ate or drank anything, I became incoherent or fell asleep, so I tried to eat and drink as little as possible. I thought the FBI knew I hated drugs, and I wanted to preserve my mind more than anything. After watching my mother's Alzheimer's disease, I couldn't bear to have that happen to me. I thought they were trying to force me to surrender and confess to something I hadn't done, but I never would.

Soon I began to fear that the new interns at *off our backs* were police plants out to get me—that a woman on the collective I had always liked before was really an FBI agent. They must have convinced her that I was a criminal and that it would destroy *off our backs* if I was arrested while on the staff, so she was trying to get me off.

My friend Tricia came from Georgia to Washington, D.C., on very short notice because I was so distraught and couldn't tell her over the phone what was happening. I begged her to share all my food and every beverage with me, because I believed they wouldn't drug anyone else; the whole point was to make *me* seem crazy. Tricia agreed, and we split all food and poured our drinks from the same bottles. I ate a little more.

Jane, my lover, looked at me with fear in her eyes. Some friends of hers from out of town had come to visit her, and I was afraid the FBI had told them to turn her against me. One morning I woke up with the terrible fear that Tricia was not Tricia, that someone was posing as her. I felt sick. That very morning, Jane told me she didn't want to make love for a while. I sobbed. I didn't want to, either, because I was afraid the FBI was watching us, but I didn't want her to distance herself from me. I went and sobbed in my bed. If the woman in the next room really had been Tricia, I would have cried with her.

During this time I had been calling psychiatrists, trying to get an evaluation from one saying that I could go back to work, but I couldn't get appointments soon enough with the few who had been recommended by feminists, and others said they didn't do such evaluations. I went to Lorraine, my therapist, and saw to my horror that she, too, had been replaced by someone who looked like her but wasn't really her. I was too frozen to talk and left the appointment early.

The next day, Jane, Tricia (I had decided she was really Tricia and apologized to her for thinking she wasn't) and my friends Jennie and Karla from *off our backs* said they had made an appointment with a psychiatrist at my HMO and would I please come with them right away. They were cheery, and I played along with them, although I was afraid to go to a psychiatrist who hadn't been recommended by feminists.

My friends said the only psychiatrist they could get an appointment with that day was a man. I had not been to a male doctor since I had become a feminist, and I didn't want to see one. I told them that I'd try him, but that I might walk out if I didn't like him and would wait until I could see a woman.

They insisted on going in with me to make sure I said what they thought I should. Jane even told the psychiatrist that I thought my food was drugged. I was very upset that they were making me tell him things I didn't want to tell him. He would believe I had a mental illness.

I didn't like the psychiatrist. He was cold, and when I asked him what his philosophy of therapy was, he didn't seem very forthcoming. He said he was a psychopharmacologist, which scared me. Jane had said that maybe I needed drugs, which had upset me. Being drugged was just what I was trying to avoid.

I told him very politely that I never saw male medical professionals, that it was nothing against him personally (which wasn't true), but I was going to wait until I could see a woman. I walked out.

My friends followed me, and all four of them huddled in the hall of the medical center. They were very upset and told me that because I wouldn't see him, I would have to go to the emergency room. I refused. "Why should I?" I asked. "I'm not shouting, I'm not hurting anyone. Why must you insist that I go to the emergency room?" I said I was willing to see any woman psychiatrist the next day (it was then five o'clock). I was telling them the truth.

My lover said she had reached the end of her rope and might break up with me if I didn't go to the emergency room. Terrified of losing her, I went, though I dreaded the emergency room above all things. I had taken my mother there for a broken arm years before and they had kept her waiting many hours and set her arm wrong, so that it was crooked for the rest of her life. I told my friends that, but they insisted that I go anyway.

The emergency room personnel showed me forms that required me to agree to accept their treatment and to stay until they signed me out. I was petrified. What if they kept me, or put me in a psychiatric ward? What if they never let me out? What if this was just what the FBI wanted? I was afraid they would let me rot there. They didn't have enough evidence to convict me, so they'd prefer to have me incarcerated in a mental institution. There were cops standing around outside the emergency room. Of course I thought it was because of me.

"You don't know what you're doing," I kept trying to tell my friends, but they kept insisting. Once I was in there, they might not be able to get me out, I explained. They said that under the law I couldn't be held without my consent for more than seventy-two hours, but I thought that a lot could be done to me in seventy-two hours.

I knew that lesbians had been abused in psychiatric wards. In the seventies, my first lesbian lover told me she had been given electric shocks at the sight of pictures of naked women by a doctor trying to force her to be straight. My friends didn't believe that she was telling the truth, but I did (and still do).

I didn't think this hospital would do that, but what kind of drugs would they give me? The nursing homes my mother had been in for Alzheimer's had given her drugs that sometimes made her dopey or made her body tremble. One drug made her aggressive and when she began hitting the other old women, the staff tied her to a chair, even though it was the drug, not her, at fault. I had had to fight with them often about overdrugging her. I had no trust in the medical profession—none.

I wouldn't go into the examination room without a friend. The nurse said that only a relative could go with me (heterosexual bias strikes again), so we said that Karla was my cousin.

I thought the doctors who examined me were police doctors. They made me keep repeating what had happened at my workplace again and again. They were trying to build a case that I was crazy. The main doctor was a woman, but she had no bedside manner at all. Karla made me tell her that I thought the police were after me. The doctor said I needed to have a CAT scan. I was wheeled off to a room where my head was stuck in a large tube with odd sounds. I was afraid that they might do something with the sound waves to make me deaf. A friend of mine had lost much of her hearing after improper hospital treatment for a case of the flu.

I clutched Karla and begged her to get in touch with famous feminists I thought might help me, such as Phyllis Chesler (author of *Women and Madness*), if my friends couldn't get me out. While I was between doctors, Karla said she thought I needed an antipsychotic drug. I screamed—I had wanted Karla to go in with me because she had written an antitherapy article.

The tough cookie doctor recommended that I be hospitalized. "No, no," I begged. She said that if my "cousin" would accept responsibility for me, she'd let me out, but only if friends would stay with me day and night. Karla hesitated. She said she would discuss it with my other friends in the waiting room. "Please, Karla, please," I begged. "Don't let them hospitalize me."

After what seemed like an eternity but was probably fifteen minutes, Karla and the doctor returned and the doctor said I was going to be released into the custody of my friends, who would take turns staying with me. I was released conditionally, and I had to sign a paper saying I was going back to the medical center to see a psychiatrist the next day. I also had to promise several other things that I can scarcely remember. Perhaps not to hurt myself? Perhaps to tell anyone if I had any delusions? I did promise to go back to the emergency room if I was in pain. I didn't know what signing the paper meant. Could I be hauled in off the street if I broke the conditions? Who could commit me?

The next morning, I went to see a psychiatrist, accompanied by Jane and Tricia. This time, I asked them not to talk, and they didn't, except to tell the psychiatrist that they loved me and that I was a wonderful person. This psychiatrist, Susan, was a woman with a gentle-seeming voice and face, but I thought she was a fake (or a police psychiatrist) because she sometimes said "um" and "er," and I thought she was mocking my speech patterns. She gave me a prescription for Risperdal, an antipsychotic drug she said would also help me sleep. I agreed to take it.

Friends spent nights on my sofa, supposedly to help me if I had any side effects from the medication, which made me afraid to take it, but I did. Since I believed that the psychiatrist was a cop, I had to take it. The cops might get me and take a blood test to find out whether I was taking the medication. If it made me unable to function, I could always stop, I told myself.

I began to think that these people weren't my friends, but other people substituted for them. I thought my lover wasn't my real lover. I sobbed and sobbed. I believed that the FBI had taken them all away as part of the Federal Witness Protection Program and substituted other people. I wondered whether I would ever see my real friends and lover again. Perhaps not until and unless I went on trial. If only they would charge me and put me on the stand. It would be better to go to jail than to live like this.

I no longer thought of calling famous feminists to ask them to help me. I didn't want them to be "disappeared" by the FBI. Perhaps this was a bigger plot than I realized. Perhaps this was happening to feminists all over the country; they were being disappeared, they were being institutionalized. I wondered whether Mary Daly was safe. Was Catharine MacKinnon safe? Who was left?

Walking to *off our backs* one day, I saw several white cars back up. I thought it was a signal that someone would take away my little white cat. If I left *off our backs,* perhaps I could keep my cat. *off our backs* was my life, and I had thought I would never leave it until it died or I did, but I was afraid that someone was going to hurt my cat. Even if they didn't hurt her, she'd be terrified if she were taken away to a strange place. So I got on the phone and resigned from the collective, asking them to take my name off the masthead. It felt like the greatest defeat of my life. But it appeared that someone had taken my cat away anyway and substituted a cat that looked like her. It was a fairly nice cat, but I wanted my Chloe. I thought the FBI was so cruel, so determined to destroy me, that they wouldn't even leave me my own cat. They were determined to show me my utter helplessness.

I believed they were even trying to take away the satisfaction of reading from me. The *Washington Post*s I got in the morning were full of fake news: For example, I thought that John Denver hadn't really died or that he had been killed to scare me. And when I started to read a book, it seemed that someone had substituted a fake version for the real one.

One night Jane (or pseudo-Jane, as I thought of her) said she was going to bring me dinner, but instead she came with two other friends to tell me I should hospitalize myself because I was so depressed. She talked about my going on permanent disability. They kept me talking for hours. I was hungry and annoyed. It felt like a siege. No, I said, I won't hospitalize myself for anything in the world. Jane again threatened to leave if I wouldn't go, but I told her that tactic would never work again. I was still angry about the emergency room and would never go there again.

Jane responded she would have to take care of herself, then. She was worn out. Fine, I said, take care of yourself, and let me be. When they suggested I should take an antidepressant, I said fine, I was willing to take an antidepressant. I'd take anything that might make me feel even a little bit better. Taking an antidepressant wasn't strange like taking an antipsychotic; many women I knew did. Finally they left.

The next day I saw the psychiatrist, Susan, and she prescribed an antidepressant, Zoloft, and said I should go to a day-treatment program for people with mental illnesses. I asked her if that was the way to stay out of the hospital, and she said yes. Susan said that Jane had been calling her, and I felt I had to ask Susan not to listen to Jane, because she wanted me to be hospitalized. I asked that Jane not be considered my spokesperson and gave Susan the name of another friend, who didn't think I should be hospitalized, as my contact person. I realized the irony in my having championed for more than two decades the rights of lesbian partners in case of illness, but now I thought my doctors were paying too much attention to Jane.

I took the Zoloft, and within hours I felt better. I was able to write, which I hadn't been able to do in weeks. I wrote bitter poetry, disguised by being about Shakespearean characters, and read Shakespeare. I was determined to keep my mind functioning. I would read my books, even if they were fakes.

I was afraid to go to the day-treatment program, but I did. Everyone was fairly nice, though they were obviously trying to brainwash me into believing I had a mental illness. I told them, as I told my psychiatrist, that I didn't have any more delusions that policemen were trying to get me, that I didn't think anyone was trying to get me. I knew what I had to say to keep out of the hospital. I knew that I had to pretend to go along.

My psychiatrist diagnosed me as having severe depression with delusions. The staff at the day-treatment program diagnosed me as having delusional disorder with severe depression. They showed me an article on delusional disorder that described feelings so much like mine that I thought it was an article the FBI had written to convince me I was delusional. I still had no idea I was sick. I was sure that all the staff at the day-treatment center were cops. So were all the other patients. But that wasn't so terrible. I could cope with that and pretend that they were the real thing.

What was much harder was pseudo-Jane. I didn't want to touch her and thus betray the real Jane, even though the real Jane had abandoned me and let the FBI take her away. Sometimes pseudo-Jane said she loved me, and I'd respond, "I love Jane" instead of "I love you." I desperately missed my real friends, who I thought I'd never see again. No matter how nice people were to me, I didn't believe they were who they said they were. I saw them as subtly threatening me.

I felt I now understood how people survived losing everyone they loved in wars. There was still some part of me that wanted to go on though I had lost everyone and everything that was important to me. I felt suicidal at times, particularly the day after I was at the emergency room, but I was afraid to try killing myself because I knew I'd be hospitalized if I didn't succeed. Sometimes I thought I was a fool or a coward not to kill myself because something much more terrible, such as hospitalization or torture, might happen to me, but I didn't anyway. I told myself that it was all right to be a little cowardly about physical things. I was brave mentally.

I wondered how I could live an ethical life while I had to lie to everyone and could trust no one. I hated pretending that pseudo-friends were my real friends, but I felt I had to for self-protection, and I hoped that my real friends would understand. And how could I live a meaningful life without working for the women's movement?

After I had completed three weeks at the day-treatment program, my psychiatrist gave me a clean bill of health to go back to work at News Pubs. I was full of joy when I went back to work. I even believed my coworkers were their real selves. The coworker who had been rude to me before left me alone, and two others who had worked with me closely proved to be true friends and wanted me back at work. I managed to work without saying or doing anything strange, even though I silently believed the FBI still controlled my world. I knew what I had to do to fit in.

It seemed that the FBI had let me live. They had let me go back to work.

Since I had started taking the antidepressant, eating didn't make me fall asleep, so I thought they had stopped drugging my food. Perhaps the FBI would even let me write for the movement. I wrote an article for *off our backs*. The collective agreed to publish it. Perhaps they would let me come to layout weekend and help with layout. I went. Everyone was nice to me. Perhaps they weren't all FBI agents after all. Perhaps none of them were.

Gradually, person by person, I began to realize people were their real selves. By that time I had been taking the antipsychotic drug for nearly two months. All along, I had been watching for signs that would tell me whether people were my real friends or substitutes, asking them questions that only my friends would know the answers to. But even when they knew the answers, I thought that they had been unbelievably well briefed. Nothing convinced me.

One day on a walk by the canal with Jane, she mentioned that on the first walk we had taken together we had seen three different species of grebes swimming there. How could she know something that specific, such a small detail, if she wasn't Jane? But the thought that she might be the real Jane was horrifying, not consoling. Perhaps Jane had been part of some plot against me all along, not a woman who had ever loved me. I suddenly thought that everything she had ever said to me and done with me had been false, that I had been a fool. How could I have believed, for instance, that anyone could think that my hair was beautiful, as she had told me, when I know it is stringy? Now I realized she had been too good to be true.

I can't remember the moment when I realized that my oldest friend, Ginny, was really herself, not an FBI substitute. She had gone out with me often to movies—always one of our favorite things to do together—during my illness. But nothing she said seemed out of character, and one day I realized that she really was Ginny.

The gentlest woman I know, Jackie, was one of the people I had most feared. I had stayed the night at her home and after eating the worst TV dinner I had ever tasted, I had believed she was trying to poison me. Because her cats were timid and hid, I believed that she was a right-wing, anti-abortion fanatic who had stolen pro-abortion people's cats, and that she would steal mine. (I had always been terrified after I heard about "right-to-lifers" killing the cats of an abortion clinic worker.) I had had difficulty finding her house, and I lay awake that night worrying that I had been kidnapped to the suburbs and would never be able to find my way back to the city. On my way home the next morning, I had heart palpitations (probably from the Risperdal) and was convinced she really had poisoned me.

One day I just knew that Jackie was really Jackie. And if she, who I had feared the most, was her real self, then I knew I must have been sick to think that she was not. She was warm and reassuring, so she was the first person I talked to about my illness, even though she was not one of my closest friends. We went out to brunch, and I told her I had been sick and hadn't believed she was her real self. She was astonished, and was very good to talk with. She had no idea that I hadn't known who she was (neither did anyone else, except Tricia, the only one I had told), but she responded with warmth and encouragement rather than fear. I felt so good after talking with her that I wanted to tell everyone else, too, about what an amazing thing had happened to me. But I proceeded cautiously, deciding which person to tell when, because I knew that some people might be more afraid than reassuring.

It was a great shock for me when I finally realized I had really been sick. For several months, everything I had thought was happening was not. I was used to trusting my own perceptions, so it was devastating to realize that I, who had always prided myself on my mind above everything, had been betrayed by it. I, who had rebelled against biological determinism, who said biology isn't destiny, had been controlled by my biology. I had a serious mental illness, probably delusional disorder. I, who had always opposed psychiatric medication, had been restored to my normal mental state by pills. Two pills a day kept my mind and body in balance.

I was stunned by my own frailty. I knew that many people had chemically caused mental illnesses and I had seen some of my friends improve their lives by taking antidepressants, but it can be hard to believe that it has happened to you. In the 1970s, most of my friends and I had believed that all mental illnesses were socially caused, that women came down with mental illnesses only because they were oppressed. We had been very skeptical of the idea that there could be a physiological cause for it and thought that people who focused on that aspect or gave women drugs were just trying to pacify women so that we wouldn't rebel.

Although I was shocked to find that I had been mentally ill, I was also delighted that the rest of the world had not changed. I had loved my life for years—loved my lover, my friends, *off our backs,* my straight job and my interests, like bird-watching. It was indescribably wonderful to know that that life had not somehow disappeared.

Throughout the illness, when people told me I was sick, I had thought, "If only I were. It would be great news if I really were just sick, and I still had my world." So it was a happy as well as sobering realization. Finally, I could say what had happened to me. Finally, I could tell the truth to my lesbian therapist, Lorraine, and my psychiatrist, Susan, letting them know that I hadn't believed in them or told them what I was really thinking. I told them that I had believed that everyone in my life was a substitute. I also told most of the people I had thought were fakes. It was wonderful to live in a world where I could tell the truth. I called all my friends, delighted that they were their real selves. Most of them wanted to talk about it, although a few were a little queasy. It was such a joy, knowing that I was with my real friends. And that my dear cat was my real cat after all. My books had always been my real books.

In recent years, I had become a little bored with writing for *off our backs.* After you have written hundreds of book reviews, it can become automatic. But after having believed I would be prevented from writing for the movement, I felt renewed excitement at realizing that I still could, and have written a flurry of articles since then.

I also began to want to be affectionate with my lover again. I hadn't liked everything Jane had done, but I also saw now that she had practically fallen apart from the strain. Jane had wanted me to be hospitalized because she was afraid I would kill myself; the truth, ironically, was that it was the thought of hospitalization that made me feel suicidal. We entered couple counseling with another lesbian therapist to help us cope with what we had been through.

Jane now understands more about what happened to my mother and why it made me distrust the medical profession and, I hope, how my passionate love for nature made confinement in a hospital seem particularly horrifying. I was used to spending every weekend taking long walks, and I continued that as much as possible when I was ill. Even at my sickest, I found some slight comfort in being outdoors. (Not as much as I had before, because I was afraid that the FBI would damage the parks I loved as a punishment for me.)

I now understand what Jane went through, for I have had the experience of seeing people I love have mental illness and know how frightening and agonizing that is. To my astonishment, I really was helped by psychiatrists. They had diagnosed me correctly and given me the right medication the first time, without experimentation, which everyone says is practically a miracle.

I am also pleased, but not surprised, that my friends stood by me and saw me even when I was ill. Only one woman, who I had not kept up with very well, was so put off by my apparent distrust of her when I was ill that she wants nothing more to do with me. None of my close friends reacted that way, nor did any other friends. Indeed, my friends were afraid I would never forgive them for trying to get me to a doctor and to take medication.

I do appreciate that intervention was needed to get me to a psychiatrist, and I am grateful that my lover pushed for it to be a psychiatrist at my HMO, where it was all paid for. Otherwise, I would have had terrible medical debts to face in addition to everything else. I know from experience what a burden medical debts can be; my family went from affluence to poverty as a result of my father's and mother's illnesses, my mother ending up with nothing but Medicaid and Social Security, which went to the nursing home to pay for her care.

I now realize that I desperately needed drug treatment and would have fallen completely apart and lost my job, my lover and most of the rest of my life without that treatment. I'm glad my friends and lover understood that. I'm also glad that my boss was understanding—in fact, he was the first person who understood what was happening to me—and that he didn't simply fire me but pressured me to get the help I needed.

However, I still think I should not have been forced to go to the emergency room, an experience that was terrifying for me and not helpful. My lesbian friends should have understood my refusal to see a male psychiatrist and believed me when I said I would see a female psychiatrist the next day without having to go to the emergency room. I'm glad they didn't leave me in the hospital when the emergency room doctor wanted to hospitalize me; it might have been hard to forgive them if they had left me. I still see no good reason for the doctor to hospitalize me. I had done nothing suicidal, nor threatened suicide; nor had I done anything even slightly threatening to anyone else. I don't believe that anyone should be hospitalized unless she is violent to others.

My friends now say that they didn't know what to do and shouldn't be judged harshly for trying to do their best and perhaps not always doing the right thing. I can appreciate that, but I would be less understanding if I had actually been hospitalized. My lesbian therapist, Lorraine, and some of my friends were determined to help me stay out of the hospital, and I appreciate that. Tricia came from Georgia especially to keep me from being hospitalized. Unlike the emergency room doctor, my psychiatrist, Susan, has treated me with respect, showing me my diagnosis and telling me what she was doing and what I needed to do to stay out of the hospital.

I believe I was very wise to do everything I could, including lying about what I was perceiving, to avoid hospitalization. As a lesbian feminist, I knew enough to have an intelligent fear of mental hospitals. I also spoke very strongly about being skeptical of drugs and of wanting to take the lowest possible dose, and, fortunately, Susan agreed. I have since spoken with a number of feminists, including those who have written very critically about the mental-health profession, who say that drugs now are very different from what they were twenty or even ten years ago, and that they can be helpful. Phyllis Chesler told me she believes failing to provide needed treatment, which can include drugs, can be as harmful as the mistreatment she has recorded in her writings about psychiatry.

Chesler asked me what age I was when I became ill. When I told her fifty-one, she responded, "Aha, menopause," and I agree. Nothing like this had ever happened to me before. I doubt this mental illness due to a chemical imbalance would have come about now unless it was connected to menopause. I was going through much stress at work, but I have gone through great stress before without becoming mentally ill. The doctors say that psychoses appearing at this late age are relatively rare. But are they just not diagnosed? I had been having hot flashes for about a year before the illness became obvious, but they became worse that spring, as I began to have irregular periods. I felt premenstrual all the time, with no relief. I became tense, more easily afraid and angry beginning in April;

I started thinking people were bugging my phone in August. I am sure there is a connection. And interestingly, since I have been taking the medication, my hot flashes have almost disappeared, as has my heightened state of tension.

I am angry more research has not been done on menopause and mental illness, angry that not one of the books on menopause that I've seen says that there may be a connection between the onset of menopause and the onset of mental illness. Who knows how many women have gone through what I did. I want more women to be aware of the possibility in case they notice they or their friends are going through something similar at menopause. Susan and other psychiatrists at the medical center seem very interested and, with my active encouragement, are looking into the connection between mental illness and menopause.

It is no coincidence that my fears were of persecution by the FBI. It's not unreasonable to believe that radical feminists could be harassed by the government, nor, of course, is it unreasonable for a lesbian to fear mental hospitals. As Phyllis Chesler has demonstrated in her research, including a fall 1997 article in *On the Issues,* women still are being abused in some mental hospitals. In some cases, other patients and hospital staff have abused the women, and no one believes them because they are labeled mentally ill.

The strain of living a double life also no doubt contributed to my stress and eventual illness. Although I have always been out as a lesbian at work and have had good support from my boss and most coworkers, being the editor of a straight though nonprofit tax magazine and being on the staff of a radical feminist newspaper can feel like a schizophrenically double life. Trying to act like a feminist with some coworkers who are anything but is a particular strain.

Although I want to encourage other lesbians to get medical help and even drug treatment if all of the friends they usually trust say they should, I hope no one will construe this essay as suggesting that it's always safe for lesbians to see psychiatrists or to take psychiatric drugs. That's far from the case, though I now think they can be helpful in some cases, and I am grateful I had this help before my illness became even worse. But in the day-treatment program, I met women who shook constantly—and always will—because they had been given Haldol. The doctors at the treatment program were very critical of Haldol, but some doctors still prescribe it. Others patients said their sex lives had been ruined for years.

Even the small doses of Zoloft I am taking have a negative effect on sexual ability, which is infuriating given that I have fought so hard to live as a lesbian. I still feel as much desire for sex as ever, but my ability to have orgasms is impaired, a common side effect of Zoloft. If my sexual response doesn't improve, I shall change medications. Susan supports me in that and is suggesting Wellbutrin as a possible alternative. Drugs are much better than they used to be, but they could be still better, and such research should be an important priority.

Being in the psychiatric day-treatment program was, in retrospect, a powerful experience. I am ashamed to say that it was my first prolonged time (three weeks, all day) of intensely personal discussions in a predominately working-class, African-American setting (the other patients, not the staff, which was predominately white). Many of the patients were on Medicaid. I thought I was empathetic before, but now seeing homeless people feels much more personal to me. I always have given homeless women money, but now I give it to homeless men, too, and am friendlier to them. They could be me. Or they could be like one of the people I liked in the day-treatment program; one had been a homeless, alcoholic man.

I also have a more personal empathy for ill people like the man who shot up the U.S. Capitol (in 1998). True, I never had the least violent impulse when I was ill, but I know what it is to feel that the government is spying on and controlling every aspect of your life and you are helpless to prevent it. I am also more concerned than ever about being a good person. I feel that I have a second chance at life. I still want to do all the things I was doing before, but I want to do them better.

My therapist and several of my friends have told me that I am more emotionally available since my illness. And, as one friend put it, "You write better since you went crazy." I hold back less, because why the hell not be emotional? What more do I have to be afraid of? Actually, I'm very afraid of the possible recurrence of the illness. Intellectually, I can't quite believe it could happen to me again. Surely I was deceived before only because I had no idea that it was a mental illness. Now, if it happened, I would know very quickly and seek medication. People tell me that it isn't that simple, however. I hope never to find out.

Certainly I think I would be readier to listen to my friends if they told me they thought I was becoming ill again. I know they would understand what was happening sooner than they did before.

It appears that I won't have a relapse as long as I am on the medications. My doctors say that I need to keep taking them at least through the menopause years, and then they'll try tapering the dose. If that doesn't work, I might need to be on them for the rest of my life. I have asked whether I might become addicted to the drugs, but they tell me that these drugs aren't addictive. I say that I could become addicted to sleeping well, because I now sleep much better than I ever have in my adult life.

After I gave a talk about my illness at the Cambridge, Massachusetts Women's Center, some kind feminists from Bloodroot Restaurant feared that I had become too comfortable with the idea of taking drugs and sent me information about naturopathic remedies, such as St. John's wort, which I may take someday when I am no longer on my present antidepressant.

Sadly, some friends are afraid that I may become ill again and, perhaps a little afraid of me as a result, watch to see whether I am doing anything unusual. I find that aggravating and frustrating. I need my friends to see that I am not ill now, as most of them do. The hardest part of my illness is not learning my own limitations, but learning other people's.

I've always been out before, so it's important to me to be out about my illness, too, with the hope I might help someone with a similar illness to recognize it. My psychiatrist asked me if I was willing to go before a group of psychiatrists to discuss my illness, and I readily agreed. After discussing my illness (apparently my cure is considered very quick and they are proud of it), they asked me what advice I would give psychiatrists. I said that they should allow people to stay in their own homes, treat them with respect, consult them as much as possible about their treatment and try low doses of medication.

I wrote about my illness in *off our backs* and received more letters in response than I have for anything I have ever written. I think lesbians and feminists are willing to try to understand mental illness because we see its political and social context as well as its biological aspects. We live in a violent, fiercely competitive society—a patriarchy—which isn't good for preserving our mental health.

Any of us can become mentally ill. Fortunately, psychiatry has changed considerably in recent years, at least in some places, and there may be a chance that we can get help for ourselves or our friends if we become ill. However, we should be cautious. I was helped by drugs, but not all drugs are benign. We should be as informed as possible about the policies of the medical practitioners we see and the side effects of the drugs that they prescribe.

Before this illness, I would have done anything I could to keep any of my friends out of the hands of psychiatrists, but now I see that some illnesses require medication. When I didn't believe that people were their real selves, there was no way anyone could reach me until the medication took effect.

Now I am horrified to think of the women and men who need the kind of medication I am taking but do not have adequate medical care to provide or pay for it, as my HMO does. I have always supported nationalized medical care, which all other prosperous nations have, and I do now more than ever.

But such treatment needs to happen in the context of a caring lesbian community that pays attention to the treatment their friend is getting and that gives as much support as possible, as my friends did. Even when one is mad, a warm, friendly tone conveys something, although one isn't sure whether to trust it.

I have just begun talking with other lesbians with disabilities as one of them. Through the Disability Caucus of the National Women's Studies Association, I have learned that there are places where we can get respectful attention for sharing our concerns. I used to report on the caucus from an outsider's perspective, but this year I attended its workshop as one of those affected. The women welcomed me, and now I have a new identity. Accustomed to being out in all my identities, I think it is important to be out in this one as well, to challenge stereotypes and speak up for our rights.

# STILL. FEMME.

## Sharon Wachsler

Autumn 1994. We sit in a conference room at the gay and lesbian health center, among salmon- and beige-toned chairs, walls and carpet: We are ten or so women, tentatively beginning a discussion of what it means to be butch, to be femme, how we arrived at these identities. We are all, in varying degrees, nervous—afraid to offend, steeled to be challenged.

For me, this group, the monthly Femme/Butch Rap, is a realization of a dream. Or, at least, the road to a dream. After several years of searching for my sexual and gender identity, shuffling through many costumes, labels and sexual partners, I'd finally come home to femme. Femme dyke. Femme woman who loves butch women. Political, capable, comfortable—and femme.

But once I had unearthed my identity, I didn't know where to go with it. I wasn't in a relationship, and it was hard to meet other self-identified femmes or butches to date or talk to. The taboo on butch/femme identity made most discussions on the topic turn into heated debates in which political positions, personal repudiations and secret desires inevitably collided, resulting in hurt feelings, confusion and more battle lines. Tired of my role as champion and educator of butch/femme identity, I sought community. Thus, with community-building in mind, I and several like-minded women started a regular discussion group for femmes and butches.

Now, at one of our first meetings, we were getting to know each other. I don't remember most of what we said, but I remember one woman in particular with soft red hair. She said she had a disability and it made her question her identity as butch. Wasn't the butch supposed to be the do-er, the protector, the one who says, "Let me get that for you, honey?" Wasn't she supposed to be strong, independent and self-sufficient? Yet, she admitted, living with chronic pain and fatigue, it was she who often sought comfort, who asked her nondisabled femme partner for help, who even appreciated it when a man held the door open for her. She wondered how to maintain her butch identity in the wake of disability.

I remember thinking, "But you're still butch; it's part of your essence. It doesn't matter what you do." I remember thinking, "I guess that's not a problem if you're femme." I remember the silence after she spoke, the murmurs. I don't remember anyone else saying that they struggled with the same issue.

I wasn't everybody's idea of a femme. Walking to the subway station on my way to a party one night, feeling tough and sexy—ultimately femme—in my black jeans, leather jacket, and motorcycle boots, I was accosted. I was wearing silver earrings that hung to my shoulders and red, red lipstick, but the man who drove his Buick slowly next to me for two city blocks jeered, "Butch! Hey, butch! Where ya going, butch?" I was more amused than scared. Femme enough for lesbians to mistake me for straight, straight people clearly had no problem discerning that I was queer.

I took to calling myself a "power femme." It accomplished what I'd hoped for—allowing other lesbians to perceive me as strong and capable, yet entitling me to wear thick lipstick, tight, black miniskirts and dance close with a butch partner. Calling myself a power femme silenced my fears about being seen as a will-less trinket and satisfied others' curiosity about how I could be a self-defense instructor in the afternoon, yet go out in heels at night.

When I was seven years old, I bought a poster that showed a frog in midair, leaping from one lily pad to another, his eyes bulging with shock; the second lily pad was too far away for him to reach. The caption read, "Just when you think you can make both ends meet, somebody moves one of the ends."

My journey to sexual/gender identity seems to have been a series of shifting lily pads. Fortunately, the water has been warm and I've been a good swimmer. When I was eighteen I came out as bisexual. At twenty I came out again, as lesbian. In between I fluctuated between flannel with fatigues and lime-green miniskirts with leggings. I'd tried to be butch, yearned to be femme and finally struggled my way into an identity: From 1991 through most of 1995 I was a power femme. Then, in October 1995, the lily pads were pulled clean away and I fell into the deep, murky waters of illness and disability.

I was diagnosed with severe chronic fatigue immune dysfunction syndrome (CFIDS) and multiple chemical sensitivity (MCS). Lying in bed day after day I watched the trees outside my window turn gold, then thin-limbed and spare, and finally become glazed in city snow, and I wondered what would become of me. I had lost almost all the control and independence I'd enjoyed when I was healthy. I could no longer work or go to school, do my own shopping or cleaning, go to restaurants or parties, nor even visit friends. As the cornerstones of my identity were ground under the relentless wheel of long-term illness, I sifted through the sands for the pieces of myself I could recognize, trying to pull myself together.

My identities as worker, writer, lesbian (or any kind of sexual being) all had to be either discarded or reimagined. Among these self-definitions was "femme."

The process of building identity can be so gradual and organic that the elemental building blocks may be invisible. But when a radical shift shakes down the foundations of identity, those individual pieces fall into the light and beg to be examined. This is one of the gifts of sudden disability—the chance to discover parts of yourself that were hidden in the flurry of "normal" activity. I had never given much thought to what exactly made me femme. But when I lost the markers of femme identity, I missed them terribly and wondered if I *was* still femme.

One of the most upsetting losses was makeup, specifically lipstick. Because of my chemical sensitivities, I had to throw out all my personal-care products, including perfumes, hair-styling aids and cosmetics. Applying makeup had been the finishing touch of my beloved ritual of getting dressed up to go dancing; I'd "femme out" in clingy club clothes, made up and bejeweled.

Since becoming ill, that entire experience is inaccessible to me. I cannot wear most of my club clothes because they retain chemical odors. I cannot wear some of my boots or dress shoes because of problems with dizziness and muscle coordination. I often cannot comply with many normal social expectations because of the physical exertion required by standing, making conversation or sometimes even sitting up. In fact, because of environmental barriers, I cannot attend most social events, be they meetings, political actions or parties.

I realized that most of my femme identity was bound up in those narrow social contexts—getting dressed up, going out, being among other queer women—and in the "props" of those contexts. Now that I could no longer attend those events or wear the clothing, makeup and accessories that went with them, was I still femme? Where is the meaning in being femme if I am absent from the queer women's community and have lost the markers of femme identity? My hair tangled, my body limp and sore, my skin splotchy, I wondered if I would ever look *good* again. Was there any point in being femme if I were unattractive and inert?

With the flashier, sexier aspects of my femme role buried, I found myself grasping for any active role that could help me define—and value—myself. Yet, I discovered that some of the more subtle "domestic" aspects of my femmeness were lost to me as well—caretaking tasks like driving a friend to the doctor or cooking dinner for a girlfriend were simply not possible anymore.

Ironically, while scrambling for evidence of my femmehood, I was also mourning the devastating loss of those traits that, before my illness, had kept me from being "too femme." Where I had previously seen myself as tough and self-sufficient, I was now physically and mentally weakened, as well as dependent on others for money, food, transportation and household help. As a nondisabled woman I had used the redeeming qualities of strong will and body to make femme identity acceptable. Left with the choice of being a non-power femme or nothing at all, I knew that I was—and must find evidence of my being— a femme. Yet how, or whether, I could find my femme self, I did not know.

❖

I was certainly not alone in this search. Adrienne Asch and Michelle Fine, in their book *Women with Disabilities: Essays in Psychology, Culture and Politics,* describe the phenomenon I struggled with as "rolelessness." They explain that the way women are able to attain social power or status is to excel in the traditionally masculine realms of workplace or academia or in the traditionally feminine (and less valued) realms of relationships and the home. While disabled men may be able to retain the benefits of maleness—and many try to be as rugged, virile and high-achieving as possible—disabled women who are unable to fulfill either gender role are left in a state of rolelessness, a psychosocial netherworld. Asch and Fine have found that disabled women tend to respond by becoming ultrafeminine, although the authors add, "Why this is true is left to speculation." My reasoning is that it's because extreme femininity is the only role possible for some of us. After all, needing assistance—whether physical or fiscal—is ultimately perceived to be girly.

Yet, as a lesbian with a disability, the solution of being ultrafemme is even more complicated. I don't get the kudos granted by mainstream society for attracting a man. Nor do I win the admiration or recognition of my lesbian sisters—I am not the strong, athletic, independent woman our subculture says we are all supposed to be. Additionally, as I am single and unable to be in public or meet new people (except in the doctor's office)—my sexuality is almost entirely theoretical—there can be little sexual reward for my femmeness.

How then have I maintained, even reclaimed, my femme identity? One important step has been to organize social events that I can participate in—low-key events that I hold in my home or the one other MCS-accessible location in my vicinity (a Jewish house of worship and study). These are enforced fragrance-free events in places with comfortable couches, where I can rest, if need be. By networking with other women with MCS I have also discovered catalogs with safer makeup and clothing. The clothes, made of organic untreated cotton, are dull and uniform, but at least they are new. The makeup, while less toxic than most commercial cosmetics, still aggravates my symptoms, but for special occasions I endure the discomfort for the pleasure of looking the way I want. Thus, every six months or so, I can play a version of the "party femme" I used to be.

I've also learned that it is possible to be a nurturer to my loved ones; I just need to do it differently—with more planning, less energy and generally lower standards. I can't drive anyone to a dreaded doctor's appointment, but I can talk to them on the phone when they get home. I can't cook dinner for the holidays; but given enough advanced planning, I can usually bake a great dessert.

Still, these solutions are the stuff of special occasions. They cannot feed and sustain an identity over the long haul of solitude and inactivity. It is a truism for any person newly disabled that constructing a new life and identity means learning how to become a *human being* rather than a *human doing*. As I lost the transformative powers of places and objects that made me feel femme, I had to find the essential femmeness within me.

That drive is part of my intense need—when so much else has been stripped away—to maintain the few things that are meaningful and indestructible: my values, thoughts and feelings. When I am in deep pain or illness, or simply wending through the endless solitary days, I cling to myself as my best and truest resource. I have had to become the essential me—pleasuring myself with my own jokes, conversations and ideas. And I've discovered that I'm great company.

One shockingly wonderful discovery of my adaptive femme nature is that I now embrace some of the very aspects of femme identity I'd once found demeaning or irrelevant. Accepting, and even asking for, help, taking care of myself and adopting a softer approach to the world—moving and speaking more softly—have all become important parts of my life. Sometimes I tickle myself with the idea that I've become the ultimate feminine stereotype of a bored, lazy housewife: I lie around all day talking on the phone and watching TV!

At the end of the day I cannot say what really makes me femme; certainly there is little enough outward proof aside from my long hair. I only know that I am. I feel that I have a femme essence or spirit. In the way that I move, my sense of style, the way I speak and interact with others: It is always there. Even when I can't express this energy as I'd like—those times when I have no energy at all—I know it is only submerged, not absent. I carry my femmeness inside me like a red satin cushion. It comforts me. It gives me a place to rest. It sets me aglow with color. And I know that when it can, my femme flare will emerge glittering. Maybe not as brightly as before but in certain ways the more precious for its survival and my transformation.

# COMPLICATIONS
## The Deaf Community, Disability and Being a Lesbian Mom— A Conversation with Myself

Vicky D'aoust

This essay is mostly about me. But it is also about how I connect to a world that includes my daughter and excludes me. While I am writing about my experience, I am also hoping to represent some of what my daughter has been through. I am a mom. I am a lesbian. I am Deaf and I have a Deaf daughter. I also have other disabilities. My identity is usually most aligned with being a mother. I often claim to have more in common with single moms than with lesbians without children. My social and political connections are primarily with people with disabilities and with the Deaf community. It is important to note that these are two separate groups I am a part of (or not a part of). Many of my friends are lesbians or bisexual women and my sexuality is a big part of who I am, especially during those times when I actually have sex.

In the Deaf community, passing on Deaf culture is highly valued. And certainly Deaf heterosexual couples who marry find themselves hoping to have Deaf children or pressured to try for Deaf children. Chances are pretty slim that this will happen because most deafness isn't hereditary. So when a Deaf person adopts a Deaf child, as I adopted my daughter Marianne, it is seen as a culturally supportive decision, especially if that child is someone who may become a leader in the Deaf community. Adopting Deaf children with disabilities, like physical or mental disabilities, is not given the same high ranking but is still valued. I don't see the same value placed on children in the lesbian community. Despite the numbers of women who want to adopt or who have children, there are a lot

115

of lesbians who don't want to be around children. This has made it hard for me to interact in social situations. I did not adopt Marianne for the status or even just because I wanted to have a child. I did not adopt her to start a family or even to share myself with someone else. I adopted her out of pure love and the desire to spend the rest of my life supporting her. I truly feel that she and I chose each other and that our adoption, though no better or worse than others, is unique. Notice that I call it "our" adoption rather than the adoption of Marianne, because I feel that it was a mutual act.

I was not disabled when I first met Marianne, nor during my early years of raising her. Her first image of me was as a mother and as a woman who is Deaf and can still talk. She also saw me as a leader, a coordinator of events, someone who was extremely well-recognized. Marianne traveled with me to many Deaf events and was the star of the party often enough to get used to national attention.

My disability, complicated by depression and a lack of mobility, changed that and put her in a very different position. I no longer traveled to those meetings. I had a hard time expressing my needs around my disabilities to the Deaf community, and some longtime Deaf friends stopped being there for us. At school, where Deaf children still don't want to be identified as being disabled, I was and am stigmatized as a mother in a wheelchair or as someone who walks funny. The Deaf kids would point and say, "That's Marianne's mom." Marianne defends me but she is hurt, maybe even more hurt by the exclusion on the basis of disability than by my lesbian identity. Not too many of her friends point and say, "There's Marianne's lesbian mom."

As the mother of a Deaf child, my sexuality is presumed to be hetero and this helps me maintain some status and privilege in the Deaf community and in society at large. Most Deaf children have hearing parents and do not learn sign language until after age ten. So when a Deaf adult has a Deaf child, the Deaf community welcomes them in a special way. It matters very little to the Deaf community if you have a Deaf child through adoption, artificial insemination or through sex with a man. Deaf children of Deaf mothers learn sign language as young children, have good role models and often excel in academic and social activities.

My daughter is adopted and although she has a wonderful social network, she is not doing that well in school. My daughter is part of a community that welcomes Deaf people as members, but does not have the same history of dealing with other differences. As a lesbian, I have found that some parts of the Deaf community are tolerant, accepting and even supportive of various sexual orientations, while parts of the leadership and the grassroots are as homophobic as mainstream society. As someone who was not out to everyone, I was nervous about the impact of my sexuality on my daughter, and how it might affect her membership in the Deaf community. I was scared to date Deaf women, and even interpreters, because the community is so small that just a single night spent with someone would be generally known by the next day. I isolated myself from a lot of potential allies because I was worried about the negative repercussions for my daughter.

There were days when Marianne came home from school saying that someone had called her a lesbian or a fag and I was terrified it was because of me. Usually it was just the typical school-yard taunt: spaz, geek, lesbian. My daughter is also a member of a racial minority and already stood out from the white kids in the school. I really resisted making it harder for her than it already was. I did date hearing women, had poor communication and even poorer relationships, and basically ended up as a nonpracticing single lesbian, unless you count masturbation.

I found my lesbian identity mainly through romantic novels and identifying with the guy, wishing that I could be kissing and fondling the woman in his arms. I found my lesbian identity through the women's movement and, more specifically, the disabled women's movement, where I met strong outspoken lesbians, but where I also met women who I became lovers with. This solidified my lesbian identity. Having sex with lesbians made me feel more like a *true* lesbian than just someone fantasizing about women and masturbating over the fantasies. I have spent years being single, drooling and lusting after women. This experience of desire always renews my lesbian identity. If I think a particular woman is cute and I want her to talk with me, then I feel like a dyke. I think having sex is important, but the lusting is also a key.

But my being a lesbian is not the only difference that has affected my identity as a Deaf person or even my identity as a woman. I also have other disabilities. There are several and they vary in severity—I have mobility, visual and respiratory impairments. I also have a psychiatric disability which most members of the Deaf community are not aware of but which has affected how I connect to the world and to the lesbian community.

When I participate in Deaf community activities, I am visibly different from others because I use a wheelchair. Deaf people are not disabled and I am a Deaf person with disabilities. As someone who was Deaf first, before becoming disabled, I can slightly understand the perspective of the "we are not disabled" motto, because when I was not physically disabled, I did not feel an affinity or common bond with wheelchair users. I did identify with French or Spanish speakers or anyone speaking a language other than English and with Blind people who read Braille or formats that are alternative to the printed word. The issues I identified with concerned information, communication and language. My experience as a Deaf person was an experience of culture, fun, partying, political networking and sometimes discrimination. It was not in my experience to feel "disabled" by deafness even though I acquired my Deafness (as opposed to lost my hearing) as a teenager. Most Deaf people do not consider themselves disabled, not because they hate disability or think disabled people less worthy, but because they do not feel "disabled" by being Deaf.

Because I had learned to talk, had been through most of my education in a hearing school and was socialized as hearing, my deafness is called late onset. The Deaf community understands deafness mostly by language and less by age. If you acquire deafness after you can already talk and read and write, you experience late-onset deafness. If you do not yet have a mastery over your home language, it's not late onset. My identity was developed while I was a camp counselor at a summer day camp. Attending a national conference with all Deaf people made me want to belong. After working for a year at a school for the Deaf in Jamaica and realizing how truly different hearing and Deaf people were, I realized how happy I was being a part of the Deaf world. It gave me a strong sense of belonging and pride. As I could not really be out as a lesbian in Jamaica, being Deaf was my strongest identity.

I am Deaf. Culturally, that means a big capital "D." I use sign language, interpreters, a TTY. I cannot hear on any phone or with hearing aids, and I am often in Deaf-only conversations with friends and my daughter. However, I was not born Deaf and this serves to lower my status in the eyes of some of the Deaf community. This is in part because I can talk (well) and interact with hearing people who do not sign. My daughter, on the other hand, does not talk and does not interact with hearing people who do not sign. She is also Deaf, but she was born Deaf and has always been in Deaf schools. She and I only use American Sign Language (ASL) and she rarely participates in mainstream activities, unless her friends are with her. Her friends are almost exclusively Deaf. Two of them are hearing people who can sign.

The easiest way to explain these cultural nuances is this: Little "d" deafness refers to loss of hearing of any degree. Some people are really deaf and cannot hear at all and others can hear with hearing aids. They are deaf. But being deaf with a little "d" does not mean you belong to Deaf culture. The capital "D" culturally Deaf people are people who voluntarily and purposefully identify as being Deaf and as feeling part of that culture. To do this they must meet certain criteria. Sign language use is the main requirement—even a profoundly deaf person who does not use sign language but who wants to hang out with capital "D" Deaf people will not really belong with them. So, fluency or good use of ASL is requirement number one. The second requirement is a sense of collectivity, belonging and community. This is something less tangible but very important, something that allows us to hug each other and recognize each other in foreign countries, and to simply connect. This includes connection with family members who are not deaf (children of Deaf parents can be considered part of the capital "D" community, as can some interpreters). The third criteria is debatable but important: Deaf culture and the members of the Deaf community do not identify as being disabled. They often refuse to be categorized with that population, even though they sometimes benefit from disability-related privileges like vocational rehabilitation or subsidized equipment. This is important because it causes a unique schism between the Deaf and the deaf. Lower-case "d" deaf often do associate with being disabled because they do not see themselves as members of a linguistic minority, but as people who have hearing loss.

I think there is a similar viewing of homophobia and lesbian and gay cultures by some Deaf communities. For those in the Deaf community who think that lesbian and gay people have a culture and are truly a community, there is encouragement and outright support. There are gay and lesbian interpreters, Deaf people, deaf people and family members. The Deaf community, like all others, is diverse and has some people who are left wing, some who are right wing and others who are moderates. But in the Deaf community there is also a strong movement of both Christian fundamentalists and radical Deaf manualists. These populations are the strongest advocates of homophobia. They spread negative messages about gays and lesbians and often ostracize Deaf members who are out or are assumed to be gay or lesbian. The Christian fundamentalists who are homophobic are usually homophobic for religious reasons; the manualists are more homophobic because they want the Deaf community to be proud and "pure" and untainted by difference or "deviance." Homosexuality is seen as similar to disability, something to be distanced from and something not to be connected to the Deaf community.

My daughter does not have any disabilities (besides being deaf if you consider being deaf a disability). Because I use a wheelchair, my daughter is also restricted to many of the places that I go, because if it's not accessible for me, it's not accessible for her. We boycott restaurants or services that do not provide physical access (like we could go in if we wanted to!) and we do not go to events where there is smoking, large amounts of perfume or cats. I have significant allergies that result in asthma. My limitations, health or mobility related, also limit my daughter. Or I should say, societal inaccessibility which restricts my participation also restricts the participation of my daughter.

Some of the places I do not go because of access issues include the local lesbian/gay bar, the local lesbian/bisexual/transgender community action center, the annual lesbian events and the Pride parade. I do not always want to take my daughter to these events and she does not always want to go, but if I did want to take her and the event was not accessible, then neither of us would be able to attend.

Being a lesbian mother is very important in how I connect to my daughter. It means there are no fathers or male lovers around, and it also means she does not have answers to the fill-in-the-blank forms sent home from school. My daughter has been exposed to women's community events and disabled women's events for so long that she assumes that all women are lesbians. If she sees a book with the word "woman" or the woman symbol on it, she calls it a lesbian book. When we head to a Women's Craft Fair, she calls it a Lesbian Craft Fair. In her eyes, and in her life experience, being a lesbian is central to being a woman. However, she does not think of herself as a lesbian even though she is quite certainly a young woman. In many ways, I think she understands lesbian to mean "strong women with short hair," because she points out women on the street saying, "dyke...dyke...straight." She is sometimes right. I have short hair now, but during the time I raised her I mostly had shoulder-length hair and was not particularly obvious about my sexuality in terms of clothing and persona.

I am out in some circumstances because a girl has to have sex sometimes. I want to be attracted to women and I want them to know I am open to having a sexual relationship. This is a harder task than you might realize when you are Deaf and sitting in a wheelchair. There is an assumption of inability and, perhaps, of disinterest. I am very politically active and usually articulate in academic settings, so some people think I am too "head" oriented to think about my body. How wrong they are! Part of the passion that drives my intellectual work is my sexuality. I want to be able to be sexual and not hide it. I want to make love, have sex, get laid, and maybe even say no to sex once in a while. I want to do these things because women turn me on, because my body yearns to be touched and satisfied. I want to be a lesbian perhaps, in some small way, because I have been told not to be. I have been told that Deaf people do not want to be associated with yet more "stigmatizing" characteristics. I have also experienced the exclusion and outright discrimination from lesbians and bisexual women who look right through me or above me.

About nine years ago, I gave up on the idea that another woman could make me come in the way I wanted. She might please me, excite me, and I would love the licking, hugging and kissing, but it was my trusty vibrator and being alone that I resorted to for my actual climax. I find it extremely difficult to meet new lovers. Almost eighty percent of the women I have ever slept with were friends or people I first knew politically and then we decided to have sex together. It's been very rare that someone who doesn't already know me approaches me for some kind of flirtation.

The one advantage I have over many people who are Deaf and disabled is that I am in a leadership position. I like power and power attracts women. For example, if I am training at an event or presenting at a conference, women feel like they have permission to approach me for "legitimate" reasons that have nothing to do with sex, and then we can flirt and feel excitement. After that, it's usually lots of Internet hot and bothered sex before the next actual physical meeting. I have found that the Internet makes it a lot easier to develop that playfulness. It helps avoid the initial questions and issues raised by disability. I have not slept with or had relationships with nondisabled women. My sexual partners have been almost all either Deaf, disabled or in some way identified with the movement (one was an interpreter).

I like being a top. I like being in control. I like being the teacher. I like showing women what I know. I can really get off by pleasuring other women. I like the look on their faces, the feel of their nipples and the wetness of their bodies when I am touching them. Because I like that control and because I like to enjoy other women's experiences, I don't really miss it too much if I am not on the receiving end. I have my trusty vibrator when I want to come. I get too dizzy, and feel too sick, asthmatic and exhausted if I have to be fucked or be on the receiving end of any kind of active sex. I admit to liking necking as long as I can come up for air, but anything that requires aerobic activity is out for me, although not for my partner.

I need to be out enough to say who I am, yet close enough to that closet to protect my daughter. She will soon be an adult, and maybe then I will be less frightened about the repercussions of my actions. Maybe not. I do know that when I am out and about and want to have sex and be openly lesbian, I want access. I want to be able to read the erotica, see captions in lesbian movies, have interpreters at lesbian festivals and have ramps and elevators and smoke-free venues. I am not being demanding or even unreasonable. I am saying I want to be who I am without fighting every step of the way.

My Deafness makes it difficult to have a decent argument with hearing people. My physical disabilities make it difficult for me to "go in anyway, despite the stairs," and my other disabilities often make it impossible for me to respond under stress. Put these together with being a mother and you get complications.

I cannot change who I am and, in fact, I don't want to. I am a whole person with multiple identities and issues and priorities. Who I am in various situations changes depending on the company I keep. Even my daughter, who knows me better than anyone else, sees me taking on the roles that different situations demand. I take on "the mother" in a parent-teacher interview or "the Deaf advocate" at a Deaf conference. She knows and I know that none of these are the whole of me. To be a happy, whole person rather than a paranoid one, society has to change. Lesbians and the queer community have to release their dogmatic attachments to who is and isn't a real lesbian. They have to accept motherhood, lesbian motherhood, Deafness, disability, ethnicity and inter-racial relationships. It isn't just the lesbian community that needs to figure this out. The Deaf community needs to get its act together and realize that disability is not a horrible thing and that being Deaf and disabled is possible. They have to get that being a lesbian or gay person is not deviant or evil but is as much a cultural minority status as Deafness. The Deaf community, which already seems to support Deaf mothers and Deaf children, has to open up more to people who are learning to sign or who cannot sign but wish to learn more about the Deaf community. This flexibility or openness is key to allowing our communities to thrive instead of shrivel.

In considering the disability community, I have a problem because I don't think there is one disability community. I identify most with the disabled women's community and the independent living communities, but there are many more. There are the political disability advocates, the sports advocates, the cultural activists and others. But in all its forms, the disability community needs to get together with Deaf people and learn what we mean by cultural identity and learn what we mean when we say we aren't disabled, as opposed to arguing that Deaf people just don't understand disability. And as for homophobia, the disability community has a vested interest in ensuring that gay and lesbian rights are enforced as much as disability rights, especially since homosexuality was once a psychiatric diagnosis. We all need to work on our relationships and our knowledge. I don't want to be a partial person. I want to be a whole person. I don't think ramps, interpreters and perfume-free environments are going to be enough. We need actual change in how communities think, behave and act. Perhaps the biggest obstacle of all is that these attitudes are what prevent us from being whole.

# TWO COMMUNITIES
## Lesbian and Deaf Cultures Meet

*The following transcript is adapted from an episode of the public television series* In the Life, *which focuses on lesbian and gay culture and issues. The issues raised by the lesbian couple interviewed define much of the debate within Deaf culture over whether deafness is a disability or simply an alternative culture, not unlike lesbianism. The interview was conducted by the show's senior producer, Katherine Linton. It is important to note that the Deaf women and their daughter communicated in American Sign Language (ASL), which was interpreted by a speaking narrator.*

*With increased funding,* In the Life *hopes to add closed-captioning services for Deaf and hearing-impaired viewers in the near future. Access* In the Life *at their Web site: www.inthelifetv.org.*

**Katherine Linton on-camera:** Sometimes we can explore another culture without venturing far from home. This segment takes us into the world of lesbians who are Deaf, people who share a language and experience unfamiliar to most of us, but see this as a challenge and definitely not a handicap.

**Narration:** Deaf lesbians and gay men were a visible part of the 1993 March on Washington, exhibiting pride in their identity and culture. Like gay men and lesbians who belong to other minority groups, deaf men and women live in more than one world. Where they feel most at home may be surprising.

Gallaudet University in Washington, D.C. is the only undergraduate university in the world for the deaf and hard of hearing. It was here that Candace McCullough and Sharon Duchesneau met. Candace is now back at Gallaudet, working on her doctorate in clinical psychology, and Sharon works as a mental health counselor. The two live in Bethesda, Maryland, and are the mothers of a two-and-a-half-year-old girl.

**Sharon:** We discussed it and we really wanted to have our own child. We discussed who the donor should be. We wanted our child to know the donor. We wanted the donor to allow our child to meet him, if she wanted to. We didn't want to keep this a secret from her. We also wanted to know the donor's medical history.

**Narration:** Sharon and Candace were looking for a donor that would enable their child to share their unique culture.

**Candace:** It was important to us that the donor be a hereditary deaf person since we would have a better chance of having a deaf child. This doesn't mean we wouldn't have wanted our child if she had been born hearing. We would have loved her just the same. So we asked him and he agreed and we worked out all the details. Everything went as planned. The day our daughter was born we felt that she was deaf. We tested her hearing by turning up the TV to a loud roar and she remained sound asleep. She was tested at six weeks, and it was confirmed that she was deaf. We were thrilled.

**Sharon:** Having Jehanne has brought us more out into the open about our relationship, our family. We don't want to keep this hidden. We don't want her to grow up embarrassed or ashamed about her family. It's our responsibility to let people know who we are and that we are proud of our family. This started with letting people at school know. We're lucky that all the parents were supportive and accepting of us. One of the teachers even wrote a supporting letter for us when one of us went through the adoption process. That was very nice, and we feel very accepted by the school and by the other parents.

**Narration:** It was important for Candace and Sharon that their daughter was born at home, surrounded by a support system of other women, women like Jan Delap, Jehanne's godmother, who lives with them and takes care of Jehanne while her mothers are at work.

**Candace:** Some people ask me what I'll do if kids tease her about having lesbian moms. I know that may happen, because kids can be cruel at times and they tease other kids about many things like wearing glasses or having divorced parents. So I'm not worried about the teasing. I expect it will happen, but our job is to teach her how to deal with it in the right way. I think Jehanne will develop a gift of sensitivity to others, because of being different. She'll be a good person, I hope.

**Sharon:** I grew up in a hearing world, struggling and feeling frustrated, trying to be a hearing person until about seven or eight years ago. I don't want Jehanne to go through that struggle over speech and feel incompetent. My whole childhood I wondered what was wrong with me, why was I different. I didn't know until I entered the Deaf world. Finally, I understood. It was all about communication. I was finally able to relate to others on the same level. That's what I'd been missing.

**Candace:** I want to say something about self-esteem. If you're told it's bad to be deaf, it's awful and very deflating to be constantly told you must be like hearing people. It's the same with gays and lesbians. If you are constantly told you must be straight, and you struggle to be straight, deep down inside, you don't feel good about who you really are.

# FLIRTING WITH YOU
## Some Notes on Isolation and Connection

### Eli Clare

All weekend we have been shouting slogans, singing songs, blockading door-ways, being rude to cops, making as much noise as possible with the intent of disrupting the national Hemlock Society convention. Fifty crips and our non-disabled allies in all, we make it known in no uncertain terms that physician-assisted suicide and euthanasia put our disabled lives at risk. We say "NO" loud and clear to Dr. Faye Girsh, head of Hemlock Society USA, who has said in support of "mercy killing":

> A judicial determination should be made when it is necessary to hasten the death of an individual whether it be a demented parent, a suffering, severely disabled spouse or a child.

We call ourselves "Not Dead Yet," and when all the other slogans and songs dwindle away, we simply chant and sign, "We're not dead yet. We're not dead yet."

Amid all the chaos—making placards, strategizing, figuring out how to get into their conference rooms, passing out handcuffs to wheelchair users so that they can lock their chairs together—you and I keep returning to each other. We flirt and joke and talk: talk about class, disability, queerness, writing, the freak show as crip history. Talk and talk and talk. You—a fat, queer, radical crip femme—as our blockade progresses, you park your three-wheeler among the jam of wheelchairs, lock your brakes and defiantly fold your arms across your chest. No one can get around you. Me—a gimpy butch, shaved head and one ear pierced, shaky hands and slow speech—I'm a walkie: a crip who walks rather than rolls. Today the cops would love to arrest a walkie, easier than finding wheelchair-accessible transportation to the police department, easier than figuring out how to unlock wheelchair brakes and steer the power chairs of noncompliant gimps. So I hang back and watch, do support work, shoot the breeze with our lawyer, scope out which entrances are still unlocked. This is civil disobedience crip style.

Through it all, you and I can't get enough of talking, laughing, trading stories about queer community. I walk you back to your van at the end of the day. You call me a gallant butch. I give you shit for generalizing about femmes. You tell me about growing up white trash. I talk about being taunted. Your eyes take me in. I smile in return, my wide lopsided smile.

Sunday, as the convention winds down, we sit outside the hotel and make noise using whistles, air horns, tambourines, our voices hoarse after two days of protesting. You and I watch Sean, a six-year-old kid with cerebral palsy (CP) in his bright red power chair. He wears a "Crip Cool" baseball cap. His brothers hitch rides on the back of his chair. His nondisabled father wears an ADAPT T-shirt and has trouble keeping up as Sean motors through the crowd of gimps. We both know he could be another Tracy Latimer, a twelve-year-old girl with severe cerebral palsy, killed by her father, who says he did it only to end her unbearable suffering.

Something about how Sean moves—his wrists bent at odd angles, arms pulled tight against body, tremors catching his head—feels so familiar to me. His CP and mine are so far apart, and yet in him I can see my reflection—hands trembling, body slightly off center, right shoulder braced. You lean over and ask, "What would it have been to grow up like Sean in the middle of crip community?" I can almost hear all the stories rise untold around us. I say, joking, "Don't push it. You'll make me cry, which I don't do often and never in public." You respond, laughing, "That's what all butches say. But I know, you just need a pair of loving arms." I try to banter but can't, feel a lump form in my throat. I just look at you and start chanting again, "We're not dead yet."

❖

In the backwoods of Oregon, in 1969, I started the "regular" first grade after a long struggle between my parents and the school officials who wanted me in the "special education" room. When I was two, my parents had taken me to a state-run hospital where a seemingly endless number of doctors, physical therapists, speech pathologists, psychologists and who-knows-who-else put me through a battery of tests, designed, I suppose, to figure out what was "wrong" with me. I didn't yet talk and so was given an IQ test that relied not on verbal skills but on fine motor coordination. And I, being a spastic little kid with CP, failed the test miserably. I simply couldn't manipulate their blocks, draw their pictures or put their puzzles together. In the end they diagnosed me as "mentally retarded."

Nonetheless, four years later my parents won their struggle with the school district. They insisted on another IQ test. And I, being a white kid who lived in a house surrounded by books, ideas and grammar-school English, a disabled kid who had finally learned how to talk, scored well. It also helped that my father taught in the same district and that the first grade teacher knew my family and liked me. The school officials relented: I became the first disabled child to be mainstreamed in the school. Eight years later, the federal government finalized the Education for All Handicapped Children Act and Section 504 of the Rehabilitation Act, the first laws requiring public schools to provide quality—and when possible, integrated—education for all disabled kids. By the mid-1980s mainstreaming happened with some frequency, even in small, rural schools, but in 1969 I was a first.

No one—neither my family nor my teachers—knew how to acknowledge and meet my particular disability-related needs while letting me live an ordinary, rough-and-tumble childhood. They simply had no experience with a smart, gimpy six-year-old who learned to read quickly but had a hard time with the physical act of writing, who knew all the answers but whose speech was hard to understand, who continually tripped and fell but wouldn't stop playing hard, who needed more time to complete everything—school assignments, chores at home, the daily tasks of dressing and eating—but *could* do those things with enough time.

In an effort to resolve that tension, everyone ignored my disability and disability-related needs as much as possible. When I had trouble handling a glass of water, tying my shoes, picking up coins, writing my name on the blackboard, no one asked if I needed help. When I couldn't finish an assignment in the allotted time, teachers insisted I turn it in unfinished. When my classmates taunted me—*retard, monkey, defect*—no one comforted me. I rapidly became the class outcast, and the adults left me to fend for myself. Still, I put as much distance as I could between myself and the kids in "special ed." I was determined not to be one of them.

In the working-class fishing and logging town of my childhood, many of the men had work-related disabilities: missing fingers, arms and legs, broken backs, serious nerve damage. A good friend of my parents had diabetes. A neighbor girl, seven or eight years younger than I, had CP much like mine. My best friend's brother had severe mental retardation. And yet I knew no one with a disability, none of us willing to talk, each of us hiding as best we could.

No single person underlines this ironic isolation better than Mary Walls, who joined my class in the fourth grade. She wore hearing aids in both ears and split her days between the "regular" and the "special ed" classrooms. We shared a speech therapist. I wish we had grown to be friends, but rather we became enemies.

*Mary, if only we had taken the boys on, those who knew the litany best— rocks and erasers, the bruising words. Instead the taunted turned: your paper-thin voice reaching across the school yard, my shaky fists answering back.*

I now understand that Mary lived by trying to read lips, and my lips, because of the way CP affects my speech, are nearly impossible to read. She probably taunted me out of frustration, and I chased her down, as I did none of the other bullies, because I could.

There were only a few things I knew about disability. The long, slow process of teaching my tongue to talk, my feet to walk, my hands to write. The frustration and shame of coming up against things I couldn't do. How the word "retard" could slice to the bone, a sharp, sharp knife. Above all else, I wanted to be normal, to not be handicapped—the "polite" word used to describe me. The rest was written in code. The code of missing arms lost in sawmill accidents. The code of I can't ask for help because then someone might notice something is wrong. The code of I want to cut my right arm off so it doesn't shake. The code of maybe I can will away the tremors.

> *Mary, I have always felt that you and I were lonely bodies, the only two. But in actuality the dangerous, back-breaking jobs of logging and mill work assured us plenty of company. Not like Ted Gromm, an African-American kid adopted into a white family, the only person of color in our high school of two hundred, our town of a thousand. We could have had each other if only we had found a way not to fight. Mary, did you feel as alone, as singular, as I did? I don't know.*

I never asked because to ask would have been to break the silence, to challenge my deep desire *not* to be disabled. Although my isolation was real enough, my attempts to pass, to be "normal," were all illusion. A crip kid whose hands shake, speech slurs, feet trip doesn't have a chance. But I tried; oh, did I try.

I remember the year my teachers placed me in "special education" for gym class. Finally they recognized that although I was a tough tomboy who climbed trees, loved my bike and slingshot and spent long afternoons at the river, I just couldn't keep up physically with my nondisabled classmates. Gym class, where I tried my utmost to play kickball, softball, tag football, had become a particularly embarrassing and shameful place for me, and so, for gym class, I was put in with the "special ed" kids.

Being with Carl Marshfield and Susie McCall, Doug Johnston and Kathy Green, mortified me. They were the "retards," not me. *Retard*—I hated that word so much. I heard it all the time, as a taunt on the playground, a curious question on the street. I know now that the politics of who becomes labeled as having mental retardation and who doesn't are complex, a politic as likely to depend upon class and race as it is upon any particular cognitive, developmental or learning disability. "Special ed" classrooms have been, and still are in some school districts, a dumping ground for poor kids, kids of color, particularly those who don't speak English, and kids with a variety of disabilities, all of whom learn more slowly or differently than kids in "regular" classrooms. I know now that my mortification is called horizontal hostility. Gay men and lesbians disliking bisexual people, transsexual women looking down upon drag queens, working-class people fighting with poor people: Marginalized people from many communities create their own hierarchies, and the disabled are no exception. I know now that much of my need to separate from Susie and Carl, to think of them as "retarded," came directly from my parents. In their scramble toward the middle class, my father, raised poor in rural North Dakota, and my mother, raised working-class in Detroit, placed supreme value on education and intelligence—not working-class savvy but academically groomed logic. So even the *suggestion* that their eldest child was mentally retarded terrified and insulted them. And as I tried to make sense of my CP, I absorbed those attitudes.

But at the time I knew only that I was mortified. I feared that the word I hated so much might stick if I hung out with Doug and Kathy. I didn't want anyone to know that I joined the "special ed" class once a day, even if only for gym. I would, come gym time, walk as casually as I could across the playground to join Mrs. Lewis's "special" section, hoping none of my classmates noticed my absence. Yet in spite of my mortification, once I was there, I had fun playing Twister on rainy days, tag and catch on sunny ones. I could keep up, even excel. No one laughed or tried to hurt me. But always at the end of gym class, I'd walk back across the school yard, relieved to be rejoining my nondisabled classmates.

The summer between seventh and eighth grades, I met my first dyke, had a hopeless childhood crush, started to know I was queer. That same summer I went to the University of Oregon for yet another round of diagnostic evaluations. After several days of being poked and prodded and asked a million questions, I got my first orthopedic equipment: heavy, leather-covered cuffs that strapped on to my forearms. They weighed several pounds a piece. The physical therapist said they would help control the tremors in my arms and hands, making tasks like eating and writing easier. I hated them because they were hot and uncomfortable, because they made my CP that much more visible, because I didn't want to have to explain.

My parents insisted I wear the cuffs at school, an idea I was utterly opposed to. But I lost those fights, and so every morning before classes I'd slip into
the restroom to strap them on, pulling cloth covers over the leather and Velcro,
unwilling to even put them on in front of other people. I spent the year, a thirteen-
year-old, trying to hide the unhideable, not knowing what I could ever say to my
classmates, teachers, parents. Years later my mother, cleaning the bin where she
stored potatoes, found one of the cuffs, misshapen and dirty. I must have put it
there one day in a fit of rebellion, pretending to have lost it, smiling quietly to
myself when everyone seemed to forget. What I would have done to dump my
CP in that same bin.

After the action is over, a group of us roll and walk and drive to the mall to find
some lunch. Sunday afternoon, an upscale mall, five crips, two service dogs, one
nondisabled lover riding on her boyfriend's lap, and one very out dyke personal
attendant: This is material for a hilarious comedy. People gawk; people turn
their heads; people get out of our way. We meet the staring head on, seven of us
taking up so much space.

Over pizza and root beer, you ask me, "Do you pass," then smile, "I mean,
as nondisabled," both of us knowing I never pass as straight. I don't know how
to answer. I could tell you about the brief moments before I open my mouth
and folks hear my slurred speech, before my hands start shaking, before I take
the stairs carefully, one by one, using the handrail for balance. In those moments I probably do pass, but then they're gone. I could tell you about not knowing why people stare at me. Are they gawking at the cripple, trying to figure out
what's "wrong" with me, or at the transgendered butch, trying to figure out
whether I'm a man or a woman? Or are they simply admiring my jean jacket, my
stubbly red hair, my newly polished boots? I could tell you about how I mostly
don't see people gawking at me. I have built the stone wall so high. I could tell
you about all the years I wanted to pass, and failed, but tried to believe that I was
succeeding.

I no longer want to pass; that much is easy. Fifteen years after answering
Mary Walls's taunts with my fists, I made my first friend with another crip, slowly

finding my way into disability community. I've come to appreciate the tremoring arm, the gnarly back, the raspy breath, the halting speech, the thin legs, the milky eyes, the language that lives not in tongues but in hands. Somewhere in there, my desire to pass as nondisabled—really to *be* nondisabled—reluctantly let go but at the same time left its mark. Today, even as I sit here laughing with you, queer humor sliding across crip humor, all my close friends, the people I call chosen family, are nondisabled. Often I feel like an impostor as I write about disability, feel that I'm not disabled enough, not grounded deeply enough in disability community. Isolation and connection tug against each other.

I never feel this way about queer community. Even as a rural-raised, mixed-class (working class/lower middle class) person in a largely urban, middle-class community, a gimp in a largely nondisabled community, even when I feel queer among queer folk, I know without a doubt I belong. My butchness, my love of dykes and queer culture, my gender transgressiveness all make my connection to queer community unambiguous. But with disability community, it's a different story.

Inside your seemingly simple query—*Do you pass as nondisabled?*—live a dozen questions. What does it mean to be disabled? Which experiences shape a disability identity? What are the differences between me and you: me a walkie and you using a chair, me disabled all at once at birth and you disabled in progressive steps through your adulthood, me securely employed right now but with a long history of trouble finding work and you fighting with Medicaid and SSI? How does my college education, shaped in part by the early decision to mainstream me, impact my experience of disability? How do I answer these questions honestly without separating myself from other disabled people?

It would be easy to call myself a privileged crip and leave it at that. After all, I have a decent job at a time when some of us work in sheltered workshops, earning only a few dollars a day, when the unemployment rate among disabled people is seventy-four percent. After all, I live in a house of my own choosing when many of us are homeless or locked away in nursing homes, group homes, state-run institutions, our own parents' back rooms. After all, I don't struggle daily with issues of accessibility—I can always get into the building, use the restroom, board the bus, use the phone without a TTD, read the signs not in

Braille. It would be easy to call myself a privileged crip, but since when are housing, decent jobs and basic accessibility privileges? Are these not rights we should all have? Instead I'm faced with finding my place in a community with a complex criss-cross of differences and similarities. Where do my privileges exist? Where do they not?

Sitting here, being loud and rowdy with other crips, our food eaten but no one wanting to leave, I feel connected. I feel at peace with being a crip. Sitting here with you, I realize I'm not the only queer gimp in the room. It's so familiar, being the only gimp in a crowd of queer folk, the only queer in a room of disabled folk, the only crip in my daily life. I catch your eye again. You raise an eyebrow as if to say, "What next?" I simply grin.

I feel connected here, but yet when I go home tonight, the action done, these rabble-rousing gimps headed back to their homes all over the country, I'll slip back into the nondisabled world with relative ease, an ease that reflects yet another difference between us. This morning before we started making noise outside the convention, you came back from Burger King fuming. Some snot-nosed manager had given you and your service dog grief about blocking the entryway with your three-wheeler, had been barely willing to serve you, a simple trip to get a junk-food breakfast turning into a royal pain-in-the-ass. Unlike me, you rarely slide smoothly into the nondisabled world.

But once I am in that world, I often feel alone, different, the only one. I am reminded over and over that I move more slowly, talk more slowly, carry myself in ways different from everyone around me, and reminded that difference is not valued but mocked, not respected but used as leverage to give certain groups power and to marginalize others. Alone, different, the only one. Me the butch so deeply embedded in queer community, me the crip so loosely tied to disability community—I feel the legacy, the legacy of being the first one in that backwoods school to be mainstreamed, the shadow of my deep desire to be "normal," even as I flirt with you, gimpy butch to gimpy femme.

# WHO CHOOSES?
## The Debate over Eugenics and Euthanasia

Victoria A. Brownworth

$D$r. Jack Kevorkian was convicted of second-degree murder in April 1999 and sentenced to fifteen to twenty-five years in prison in the euthanasia death of Thomas Youk, a fifty-two-year-old Michigan man suffering from ALS (Lou Gehrig's disease). Kevorkian had videotaped the euthanasia and had given the tape to the CBS News program *60 Minutes*. The day after the program aired, Kevorkian was arrested and charged with murder in Youk's death. In the aftermath of the trial, many (including Youk's family, who had contacted Kevorkian at Youk's request) argued Kevorkian's conviction would set the right-to-die movement back decades.

The right-to-die movement has spread throughout Europe and the United Kingdom over the past thirty years and also gained strong support in the United States, which now has its own branch of the Hemlock Society, a right-to-die group founded in England by Derek Humphry. Concerted efforts by members of the Hemlock Society, AIDS and cancer activists, hospice workers, nurses, health care professionals and many others in the United States have resulted in a series of attempts to legalize euthanasia through getting the issue on the ballot. Thus far, only Oregon has enacted right-to-die legislation. However, public opinion polls consistently indicate Americans favor choice when it comes to determining how and when they die should they be suffering from terminal disease or intractable pain. Further, several reports in major medical journals, including the *New England Journal of Medicine* and the *Journal of the American Medical*

*Association (JAMA)*, show many physicians are already performing covert forms of euthanasia with terminally ill patients by increasing morphine dosages until a patient dies.

For over a decade Kevorkian, a former pathologist who has not been licensed to practice medicine for over a decade, has been performing what he has termed "assisted suicide" for people who are seriously ill or disabled and have chosen to die but who are unable to access the means with which to commit suicide on their own. Kevorkian provides the lethal cocktail of several drugs for a client choosing to die but does not administer the lethal cocktail himself—the client does this with a machine Kevorkian invented that injects the drugs into the client's bloodstream. By his own admission, Kevorkian has conducted nearly a hundred such assisted suicides, most in the last five years. The majority of his clients—predominately women—have suffered from progressive diseases like rheumatoid arthritis and multiple sclerosis (MS); a few have been cancer patients and one, a former high school football star, was a quadriplegic. Kevorkian's clients seek him out; he insists he interviews each potential client before determining whether or not to provide his services; he claims to regularly turn clients away if they do not meet the criteria he has established (but has never actually revealed). Nevertheless, at least one of his clients was found after her death to have no actual physical disease, though she was severely depressed and under treatment for depression at the time Kevorkian assisted in her suicide. Kevorkian, who operates in his home state of Michigan, had been arrested and tried several times for his role in these assisted suicides, but never convicted. He has repeatedly asserted that the state's failure to convict him remains the strongest indicator of the public's desire for assisted suicide. Prior to Youk's death, he had never been charged with murder. Unlike previous trials, in the Youk case Kevorkian was unable to call witnesses to testify either to the victim's wish to die or to the extent of the victim's suffering. However, Youk's widow, who had hoped to testify at the trial but was barred by the judge from doing so, spoke at Kevorkian's sentencing and pleaded for leniency based on her assertion that her husband had chosen his death and begged for Kevorkian's help.

During Kevorkian's murder trial I had a conversation with a disabled friend who has long been involved in Not Dead Yet, an activist group comprised almost exclusively of disabled people adamantly opposed to euthanasia. "I feel very conflicted about this trial," I told her. "What's to feel conflicted about?" she asked me, an edge creeping into her voice. "He killed someone on national television. He's a murderer." Utterly succinct, her response brooked no argument—especially not from the vantage point of the disabled. And I wasn't quite certain what argument I might pose to counter hers, regardless. Still, the case had left me unsettled, even as my friend steadfastly stood her political and moral ground. Pro-life in the true sense of the word (rather than the political, right-wing usage), I am morally and ethically opposed to abortion and euthanasia (as well as the death penalty). Watching Kevorkian's videotaped euthanizing of Youk on *60 Minutes* in November 1998 disturbed me deeply. That week I devoted my weekly newspaper column on national politics to the event and its impact on me.

What had struck me at the time was the sheer mundanity of Youk's death—the utter lack of drama attached to it. I have seen people die before, in a variety of circumstances, some quite brutal. I have also watched animals die, through accident as well as euthanasia. I have never failed to be moved by any of these deaths, often greatly so. What disturbed me most about the death of Thomas Youk was its abject bloodlessness—emotional as well as literal. It stirred absolutely no feeling in me; I didn't cry or feel shock or even shiver. I watched, it happened, it was over. A man was dead—that easily—yet it evoked nothing in me. (Conversely I can remember with total clarity the execution over thirty years ago of a Vietnamese man whose brains were blown out by a Viet Cong soldier on national television and the horror it evoked—and still evokes—in me.) But Youk's death obviously had stirred my friend. The terse immediacy of her response told me where I should stand morally as well as politically on this trial of the man responsible for Youk's death. Would I, I wondered, have felt differently if Youk had been shot or knifed or died in an obviously violent manner? Or was the impediment to my outrage the fact that death was his stated choice? Did that make me queasy about the trial, despite my firm belief that Kevorkian is a soulless ghoul with a political mission that supercedes conscience or even the humanity he invokes when he discusses his "work"? And what did it mean that I had no visceral response to watching this televised death of a real human being? Should death ever be so seemingly simple, bloodless and uncomplicated?

I have had a series of major surgeries in my adult life. Some have incurred pain so intense that I didn't think I could survive it and wasn't sure I wanted to. But one recovers from surgery eventually and, as one recovers, presumes the pain will lessen and finally abate. Chronic, progressive or terminal disease differs; one knows pain will be a constant—in fact, may be the predominate element—of one's illness, usually for the rest of one's life. For years I have been in severe pain on a daily basis. Some days the pain overwhelms every other aspect of my life; it is incapacitating. Several years ago I spent the majority of a four-month period curled in a fetal position in my bed, overwhelmed by the constancy of the pain and seriously wondering how long I would be able to maintain any quality of life were it to continue. In addition I have an aversion to most pain medications because the side effects I experience—particularly nausea and mental impairment—are so pronounced and can interfere as much with my daily life as the pain itself. My experiences with severe pain—what I would call intractable pain, the sort of pain that causes one to scream or shriek or moan involuntarily—have made me fearful. I have come to realize that there are certain kinds of pain I can live with and others the prospect of which make me terrified.

But pain is not my only fear. Since 1996 I have become progressively more disabled. Vertigo, muscle weakness, paresthesia and overwhelming fatigue keep me mostly bedridden. With the aid of a cane or another person, I can walk a few feet without falling, but my predominate means of transport is a wheelchair. Because I no longer have enough muscle strength in my arms to propel a wheelchair on my own, I must be pushed by someone else. I have lost much of my fine motor ability; this, combined with a growing spasticity only partially relieved by medications, means that fairly simple procedures like brushing and flossing my teeth can become terrible and often bloody events as my brain short-circuits the message to my fingers and hands. Similar problems occur when cutting food or getting the fork from plate to mouth. I have learned to favor foods that come in discrete pieces easily delivered from fingers to mouth—and thus less likely to end up flung across the table, bed or onto my clothing. Brushing my shoulder-length hair can be arduous; washing it even more so.

The sheer exhaustion caused by mundane activities—bathing, dressing, eating—as well as the progressive nature of my disability have made me fearful of the days ahead. What if my partner of the past twelve years—who fell in love with a woman who danced till dawn, rode a bicycle everywhere and walked miles with her all over England when we were first together—decided the woman who could no longer dance, bicycle or even walk (not to mention cook, clean or do laundry) was no longer a viable love interest and decided to leave in search of a nondisabled partner? How would I, the woman whose fierce independence has been replaced with an involuntary dependency, who now needs help with many of the basics of daily living, manage without her? So I had an inkling of what Thomas Youk might have feared—increasing debilitation, abandonment, burdening those he loved with his own disability. All these things might have caused him to choose death over an increasingly uncertain life. And thus, my own hesitation in response to Kevorkian's actions. If Youk *wanted* to die, if Youk *asked* Kevorkian to kill him, then should Kevorkian be charged with murder? For my friend, the one whose reponse to the Kevorkian trial had been so succinct, herself severely disabled and often at the mercy of sadistic attendants, the question had only one answer. My trepidation and queasiness were born, she implied, out of fears about my own situation. Where was *my* moral outrage over what *she* saw so clearly as murder?

My pro-life politics, predicated as they are on my religious, moral and ethical beliefs, define my perspective on abortion, euthanasia and the death penalty. But these are *my* beliefs, so just as I don't think I have the right to impose my anti-abortion politics on other women, I also question my right to keep others from choosing euthanasia. My preference would be that no woman chose abortion, but I would never be found outside an abortion clinic attempting to prevent another woman from making that difficult choice. I feel similarly about euthanasia. Disability impacts and alters one's viewpoint on many things. Sometimes the closer one is to an issue, the more difficult to discern the variant perspectives—one *becomes* the debate, rather than merely a party to it. It is impossible to be disabled in the United States and *not* consider what abortion and euthanasia mean to one *personally*, because even if one never makes either choice, a significant part of the argument for both *is* disability. What has not entered the national discourse on the consanguineous issues of abortion and euthanasia is this: The right to die necessitates definition of who does and does not have the right to life—from birth to death.

Theories of eugenics have always been predicated on the concept that disability, physical or mental, is a scourge, weakening the very structure of society. Various cultures have practiced it over the millennia: In this century the most defining example has been the Nazi quest for a "master race" that meant exterminating all social undesirables, including "defectives"; Sweden covertly utilized eugenics to force sterilization of those with mental and physical defects until the practice was exposed in the 1980s, when a series of lawsuits by women and men who were forceably sterilized was instigated; in the United States, forced sterilization of the mentally and physically disabled was common until the 1970s and still occurs on a case-by-case basis; and China legalized eugenics in 1973, enforcing sterilization policies against families with genetic predisposition to mental or physical disease.

Discourse—legal and political—on reproductive rights in the United States has been limited to a woman's right to choose contraception or abortion. Regardless of political stance—left, centrist or right—no debate has been generated on a woman's right to choose to *have* children or to access medical procedures (artificial insemination, in vitro fertilization) that allow her to have a child. That debate would necessitate including those women most often marginalized in our society—poor women, women of color, lesbians and disabled women—and arguing their equal right with white, middle-class, heterosexual, nondisabled women to bear children. Many states impose restrictions on medical techniques to impregnate women. Single women are frequently barred from such procedures—which impacts lesbians and disabled women. Prohibitive costs for such procedures—rarely covered by standard medical insurance—renders them inaccessible to women with limited incomes. This means disabled women, lesbians and women of color are all restricted from access to these procedures and thus, inevitably, from bearing children. In addition, women in these minority groups—particularly disabled women and lesbians—may have their children taken away from them by social service agencies if they do not meet the criteria set for normalcy by the state. Case after case has come before the courts contesting the rights of disabled women and lesbians to maintain custody of their children on the basis of their "fitness" (a vague legalistic term usually defined by the politics of individual judges) as parents. Thus eugenics alone doesn't determine who is and is not allowed to bear children, but such theoretical concepts seep into the general culture, influencing not just public sentiment, but the laws that evolve from such sentiments.

This societal aversion to certain women giving birth may explain the lack of support they have received from either left-leaning feminists or right-leaning family-values proponents. Mainstream feminists have routinely supported the right of any woman, including young and poor women, to choose abortions, while the self-proclaimed pro-life movement purports to support the right of any woman to give birth as well as the right of any fetus (regardless of genetic or other anomalies) to be born. But although the abortion rights movement has been euphemistically termed the reproductive rights movement, no attempt either within the ranks of national organizations or by feminist leaders has been instigated to broaden the debate on childbearing to include anything other than termination of pregnancy. Yet, as the United Nations Committee on Women and international human rights groups report, many countries force women to have abortions for a variety of culturally prescribed reasons. According to United Nations and World Health Organization data on women and children throughout the world, second and third trimester sex-selection abortions are routinely performed throughout India, Asia and Latin America. Sex-selection abortions are also common in Muslim cultures worldwide. Sex-selection abortions have become so common in Asia that the ratio of male to female births, about even in the United States, can be as wide as ten to one in some nations; in China, men seeking brides now find sex selection has created a serious shortage of women. Because China's population-control laws restrict women to one birth per lifetime, cultural biases mean male babies are prefered; female infants are frequently abandoned and even killed. Fear of giving birth to a disabled child combined with eugenics laws forces many women to choose abortion; disabled children are nearly always abandoned—to orphanages or even in fields or along roadways.

Lesbians, who have long been in the forefront of the pro-choice movement, have most often taken the mainstream feminist view that abortion is every woman's right without voicing concerns about broadening the discourse to include other elements of the reproductive rights debate. However, the abortion debate, as currently framed, pits disability rights activists against feminists—and ultimately nondisabled lesbians. Not only has feminism failed to extend the discourse on reproductive rights to include issues beyond abortion, but feminists have consistently maintained what can only be termed a politically and humanistically insensitive stance on the subject of eugenic abortion. The feminist position on abortion remains focused solely on the rights of the woman; the fetus is continually refered to as a cluster of cells, never in human terms. This refusal to acknowledge the humanity of the fetus actually impedes the feminist argument for abortion and limits the possibility of extending the movement for reproductive rights beyond abortion alone. For it is the very factor of the fetus's humanity—or at least *humanness*—that raises the question in the first place of whether a woman should be given a choice about bearing a child or not. She never bears a cluster of cells; she gives birth to another human being—a being who requires care, nurture and financial support for many, many years. Were this not the case, there would be no need for the option of abortion, of stopping that process before a birth ensues. In denying the humanness of the fetus, one also ignores—and even rejects—the quest so many other women have to reproduce. If the most important feminist task as stated is to give women a *choice* about reproducing, then that choice must necessitate inclusion of the option of bearing children. This means one must consider the totality of the reproductive rights question and also redefine the fetus as human, not the nonhuman cluster of cells so frequently referred to by feminists in an effort to stave off attacks from the political right.

Particularly dicey is the question of selective—usually eugenic—abortion. Many disabled activists view such abortion with the same ferocity as euthanasia: taking the life of a human considered less than viable by nondisabled society. The language used by feminists when discussing eugenic abortion has consistently been extremely offensive, often referring to the horrors attendant to bearing a disabled child with an intensity reminiscent of Nazism. References to suffering again pertain only to the woman; the fetus/child is described as both burden and horror. And just as the feminist polemic has defined the fetus as a cluster of cells in order to minimize the negative response to the concept of taking life that is at the foundation of all abortion, in the case of eugenic abortion the "defective" fetus is defined as a monstrosity, an incubus that will suck the very life out of a woman forced to care for it, thereby once again dehumanizing the fetus in an effort to rehumanize the quest for abortion.

Such political and cultural insensitivity further narrows the scope of a reproductive rights discourse, defining abortion as the only viable consideration when a child might be born disabled. This contextualizing of disability—within a feminist polemic—as something to quell or even kill pits disabled women against nondisabled women. One in six Americans has some form of disability; do we rid society of all disability *in utero*? Or do we wait and euthanize? And what of lesbians? As discussion of a genetic basis for homosexuality has become more intense and entered the mainstream, so too has discussion of selective abortion. Just as many nations throughout the world utilize sex-selection abortion on a routine and overt basis (the practice is more covert in the West), there can be no question selective abortion would be utilized were a gene for homosexuality discovered. Embedded in the call for a woman's "freedom" from an unwanted pregnancy—particularly a pregnancy in which the fetus is "defective"—is eugenics; again the question of who has the right to life in the first place and who makes that determination—and how?

What disabilitity qualifies a fetus for eugenic abortion? In Nazi Germany simply not having the so-called Aryan features—light hair, light eyes, light skin—would have brought about destruction of the fetus; mindful of the horrors of the Holocaust, most of us shudder at such theories of physiological "perfection." But sex selection remains the single most common eugenic rationale for abortion in the world, from the United States, where it occurs covertly, to the streets of major cities in Asia, where "clinics" offer sex-selection abortion through the third trimester. Needless to state, these abortions are performed on otherwise healthy fetuses whose only "defect" is their female gender. But what of true anomalies—relatively common birth defects such as cleft palates, spina bifida, Down syndrome, deafness or sickle cell anemia? Each of these defects carries some measure of disability with it and there can be no way of knowing the severity of that disability until the baby is actually born. Will the spina bifida be so extreme as to render the child paralyzed or merely a little spastic? Will the deafness be profound or allow for some hearing? Will the Down sydrome be minimal, meaning the child could grow to self-sufficient adulthood, or be extreme, requiring constant care? These questions must be asked by the prospective parent, but as we know, the majority of children born with these particular defects are quite capable of living relatively "normal" lives: Should they be denied that option because of eugenics? Disabled activists like my friend would say, emphatically, not, but feminists would counter that the choice can only be made by the woman who will have to care for and nurture that child. Which in turn raises the specter of privilege, including reproductive privilege, because the choice often depends on a woman's economic or social status.

Within this query over eugenic abortion, however, lies another debate: Where does the line on eugenics get drawn? Which disabilities are "acceptable" and which are not? We see that in many countries merely carrying the wrong chromosome results in sex-selection eugenics. We have heard numerous proponents of family values and pro-life positions advocate abortion of queers if a socalled "gay gene" is found. We recognize the Nazi attempt to orchestrate a race of *Ubermenschen* as a horrifying extreme, but many disability activists view eugenic abortion as a slightly more subtle form of Nazism. One might understand the abortion of a fetus carrying a deadly disease such as Tay-Sachs, where the child literally is dying from birth and quite horribly. But what of the disabilities mentioned above? Deaf activists view themselves as a linguistic minority, *not* as disabled, yet they claim that eugenic abortion by hearing parents happens on a regular basis. It is not inconceivable—especially given the Asian construct of sex selection and its resultant alteration in the demographics of whole societies—that whole groups of people will be selected out of society either because they are deemed "defective" by the society in which their parents live or from the more benign desire of well-meaning parents not to bear children who might have a more difficult struggle than a "normal" child. Legislating abortion necessitates legislating eugenics.

The question of what society does with its disabled or marginal members can be answered by abortion or euthanasia—or by granting full social membership to disabled and nondisabled alike. This debate holds particular resonance for lesbians because they continue to wage a battle for full social membership—both as women in a patriarchal society and as queers in a straight society. Nondisabled lesbians may be influenced in their perspective on disability issues like abortion and euthanasia by their political and social involvement in other groups. For example, despite the deep political involvement of lesbians in the reproductive rights movement, the abortion debate has been thoroughly defined by heterosexual feminists. And the impact of AIDS and cancer on the queer community has charged debate over euthanasia and the importance of the autonomous option of the right to die. Thus lesbians have been in many respects programmed by their links to heterosexual feminists and gay men to approve the concepts of abortion and euthanasia without actually considering the larger ethical—and nontheoretical—issues involved and how they may impinge on lesbians *directly,* rather than as adjuncts to other groups.

The conviction in the Kevorkian trial qualified the right-to-die debate to a certain extent. Juries had previously been sympathetic to the concept of choosing death; actual euthanasia pushed the ethical and moral envelope. Perhaps what decided the jury was Kevorkian himself, with his abrasive and unrelenting polemic. Because he chose to represent himself, rather than have an attorney tease out the quasi-humanitarian spin Kevorkian attempts to put on his actions, the Youk jury saw an unvarnished and highly unromantic version of a euthanizer; in that context, Kevorkian appeared more like a conscienceless demagogue than a former doctor with a deep and abiding concern for the suffering of those with terminal disease. What the jury saw in Kevorkian's behavior at trial may have alarmed them and raised questions that could impact every one of them; what controls are there for euthanasia after all?

The answer thus far is not many. Right-to-die advocates commonly cite the Netherlands as a veritable utopia for those who choose to die. Assisted suicide has been legal in the Netherlands for over a decade and euthanasia is common, though still somewhat hidden. Nevertheless, concerns continually arise over the stringency of rules governing such practices, despite the fact that these practices are now commonplace. Apparently everyone wants the option of assisted suicide or euthanasia, but everyone also fears what could happen if such practices are not strictly regulated.

What could happen seems clear enough, if one looks at abortion. Federal legalization of abortion with the 1973 United States Supreme Court decision in the case of *Roe v. Wade* allowed for first trimester abortions basically on demand and in a range of environments—clinics, private doctors' offices, hospitals; second trimester abortions required the intervention of physicians and a hospital setting; third trimester abortions could only be performed if a panel of physicians determined continuation of the pregnancy would cause grave physical or emotional harm to the woman and then, due to the physical dangers, the abortion must be performed in a hospital. In addition to these federal regulations, individual states have added their own restrictions, including parental and spousal consents, twenty-four-hour waiting periods and so forth. In framing the argument for abortion on demand, feminists have used certain images to bolster the urgency of the need for legalized abortion. Rape and incest are routinely invoked, as are poverty and youth. This continued use of provocative language to stoke interest in a waning movement has also taken a paternalistic turn: white middle-class feminists calling for abortion rights for those other than themselves—the poor (often women of color and rural women) and young, the rape and incest victims. But the reality of who obtains abortions in the United States projects a quite different image—one that signals an incipient casualness regarding contraception as well as human life; one that suggests the euphemistically termed "reproductive rights" movement is merely another arena of privilege for the privileged. The percentage of abortions due to rape and incest have been negligible since 1973; abortions for those under eighteen without parental permission have been outlawed in a majority of states; federal aid for abortion was eradicated in 1983 (and with it federal aid for family planning; that is, free contraception in federally funded health centers and clinics) and violence against abortion providers has closed many clinics in poverty-stricken areas—particularly rural America. As a consequence, abortion is not readily available to or accessed by the very women the abortion rights movement portends to be concerned about; rather, adult women, largely middle class, with ready access to viable contraception remain the main consumers of abortions. Maintaining the ease of obtaining abortions for women with economic privilege has motivated the abortion rights movement for well over a decade; the specter of the back-alley abortion raised repeatedly by the movement has not been eradicated by that movement: The women most likely to turn to back-alley abortionists are still likely to fall into their grasp because they have few alternatives for coping with unwanted pregnancies. Abortion may be legal in the United States, but it is only available to certain women—predominately middle class.

If abortion can be reduced to a commodity accessible primarily to the privileged, despite stringent and ever-more restrictive laws, then can we reasonably expect euthanasia to be any different? What is to prevent the privileged (nondisabled, white, middle class, heterosexual) from becoming the primary consumers of euthanasia—and wielding the power to decide who lives and who dies?

All we know of Thomas Youk's illness and death comes from others: Kevorkian and Youk's family, all white and middle class. They have all spoken of Youk's fear of his disease, its symptoms and effects, though Youk's doctors stipulate that there were treatments not yet tried to minimize some of the symptoms—like choking on food—that most worried Youk. Kevorkian and Youk's family also spoke convincingly of Youk's desire for death—and of his *fear of being a burden to his family*. Youk's euthanasia, arranged by his family and carried out by Kevorkian, spared Youk's family what might well have been years of caring for a severely disabled husband and father—with all the concomitant stress, emotional pain and financial burden.

My friend, so adamant in her response to the Kevorkian trial, told me that when queried, most disabled people, particularly those dying slowly from progressive or terminal disease, fear burdening their families more than anything else—more than pain or even death. "You love these people, but you're also dependent on them for everything," she explained. "You're terrified they'll abandon you. Death can seem preferable to the endless and unrelieved fear of being left sitting in your own excrement or choking or suffocating." She articulates one of the most worrisome aspects of the right-to-die debate: Who decides?

Who wields the power to determine when life is no longer "viable" for the disabled or ill person? Is it that person or is it those who are that person's caretakers—family, friends or the state?

Youk was totally dependent on his family for every aspect of his care. Many disabled and terminally ill people are. Others are at the mercy of strangers—in hospitals, hospices, nursing homes and other care facilities. What happens when it becomes too stressful—personally and financially—for family, friends or other caregivers to maintain the life of a disabled or ill person? The long struggle by Karen Thompson to gain legal custody of her longtime partner Sharon Kowalski after Sharon was severely brain damaged in a car accident and the steadfast love and disability rights activism of Dana Reeve, wife of spinal cord–damaged actor Christopher Reeve, have gained much media attention in recent years. But these examples are, unfortunately, exceptions to the rule of care for the disabled in America, where spouses and partners frequently desert their disabled lovers when disabling disease or injury strikes. What happens to the disabled who have no one to fight for them—or even care for them? Just as legislation of abortion has led to eugenics and other extremes, like sex selection, right-to-die/assisted-suicide legislation may eventually lead to euthanasia for people who become, like Youk, severely disabled as a result of accident or disease and a burden to their families. One of the perils of physical disability has long been the misperception that physical disability implies mental disability—and as a consequence, the inability to make informed choices. However, the majority of disabled people can indeed make their own choices; but economic, social and other pressures may restrict those choices or lead people to make decisions predicated on the needs and desires of others, rather than their own. And some settings are more conducive—one might even say coercive—to forcing a disabled person to do what's best, particularly financially, for others, rather than for herself.

How then do we ensure the right to life for those without privilege, whether that is from the womb or much later in life? How much of the debate—from Kevorkian as the symbol of the right-to-die movement to abortion with its pro-choice/pro-life arbiters—is indeed about privilege? For example: Who is allowed to bear children? Who gains access to the kind of medical help and treatment that might mitigate the need for euthanasia or vitiate the desire for it?

Christopher Reeve has become a veritable poster boy for disability in America, yet his experience couldn't be further from that of the average disabled person—like the quadriplegic former football player who was "assisted" by Kevorkian. This young man told Kevorkian his life was an unrelieved agony because he was trapped at home, had none of the equipment that might have made him feel his life had value and *felt he was a continual financial and physical burden to his family.* Access means life can be far more livable, regardless of the extent of disability. Dana Reeve has stuck valiantly by her husband since his accident five years ago and has been deemed a virtual saint by the media for doing so. But Dana Reeve has extensive privilege and a massive amount of help; there is little she is actually responsible for in Reeve's care. Such is not the case for the majority of spouses or partners of severely disabled people. That privilege makes a huge difference in the ability of a couple to maintain their relationship beyond the problems of the disabled partner.

But economic privilege isn't the only chasm the disabled must bridge. For disabled lesbians, heterosexual privilege can be equally daunting. For example, Dana Reeve never had to fight to maintain her relationship with her suddenly disabled husband while also planning for his care; Karen Thompson waged a decade-long battle to return her brain-damaged partner to her care, delivering Kowalski from the sterile nursing-home environment in which Kowalski's parents had incarcerated her.

Thus privilege defines the treatment disabled lesbians can expect within heterosexual nondisabled society, where standards of care are predicated on a heterosexual model and where even feminists have yet to embrace the needs and concerns of *non*disabled lesbians, let alone their disabled sisters. How then do disabled lesbians broaden the discourse among feminists to include them in terms of reproductive rights? How do disabled lesbians get themselves included in the "pro-life" discourse that has excluded them because of both their disability and their "defect" of lesbianism? How do lesbians protect themselves from a society that would, given the option, practice genocide against them through genetic testing and eugenic abortion? These are questions that must be addressed.

When we debate the so-called "options" of eugenics and euthanasia at the turn of the century, we do so with the full knowledge that technology and expanding scientific resources can and perhaps will render whole segments of the population extinct. We have only to look to China with its melding of population control and totalitarianism—and mass annihilation of girl children—to see how easily (and insidiously) this can occur. It is not mere hyperbole to invoke the evil shadow of Nazism in this context. When, as a society, we have the means to do something—such as eugenic abortion or euthanasia—only ethical and moral considerations can provide deterrents. But often polemic and intellectualizing supercede ethical considerations, even when it concerns who will live, who will die and who will, ultimately, decide. Exclusion of the disabled from the discourse has kept it centered on the needs and desires of the nondisabled. But without the inclusion of the disabled in this debate—which is all about disability—how can there be any real discussion?

# PRIVATE DANCER
## Evolution of a Freak

### Nomy Lamm

I'm straddling her legs, wearing a black lace push-up bra, black half-slip, leopard granny panties and thigh-high fishnets. Her blue silicone dick is out of her pants, and she's thrusting against me while I lip-synch to "Private Dancer," fumbling at my crotch to undo a buckle. *I'm your private dancer/ a dancer for money/ I'll do what you want me to do* . . . I pull my leg off, sling it around her neck and pull her close with my tits in her face. The audience applauds, and I crawl offstage as she jerks off, fucking the leg I left in her lap.

This is a drag show on the night before Halloween in Olympia, Washington. The audience is full of freaks, and I feel pretty confident they'll think my leg coming off onstage equals hot. Our routine is about a dude who goes into a strip joint (the "Lusty Lotus") to see "Sweet Sextina" (me). I dance for him and the audience, writhe on his lap and then pull off my leg while he gropes me and jerks off.

While I don't necessarily want to attach the performance to some overt "message"—I would rather just let it be sexy and leave it at that—I will say that this is the kind of thing you would only see in certain communities. For one, this is not the goddess-centered, womon-loving-womon erotica you're supposed to find in the "lesbian community" (although I'm thinking that idea is getting pretty much outdated). For another thing, it's uncommon—in any community, be it gay, straight, queer, whatever—to see disabled women portrayed as sexy. Whether or not an audience would think that a disabled (and, let me add, fat)

152

woman doing a striptease was sexy, we usually would never know because the environment is not supportive or inclusive enough to make a disabled woman want to expose herself in that way.

The audience reaction is amazing. They're going crazy, giving us so much energy, screaming the entire time we're out there. This is an unusual drag show—drag queens and kings and everything in between and beyond, all performing together. The thing that binds us together here, which is repeatedly pointed out throughout the night, is that we are freaks—the drag part is incidental. There's scary rocker-chick drag queens, astronaut drag kings, serpent queens and croco-dile kings, a live sex act, a pornographic reading about alien sodomites, a touch-ing and heart-wrenching performance based on a Lynda Barry comic called "What Is Weirdos?" This is queer community in the truest sense of the word, and the audience is amazingly supportive of everybody.

What does it mean to be disabled in a community like this?

Like I said, this is a community that prides itself on its freakiness. That freakiness takes on a lot of different forms, having to do with gender, appear-ance, sexuality and, at least in my group of friends, disability. There is also a lot more acceptance for variance in body size than there is in most of the world, and I happen to be lucky enough to know a lot of totally sexy fat girls. So, some-times, I really do feel accepted and included in this community of freaks. Sometimes I feel that being a fat, one-legged Jewish dyke is the most natural thing in the world and feel absolutely included and at home. As my friend Hilary, a double below-knee amputee once put it: "You are all my freaky family, because when I'm with you, I don't feel like a freak."

But, of course, sometimes I don't feel that way. Sometimes I get annoyed and pissed off at people who identify as freaks when I don't think they really know what that means. Sometimes being a freak doesn't make you feel like a rebel, it just makes you feel gross and untouchable. It means having people stare at you and be afraid of you. It means really feeling like a *freak,* like the kind of person people gawk at and feel sorry for, meanwhile thanking the lord they get to have a normal body.

A lot of my friends call themselves freaks because they are pervy smelly anarchist dykes who have as much of a problem with mainstream gay (and lesbian) culture as they do with mainstream corporate america. I feel the same way. And I know that when you're out in the real world, being queer is reason enough to be labeled a freak, let alone being a sadomasochist or a serious gender deviant. But sometimes when we're in a group and everyone's in full-swing flirt mode, I get this horrible feeling that I'm still the freak. I'm still the outsider.

I was born with a condition called proximal femoral focal deficiency. It's a congenital birth defect, and it means that the femur in my left leg is only a couple inches long, my hip isn't fully developed, and the growth rate is half that of my other leg. When I was three, I had my foot amputated so that I could wear a prosthesis. It's obviously not the most extreme kind of birth defect you could have—I can still walk, it's not on my face or somewhere else where it would be completely obvious, but it's enough that it's always made me feel like a freak. It draws stares and questions and makes me self-conscious about taking off my leg in front of people to go swimming, have sex, put on my pajamas at slumber parties and so on.

The story of my birth is a traumatic one: My parents were young hippies who tried to do a home birth in their one-room house in Dunmire Hollow, Tennessee. Forty-eight hours after my mom went into labor, I was born by C-section at the Wayne County Hospital. I had a big blue bruise on my forehead from knocking around in there for so long. The doctor took me away and then came back to tell my dad that I was probably a German measles baby—that one of my legs was deformed and that I was probably also blind and retarded *(sic).*

Well, I ended up not being blind or having any mental disabilities, but the leg part turned out to be true. Nobody knows any specific reason for proximal femoral focal deficiency. What I do know is that it's something that happens randomly during development in the womb, that it's always on the left side, that there are four different levels of it (I have the second-to-lowest level) and that, according to my dad's account of what a doctor once told him, people who have it tend to be really smart.

When we moved to Olympia from Tennessee, my parents hooked up with the Shriners Hospital in Portland, Oregon, which provided free care for low-income "crippled children." I had my foot amputated there, and after that I would stay there once a year for a couple weeks at a time while my legs were getting made—clunky ectoskeletal prostheses made of hard plastic, a big hole in the back, hinges on the sides.

All of my memories of that place are horrible: Up until I was five or six they made me sleep in a crib, and they put a big plastic bubble over the top of it so that I couldn't stand up and talk with the other kids. We were in our beds almost all the time, they never let us go outside; they were Christian and sent weird Bible people around to pray for us; the other kids were mean to me (I still think about Stephanie, the cute girl with short curly hair who I named my bear after, who told me she "hated my guts"), and my parents hardly ever visited me because I was so cranky and awful whenever they did come to see me.

My mom said that I probably only spent a total of seven weeks of my life in that hospital, but a good portion of my early childhood memories have to do with that place. I am grateful that the Shriners exist, and I know that my life probably would have been a lot harder without them, but I still kind of shudder whenever I think about it. I can only think of a couple good memories having to do with the Shriners Hospital: 1) the prosthetist once let me have a bite of his Egg McMuffin, and 2) once I was there over Christmas (we're Jewish) and we got to see a fun Christmas play. This bit of revelry backfired, though, because after that I thought this was a regular occurrence and was always wondering when the play was gonna happen again. Of course, I was always disappointed and had to be content to sit in my crib and occasionally have the pleasure of watching *The Flintstones.*

It's funny how things will make an impression on you as a kid. To me, being taped to the x-ray table because I wouldn't lie still and being made to eat beets by the mean nurse who never should've gotten a job working with kids seemed equally traumatic. All of these incidents were proof to me that the hospital was a horrible place. I actually made myself sick one time because I was so afraid my mom was gonna leave me there. On the two-hour drive to Portland she kept saying that I probably wouldn't have to stay, that they were just going to do a checkup. When we got there the people said I needed to stay and started going through the process of checking me in until they took my temperature and realized I was sick. They wouldn't admit me because they said I'd get the other kids sick, so we went home and I had to come back another time. I can't even describe my relief, even though I knew it was only temporary.

I was a weird kid. Being disabled (which I never called myself up until a few years ago) was only a small part of it. I spend a lot of time and energy thinking and talking about my childhood because I think it's interesting how certain themes have carried through in my life. Example number one: my obsession with pop/teen culture. I always loved anything having to do with teenagers, especially punk rockers. Of course, I didn't know what a real punk rocker was at age eight. I had never heard of the Sex Pistols, X, Black Flag or even Siouxsie and the Banshees; to me, Cyndi Lauper epitomized the mid-eighties punk aesthetic. But I loved the idea of punk, of rebels, of smokin' in the boys' room, drinkin' in parking lots, driving fast cars and fucking shit up.

Another example is my extreme girlyness: the fervor with which I played with Barbie dolls, my adoration of anything pink and frilly, my love of all things prissy and princessy. Of course I have always known that I'm also a tough-ass bitch (I would have put it in different words back then), but the femme thing has been a constant in my life, a fetish since the age of five.

The biggest carry-over, though, and the one that I think is most significant, is the way I learned to identify with outsiders, starting around the age of five. This is probably, at least on some level, a result of my disability, but it extended far beyond that. I always had an awareness of being "different," and I often did things that purposely set me apart from other people. The clothes I wore, the way I interacted with other people at school, the music I listened to, the activities I was involved in, often reflected this kind of rebel/freak/outsider consciousness.

Even though I was associated with different "alternative" subcultures throughout my teen years—I was a goth, then a punk, then a riot grrrl—it has only been in the past couple of years that I've been involved in a community that really identified as freaks in a way that I could relate to. Sure, when I was a goth we called ourselves freaks, but this just meant that we wore a lot of black, painted spider webs on our faces, listened to The Cure and gave people spooky looks to try to weird them out. There was very little political consciousness attached to it, and hardly any sense of inclusivity in terms of identity factors like disability. Sometimes I think it's almost my fault that I didn't feel included in things as a crip up until recently. I rarely identified publicly as disabled, I made no demands for inclusion, I didn't seek out a disabled community or read literature by or about disabled people.

I have a few isolated memories of connecting with other disabled people. When I was around eight years old, my parents set me up to hang out with another amputee girl. It felt stupid, like we were supposed to like each other just cuz we both had fake legs. We weren't at a point where we could have deep conversations about disability, so we kind of showed off to each other the different things we could do despite our fake legs, and that was that. When I was twelve I met a double above-knee amputee at the swimming pool. She was an adult, she had lost her legs in a car accident, and I was really interested in her suction sockets that stayed on without any straps. I would play with her six-year-old daughter in the pool, and it was cool because I didn't have to worry about what she would think of my leg. When I was a goth alterna-teen there was one girl I sometimes hung out with who had cerebral palsy. When walking around downtown with groups of friends we would sometimes complain to each other about how fast everybody walked, and I remember her telling me once about how she lost her job because she was disabled. At that point, to me, having a fake leg was merely a piece of trivia. While I knew that it affected me, it was all very surface and I didn't even allow myself to think that not having a leg had been hard on me. When my friends told me, "I always forget that you have a fake leg," I was flattered. I said that sometimes I forgot, too.

I don't know if "forgot about it" is really the right way to put it. On one level I did forget about it because it was so normal to me. I never had a leg in the first place, so having a fake leg seemed just the same as anything else. I didn't have the language to figure out what it really meant. To me, disabled meant something a lot more severe than having a fake leg. It meant being laid up in a room, unable to move. Or it meant giving up, trying to get people's pity. Neither applied to me. I could walk, I could do a lot of the same things that able-bodied people could do, and what I couldn't do I shrugged off and didn't talk about. Plus this "you're not a cripple" mentality had been so ingrained in me—my parents never allowed me to say I couldn't do something because of my leg (even sometimes when it was true), and I didn't have a lot of opportunity to feel sorry for myself (even though I would have liked to sometimes).

It wasn't until late in high school that I realized and admitted to myself that things actually are a lot harder when you have a fake leg. That sounds silly, but my disability was so downplayed for most of my childhood, I never would have thought of saying, "Can you please slow down for me? I have a fake leg, you know." Instead, I felt bad for slowing people down and would do my best to keep up. It's weird, this issue of "passing" as able-bodied. On one hand, it can save you a lot of alienation, because people assume you're the same as them. But it can also be really difficult because people don't know or understand your limitations. If people don't think of you as disabled, and you are, it means they make no allowances for you, they think of you as lazy.

During my senior year in high school, I got involved with riot grrrl, a grassroots network and support system for feminists in the punk scene. Riot grrrl was where I was first introduced to the idea of women-only space. This was where I first started meeting girls who talked about really heavy shit—things like incest, abuse, rapists in the punk scene, mental illness, fat oppression and body hatred. This was where I got my introductory education about the evils of capitalism and the interconnectedness of all forms of oppression. This was where I first started meeting queer girls my age. Basically, as a result of my involvement with riot grrrl, I became a vocal spokesperson for fat liberation and feminism at the age of seventeen.

But even as I was putting out zines about fat oppression and becoming well known as a fat activist, I hardly talked about disability—as a personal issue or a political one. I once did a spoken-word piece where I pulled out all my various legs from throughout my life and talked about them, telling little anecdotes and then answering questions, but that's one of the very few times I can remember publicly making an issue out of my leg.

My coming out as an amputee pretty much coincided with my becoming part of a community of freaky anarchist dykes. Like riot grrrl, which grew out of the feminist movement and the punk scene, this was a community that had grown out of a couple larger ones—specifically, the queer and anarchist communities. Like riot grrrl, it's often more of a network than an immediate community, based more on gatherings and major events than on day-to-day interactions (although it's got a pretty big contingent here in Olympia). In large part it's a community that has formed in reaction to the political apathy and assimilationism of mainstream gay and lesbian communities, and in reaction to straight-laced, straight-faced heterosexist attitudes in the anarchist community.

That I started being more open about my disability when I came into this community does not necessarily mean that it was a community that had dealt extensively with the issue of disability. It was more just a matter of coincidence. Basically, my coming out as an amputee was a result of a singular event: A girl I knew only slightly but really liked and respected (Hilary) lost both of her legs below the knee in a train accident. This new thing that we had in common bonded us immediately. In February 1997, we went to a radical women's gathering called "Badass and Free." Hilary had just gotten her fake legs but was still in a wheelchair or crawling around on kneepads most of the time. She and I and another crip named Diana talked with each other late into the night and ended up doing a workshop together on the last day there. We talked about our specific experiences with disability and about problems we had encountered within the anarchist and activist community. We all admitted to feeling somewhat guilty for having to rely on cars and pavement and other technological and industrial evils—things that are generally scorned by our community. Of course, we said, we agree that some types of development and technology are bad, but to stereotype people who rely on things like cars, pavement, computers and technology in general as lazy overconsumers is to basically ignore the existence of disabled people. Technology isn't always just a matter of convenience; it can be a matter of freedom.

Talking about this stuff with the support of two other freaky crip girls made it real to me. I knew it was wrong that I had been made to feel lazy or less committed for choosing to drive rather than march to rallies and protests. I knew that I had every right to feel alienated by things like Critical Mass and Earth First!, where participation relies on physical ability. I knew that I had reasons for having to pay to travel rather than trainhopping or hitchhiking. But I had never found a place where these feelings were reflected.

It was also at that gathering that it first occurred to me that prosthetics and amputees could be sexualized. Hilary was a total sexpot, on a mission to infuse our scene with hot dyke amputee smut, and she insisted that I be a part of it. She had plans for photo shoots, performance art pieces, amputee pageants, zines and all sorts of other projects that would involve the two of us, doing it up amputee style. It was kind of a shock for me, trying to quickly change my attitude from "I'm not really disabled, and even if I am, nobody notices" to "I am a foxy one-legged dyke, and you will love it, or else." It's been a kind of difficult transition, but I find that, like most things, it's just a matter of doing it. And it makes it so much easier when I have a partner in crime.

I've always been a performer and an exhibitionist—always loved being in the limelight, which has often meant dealing with issues in public before processing them on a personal level. My transformation at age seventeen from a typically self-loathing fat girl to radical fat activist took place within a span of maybe two weeks. Before I knew it, I was blabbing about fat oppression to anyone who would listen, standing on stages declaring myself a loudmouth proponent of the "fat grrrl revolution." Of course it was difficult, but it was above all liberating. It's been pretty much the same with my leg. There are things about my disability that are really frustrating and difficult, but like anything else, it's a lot easier to deal with when it's out in the open.

And as a performer, I've found that having a detachable leg is a real asset, something to take advantage of whenever I can. When Hilary and I mudwrestled each other last summer, we made a big production of taking off our legs before getting in the mud, waving our prosthetics in the air above our heads, screaming, "I'm gonna tear you limb from limb!" When I played a zombie in a drag reenactment of Michael Jackson's "Thriller," it felt like a wonderful gift that my leg could actually *fall off* at the end. And a couple months ago, when my friend and I started talking about doing the "Private Dancer" act for the drag show, I didn't even think about it as a political statement when I suggested taking off my leg at the end.

I realize that not every queer community has people like Hilary, Diana and me in it. But I like to think that any truly queer community at least has the potential. Being queer means a whole lot more than just being gay—it literally means being a freak. It means not caring about fitting in, assimilating into mainstream het culture. For me, I guess, that means using the challenges I've been faced with as gifts rather than burdens. It means that I can be a fat freaky one-legged Jew dyke, get up in front of people, dance, strip, take off my leg and leave the stage feeling like I've really done something right. And sometimes I think that's the boldest political statement I can make.

# IN A NEW LIGHT

Erin Lawrence

It's hard to imagine my world or my generation without HIV and AIDS. October 23, 1998, marked the end of the sixth year of my carrying the virus that causes AIDS. However, HIV/AIDS has been a part of my life since the mid-1980s.

In high school, my best friend, Chris,* shared a secret with me—he liked boys better than girls. He had been seeing older men for about three years; men that he met at parties or in West Hollywood at the clubs. However, our sophomore year, Chris had met a boy who attended another local high school during a gay dance sponsored by the Lambda Youth Council. Their relationship blossomed and Andy and Chris saw each other regularly. I was happy for Chris and supported his love for Andy, even though he still struggled with his sexual orientation. He had tried to tell his family; they threw him out.

Our junior year of high school, I was having problems with my own family, so Chris and I got an apartment together. Then Chris got sick. First, a flu that never went away—he was in the hospital for over two weeks. Then he lost twenty pounds, which he never gained back. When he finally returned to school that year, rumors of his orientation made him a target for hate and ignorance, and Chris ended up in the hospital again, this time with three broken ribs and a broken jaw. The summer between our junior and senior years was filled with

---

* All the names in this essay are pseudonyms.

good times, however. Andy and Chris were back together, and we became a three-some. Venice Beach became a routine hangout, as did watching summer sunsets and sunrises together. Every Sunday night we could be found at a club, dancing and enjoying life as most teenagers did.

Our senior year was better for Chris, as he was comfortable with his sexual orientation, and had decided that if Andy agreed, they would attend our senior prom together. In the second semester, however, Chris developed purple lesions on his torso, lost more weight and developed a flu that made it all but impossible to breathe without the assistance of an oxygen mask. With less than five weeks left before the prom and graduation, Chris withdrew from school; he was just too sick to attend and did not have the energy needed to complete assignments.

My life became a balance between attending classes, working thirty-plus hours a week, staying active in varsity sports, working on the student senate and serving as a caretaker for Chris. It was 1986, only one year after an HIV-antibodies test had been developed; Chris tested positive. Andy left once he knew Chris's HIV status for sure; he could not deal with the pressure of his orientation and losing the only person he loved—I could not blame him, and neither did Chris. Amazingly, Chris seemed to get better as quickly as he had gotten sick. We attended the prom together and afterward watched the sun rise. My friends were there to support me, and I became Chris's only support—his parents still rejected his homosexuality and blamed him for his illness.

Chris promised to finish his courses in the summer, so the administration allowed him to walk with his class at graduation. We had both been accepted to the state university; he was going to study English, and I, business. But Chris never made it to college. Three weeks before classes were to begin, Chris spiked a fever of 103. Before taking him to the hospital, he asked me to take him to see the West Coast sunset one last time. After watching the sunset we just sat there, and I held him so that he knew he was loved. He fell in and out of consciousness and mumbled during the night. The air was warm, and although I tried several times to take him to the hospital, Chris seemed to know and would stop me each time. We sat and watched the waves under the full moon until sunrise. Once the sun was above the horizon, Chris whispered for me to take the red ribbon from his sweater. Somehow I knew that this might be the last time I'd have the opportunity to be alone with Chris, and I said goodbye.

At the hospital, Chris's fever continued to rage and the doctors put him on a respirator to help his breathing; eventually he fell into a coma. Chris never woke up—he died a month after I had turned eighteen.

HIV/AIDS became a haunting memory for me during the next three years, the pain was hidden deep within my soul. I spent my first year in college working too much and not studying. I tried to stay busy all the time to try to erase the pain, the loss, the loneliness. I became a very different person than I had been in high school: I saw life as an enemy rather than as an educator. I hit rock bottom when I was academically disqualified from college after only one year. My father had been paying for my classes, so my reality check was having to tell him of my failure. During the summer, however, I found some inner strength and decided I wanted to go to college for me. In the fall, I enrolled at a community college.

Within two years, I transferred to a prestigious private university. During my first semester, one of my classes required a community-service component, and I became involved as a peer HIV pre/post-test counselor on campus. The pain from the loss of Chris was lessened by the opportunity to help educate my peers about HIV, through referrals, talking about the pros and cons of being tested and developing support systems on campus. Later, I became involved with The NAMES Project's AIDS Memorial Quilt and served as co-logistics coordinator for our campus's display the following year. My involvement in HIV/AIDS issues on campus helped me begin to work through the impact of losing Chris and the relationship we had.

By my second year at the university, I had begun to question the relationships I had had with men. I had been in a couple of long-term relationships during and since high school; however, the relationships never seemed to move past the "best friends" stage. I began to consciously question my sexuality in the same way that I remembered Chris had done during our freshman year of high school. At this point I had no lesbian role models; in fact, I did not know any lesbians—my gay friends were exclusively men. I felt comfortable in the gay community, going dancing, watching drag shows, and I had convinced myself that my comfort grew out of a sense that I could be flirtatious and bold without fear of miscommunication, since mainly gay men were in these places. I saw myself as an ally of the gay/lesbian/bisexual/transgendered community.

The summer before my senior year of college, I was suddenly presented with an opportunity to learn more about myself as a gay person. I was selected to attend a weekend retreat to discuss diversity, and at this retreat I learned more about Renee, a full-time staff member in the office where I volunteered as a student government officer. In addition, she was best friends with my advisor for the peer conduct board. I knew she was an ally for gay and lesbian issues, but I had made no assumptions about her sexuality. At the retreat, however, I listened to her story—life as a lesbian on our campus.

The stereotypes, the fears, the talking behind her back, the jokes by other students—her experience. She talked about growing up knowing she was different from other girls in school and never knowing why. She talked about having crushes on her female teachers versus the male ones, like her friends. She talked about the silence and fear she had of others finding out the truth. Her words made me remember my many conversations with Chris and his struggles to hide his secret from others, yet knowing who he was inside and feeling comfortable with the truth.

My senior year of college was my "big party" since I did not have a sweet sixteen or a bat mitzvah. At the beginning of my senior year, I sought out the new counselor on campus, who was bisexual. Her dissertation was on internalized homophobia, and I felt if I could talk with her, it might be easier for me to make sense of my issues with the label of "gay" or "lesbian." Each week, however, we danced around the issue and talked about my self-esteem and self-confidence as a woman, my fears of graduation and not knowing what lay ahead, and my feelings of loneliness.

In October, my life changed dramatically when I was sexually assaulted by someone I knew. I now see this as both a gift and a curse. The gift was that, as I pieced my life together afterward, I began to accept the lesbian identity I had buried deep in low self-esteem/confidence and years of stereotypes about "dykes." The curse is that I became HIV-positive as a result of the rape, so my status continually reminds me of that trauma.

I didn't come out as a person living with HIV until almost a year after I had become infected, partly because of the timing and partly because of my own internalized fears of what being infected meant. I did not realize my status until three weeks before graduation, and my reaction was to move far away from the new pain in my soul as if to outrun the inevitable. In the film *Boys on the Side,* Robin, the young woman with AIDS, has a similar thought as she is lying in a hospital bed: "I thought if I only made this trip again that we would all be together and things would be different. I wanted to forget [that I had AIDS]." I had all the facts about HIV and AIDS, I was an HIV/AIDS peer educator, I had helped care for my best friend who died of AIDS, but now it was happening to me. I was overwhelmed—it was as though I knew nothing.

Disclosure became a necessity of life after I moved across the country to attend graduate school at a public university in the South. I was employed as a graduate student and, because of the type of work I did, I felt it was important to disclose my HIV status to my supervisor in case of excessive absences, sickness or other concerns (i.e., injuries and universal precautions). Then I was challenged further to share my status with others.

One of my closest friends at the time and one of my few confidants stated that she could not be my only support, that I needed to reach out. Her mentor had died of AIDS, and her loyalty and compassion gave me the strength to reach out to others. My disclosures were purposeful and deliberate, and I tried to educate and enlighten. On December 1, 1995, World AIDS Day, I gave my first public speech about living with HIV to over five hundred students, faculty and staff at the university. I have spoken every year since.

All of the fears of rejection, discrimination, lack of compassion and misunderstanding I had come to expect with disclosing my lesbian identity were there again as I disclosed to others that I was living with HIV. From my perspective, the added challenge with identifying as a person living with HIV was encouraging others to move past the "How did she get it?" syndrome. Many times it was obvious that the person receiving the information was wondering how I became infected.

It is my opinion that humans have been socialized to compartmentalize and label aspects of life to understand them more fully. When we teach little children, we compare elements of a situation with other elements that they have experienced as a way of making them feel comfortable with that which is not familiar or recognizable. Part of this socialization feeds into our desire as humans to want to know the hows and whys of things. This may be the reason why news stories are made up of more than the five Ws (who, what, where, when and why), but also the hows. Usually we feel differently or make judgments based on the hows and whys—for me the *how* I became infected with HIV is important only as an educational element. It is not a focal point of my story. I do not want the rape to overshadow how I feel as a person living with HIV, nor do I want the *why* to be used to entitle me to "innocent victim" status. No one deserves to live with HIV or AIDS, and to compare one person's *how* with another's disrespects both individuals.

Another challenge for me in disclosing my HIV status is the silence. Every region has a different name for it—"Minnesota nice" and "southern hospitality" are two examples—all ways we are taught to respond with compassion. In my experience, compassion comes in the form of silence. Too often, concerned that what we might say may not be supportive or not be what the other person needs to hear, we say nothing. One technique I have used to encourage questions is to create a visual image—the "couch of no stupid questions." I inform audiences or individuals that, at any time, a person can elect to sit on the couch and ask me a question. This has helped others to feel less awkward in asking "simplistic," "basic" or "stupid" questions—as they describe them—or even the "how" question. One of my closest friends used to say that she was not comfortable putting me in a space that I didn't want to be in. She was conscious of asking me about a doctor's appointment or of noting that my energy level was down or that I appeared sick with a cold or flu. She often remained silent until we developed a "script" that allowed her to feel comfortable asking questions and me to be comfortable answering or not.

The last challenge of disclosing my HIV status is balancing my need to receive support from others and my need to make those receiving the information comfortable. My socialization as a woman has led to this concept, but the reality is that it seems like an oxymoron. Far too often I have given a hug of reassurance to another when I really needed one, or have asked the other person how she is feeling about the disclosure rather than being asked about or tending to my own emotional needs. It is always harder to tell those closest to me than to tell a room of strangers. I don't need to tend to strangers' emotions; with those I know, it's more difficult to be open. Telling the students I work with has always been the hardest for me because I am never sure of their maturity level or what impact my disclosure will have on our working relationship. The experience of sharing with student staff has been both painful and empowering for them and me.

From my perspective, more challenging than living with HIV—or in my case, living with AIDS—is coming out and identifying as a lesbian *and* as being HIV-positive. Both have significant negative ramifications within the general society and gay community, and both identities are seen as unrelated. "How can you be a lesbian and be HIV-positive?" someone might ask. Perhaps an even larger issue for me is in my role as an educator—the question of which cause do I put at center stage has always been a personal challenge. My dual identity is as a lesbian—a member of the GLBT community—and as a woman living with AIDS. Neither identity defines me more than the other, and each helps to define my view of the world, my values and beliefs. However, living a dual life has been a struggle.

For example, over the years, I have received e-mails to join online support groups for women living with HIV/AIDS. I have been involved with three different ones and have yet to meet another HIV-positive woman who also identifies as lesbian or bisexual. I share many issues with other HIV-positive women related to medical care, family obligations, hopes and dreams. However, I also share the struggles of my gay male counterparts: I am discriminated against as a gay person and for having AIDS—in fact, the religious right would say I deserve AIDS for being gay. My struggle has been to find others who lead this dual life.

Being a lesbian and a person living with AIDS makes intimate relationships more complex. While writing my thesis for graduate school, I interviewed young undergraduates who identified as lesbian or bisexual. Several questions were asked about lesbian safer sex—its practice, protection methods, how to talk to your partner about safer sex, and so forth. My data showed that the women who had been intimate with women only did not practice any type of safer sex (for example, using a latex barrier). The women who had been with men, even once, used some type of barrier on occasion or rarely when intimate with another woman and more often when intimate with a man. Within my thesis I labeled these women as primary and secondary lesbians, respectively. Needless to say, safer sex within the lesbian community is not a priority—most lesbians ask, "Why do I need protection?" And it is not just the lesbian community that is acting out of ignorance: The media also support the myths about no risk of HIV and STD transmission among lesbians, and governmental agencies, in ignoring female-to-female transmission of HIV, promulgate that myth.

The Center for Disease Control (CDC) oversees the collection of data related to the spread of diseases in the United States and categorizes transmission rates based on a variety of demographics. The CDC does not recognize lesbians as an at-risk group for HIV transmission, which is evident in the educational materials it has produced for HIV/AIDS. This lack of concern for the risk of transmission between lesbians is also portrayed as a result of its definition of a lesbian, "a woman who has sex exclusively with other women since 1979." Using this definition, to date, the CDC has not documented any cases of HIV transmission between lesbians with no other risk factors. Using this as a definition, "secondary" lesbians, as described in my thesis, are left out of the "lesbian" definition; yet in my study, they accounted for eighty percent of the respondents interviewed, and this number would be similar for the population at large.

One factor in the closeting of HIV within the lesbian community is that question of "How did you get it?" If you got it from a man, then you must not be a lesbian. I can still see the images from the movie *Go Fish*, when one woman is confronted by her peers for sleeping with a man. "How can you call yourself a lesbian?" she is asked. Our community seems to pigeonhole as much as the society at large—if you are a lesbian, then you are intimate only with other women.

The biggest impact that this has for me is the inability to date other HIV-positive lesbians. The odds are small because of the closeting of this issue within the lesbian (and overall gay) community. Primary lesbians see no need for safer sex—they believe they cannot transmit STDs and HIV to other lesbians. And secondary lesbians, although they may have had safer sex with men, also feel immune when intimate with other women.

Numerous books are available on the theme of HIV-negative gay men staying negative in the age of AIDS, negative men dating positive men, gay erotic sex in the age of AIDS, and so forth. However, there are virtually no books (at least I haven't found any) about HIV-positive lesbians and their relationships. It is even difficult to find lesbian safer sex books (I have found three, all published outside the United States, and one video, produced in England). Even AIDS service organizations (ASOs) have only recently developed information about safer sex for lesbians. Gay Men's Health Crisis in New York, for example, has published "Lesbian Safer Sex" in a brochure and on its Web site, information that refers to the transmission of HIV between women. Web sites that focus on lesbian safer sex—let alone sex in general—are minimal, however, when compared to the number of Web sites for gay men. One issue not addressed in lesbian safer sex materials is that the HIV-positive partner is at higher risk for long-term consequences from STDs than the HIV-negative partner is. While the HIV-negative partner can take antibiotics or use some other treatment for infection (for example, Monistat for a yeast infection), the HIV-positive partner, because of her weakened immune system, may not be able to fight off any new infection(s).

For all these reasons, leading a dual life as a lesbian and as a person living with AIDS is complex and, at times, difficult to manage. Sometimes I am caught in the middle of being honest with myself and honest with another person at the risk of losing that person. I think the hardest thing I ever have to say to another person for whom I care is, "I am HIV-positive; I have AIDS."

Although there is tremendous closeting within the lesbian community about HIV and AIDS, I believe a significant number of lesbians are HIV-positive. With recent improvements in medication management and a more concerted effort to develop drugs for women living with HIV, more women are living longer with this disease (approximately five years ago, a woman with AIDS died three times faster than her male counterpart; in other words, the life expectancy of a woman with AIDS was six months, whereas a man with AIDS lived for eighteen months). The increased life expectancy will have an impact on how the lesbian community addresses HIV/AIDS.

Lesbians have always played a significant caretaking role within the AIDS community, but soon we will need to accept our sisters living with AIDS and care for them as we have for our gay brothers for so many years. To this point in time, HIV has only separated us.

As a lesbian with HIV, I lost three women I loved because they could not deal with the realities of the disease, the isolation of loving a woman living with HIV and the stereotypes associated with a woman living with AIDS and her partner. Many of the same issues our gay community allies have negotiated— for example, guilt by association—have plagued my relationships with women. The biggest challenge, perhaps, is the impact HIV has on sexual intimacy. Imagine hearing your lover say to you one night, "The only way I can protect us both is by never making love to you." It's similar to being raped again—but this time, raped of dignity, hope and a future with another person.

I face discrimination by the ignorant within the general public because I am gay, and discrimination within the lesbian community because I am living with AIDS. How will we address this new closet in our community? Where is the support, understanding, compassion? How can we begin to develop safe places for lesbians and bisexual women struggling to be women loving women and living with HIV/AIDS? Does it always need to be women like me, educators speaking out in the hope of being offered a hug and a pat on the back for comfort?

These are questions that must be asked and answered. We as a community can never be free until we accept all members of our community. Not for what they are or present themselves as, but for who they are inside. It is also important that, as a community, we raise concerns related to the treatment of all women living with HIV/AIDS—by the medical and health care fields, within the legal system and within the general public. HIV and AIDS are not going away.

Students entering college this year have never lived in a world without AIDS: Simply ignoring HIV/AIDS will not make it disappear. The lesbian community must acknowledge, embrace and support those living with the disease. Our community should be one of acceptance because we have experienced ourselves what it is like not to be accepted. However, to this point, the lesbian community has ignored our own who struggle with HIV or AIDS. The time has come to unite, fight and celebrate life in an age of AIDS, in a new light.

# EVIDENCE

## Sue Russell

Let me tell you about my cousin Harvey, who disappeared. No sign in his New York apartment, no body identified in the morgue, no headstone in the Jewish cemetery where his parents now lie. Like me, Harvey was manic-depressive. I remember hearing that he did not respond to lithium treatment, but I don't know the details about his compliance, or the lack of it, to a drug regime. At that time, lithium was the gold standard in treatment. Alternatives like Tegretol and Depakote were yet to be tried. Research indicates that, untreated, or treated unsuccessfully, manic-depressive illness worsens with age.

No significant genetic link exists between Harvey's illness and my own, but we are connected nonetheless. Both bookish types with Depression-era parents who never had leisure for intellectual pursuits, from an early age we were made to feel our difference. My mother solicited Harvey's advice for dealing with my lack of social success. He wrote me a long letter and told me about how his parents had made him read Dale Carnegie.

When I was in sixth grade, Harvey was busy accumulating assorted academic credentials, including an undergraduate degree in philosophy from Princeton and a stint at Harvard Medical School. With a Ph.D. in psychology (irony lost on no one) and a new wife (much to the family's surprise—nobody imagined him having a sex life), he landed his first academic position at Brandeis University, stayed a few years and was passed up for tenure. After his third tenure loss at a descending scale of colleges and universities and his subsequent

172

demotion to adjunct status, our family began to hear stories about Harvey's manic episodes.

As a college sophomore, I visited Harvey and his wife, Jane, in their Brooklyn Heights apartment. They took me out to my first Japanese restaurant for dinner and to Top of the Sixes for drinks. I sensed some strain in his wife's reaction when Harvey mentioned that a student might be calling at home that night. Eventually we heard that his wife left him. No surprise there. Later, a woman called his parents to report that Harvey was stalking her. She wanted them to exert pressure to get him to stop. On an emergency visit to Cleveland, Harvey called our house from the airport after trying unsuccessfully to reach his mother and father by phone. "My parents are dead in their apartment," he told me, a conclusion based solely on their failure to answer. Very soon after this incident, Harvey was gone from our lives for good. Twenty years later, we still don't know if he's dead or alive.


During a manic episode, a minute can seem like an hour as the tumble of ideas and images fight each other for ascendancy. Afterward, the broad sweep of historical time allows larger patterns to emerge. It is then that I scrutinize my own mental history for symptoms and signs—insomnia and easy tears, a sense of being tuned in to the moods of others, the code word "sensitive." I can easily trace the illness through family lines, but no diagram will ever give me the exact ratio of nature to nurture.

It is the season of anniversaries. From early August until Rosh Hashanah, the Jewish New Year, I am in a state of psychic readiness. Every physical malady I am prone to seems to escalate—from sinus headaches to irritable bowel syndrome, a nagging ache in the gut. My neck, back and shoulders cry out for aggressive massage. Work pressures mount, and nightmares make me jump in my sleep. School is starting, and God (the male one with the long white beard) must decide whether to inscribe me for another year in the Book of Life. The humidity breaks.

❖

Shift to early August 1984. Look at me there on the porch swing at Robert Frost's homestead in Franconia, New Hampshire, staring out at the White Mountains. It's a perfect late-summer day, and I watch the brightly colored gliders from the local airport swoop and play. I want to rise up from the ashes of my urban childhood, become a nature poet, learn names for all the wildflowers.

I had been eager for the start of the annual Frost Place poetry festival, nervously awaiting the flight to Boston and the three-hour drive with a fellow poet to Franconia. A week later, I returned home to Pittsburgh with a urinary tract infection, a sore throat, a decimated biological clock and a burning desire to change my life. The stimulation of being among a bunch of talented, free-associating poets in a setting of natural splendor had felt like a godsend after an especially hard year whose inventory included a major car wreck, a broken right foot, an adjunct teaching overload and the long silences of a dying marriage.

Like just about everybody who goes to "poetry camp," I had been too nervous and excited to eat or sleep. By the end of the week, my sleep was down to two or three hours a night, and I was hallucinating Christ on the Cross. I couldn't stand still for more than five minutes, and people were whispering "nervous breakdown" in my presence. I got a ride to the local emergency room for sleeping pills and a prescription for antibiotics for the infection, and then hopped on a plane to Pittsburgh for a month of late-night phone calls, long early-morning walks, 5 A.M. breakfasts with the cops and compulsive talkers at the "Eat 'n Park," scribbled poems and sex on the brain.

This manic period, which came in my twenty-eighth year, split my life into a "before" and "after" as definitively as a religious conversion. The clarity of outlook that accompanies any near-death experience is equally potent for survivors of deep depression, of which mania is merely the flip side. Every impulsive thing I did or said was powered by the feeling of last chance, now or never. Although I would not have called myself suicidal at the time, I was making preparations to leave this world.

On the last feverish day before my parents (summoned from Cleveland) and husband drove me to the emergency room of the local psychiatric hospital, we talked in figurative language about eating and fruit. I was surprised at my parents' capacity for metaphor. They looked through the Yellow Pages for nearby psychiatrists. It was the first day of Rosh Hashanah, so all the Jewish doctors were off. My father tried to pick out the Gentile doctors by name, but could not find one who was available to see me on short notice.

During my intake on Yom Kippur (the Day of Atonement) at the Diagnostic Evaluation Center, I refused to sign my name for voluntary admission until somehow they convinced me that it was just "procedure" and that after I signed I could be anybody I wanted. Upon arrival on "the floor," I was received by a group of patients masquerading as doctors, just like the famous scene from Ken Kesey's *One Flew Over the Cuckoo's Nest.* Everyone looked vaguely like other people I knew, but always with a slight difference—another hair color or perhaps a sex change—and of course a different name. I was given a single room with a sink.

I stayed for two and a half weeks. During the first week, I followed a maid out the door and down the back stairs and "eloped." I walked several blocks to the student union of the University of Pittsburgh—quite a feat with my wobbly Thorazine legs. The "white coats" found me there, sitting on the floor in the ladies' room. They brought me back to the unit by ambulance, where I received a megadose of Thorazine by a shot in the rear. I slept for two full days, after which my head felt clearer, but I had trouble believing that Wednesday was truly Wednesday and not Tuesday by another name. I was getting better, but I suffered intense side effects from the antipsychotic medication. With blurred vision and inner restlessness, I could neither read nor watch television. I could not use a tape player with earphones because I might strangle myself. I went to group therapy and found myself outnumbered by the smokers and religious fanatics. I played Ping-Pong with a depressed woman who was unresponsive to treatment and eventually got her to laugh. Like everyone else, I looked forward to trips to the patient cafeteria. I had never seen so much concentrated eating in my life.

After my initial relief at being out of the hospital, the manic period was quickly swallowed by the most crippling depression I had ever experienced, six parts biological balancing act, four parts guilt and shame over my own embarrassing behavior while manic. I got through most of it with no medication at all and with the help of a few kind friends and neighbors who found ways to keep me busy. I bought coloring books designed for adults, with marking pens to match. I played Centipede on a neighbor's arcade-sized machine in her basement. I tried bowling and needlepoint.

Nothing worked until one day I began to notice that the world was no longer drained of color. Slowly, I geared up to do the things I needed to do to get my life back in order. It was time for me to find a new job where I could make enough money to live on my own. Although my husband had been gentle and supportive throughout my long illness, we both knew it was time to move on. I got a job, an apartment and a no-fault divorce, in that order. I bought a few pieces of furniture and had friends over for dinner. I fell asleep in front of the television and had nobody to put me to bed. I was celibate for six years, not entirely by design. Then I was invited to join the board of directors of Pittsburgh's now defunct women's restaurant, and after a period of lesbian quasi-dating and hopeless long-distance crushes, my friendship with Lynne started to inch its way toward romance and love.

Coming back from a major illness, whatever its cause, it is only natural to assess one's direction. For me, part of that self-searching led, however meanderingly, away from a conventional heterosexual marriage and toward a long-term lesbian partnership. I began to realize that the desire for safety and acceptance that had landed me in a conventional marriage to a nice Jewish boy had also caused me a great deal of pain. Having a manic episode teaches you to pay attention to the signs, whether for good or for ill. It took me years to know love when I found it. I am still learning to balance that need for intense human connection, sexual or otherwise, with the pleasures and reassurances of the everyday. This may take a whole lifetime to learn.

As a lesbian with a disability, some might say I have two strikes against me in dealing with the "real" or "straight" or "normie" world. I have found that the stigma of mental illness has a more direct effect on my daily life than my sexual orientation. It feels easier these days to be an out lesbian than to be an out manic-depressive. At my new job in a new city, I've been upfront that my move was due to a career and job change for my female significant other. My colleagues politely refer to my significant other at the appropriate moments in conversation, and she is welcomed at the occasional "couples" event. Whatever unease some may feel about the presence of queers, at least they behave themselves in public. On the other hand, I know very well from past experience that if I were to drop into friendly conversation a reference to being manic-depressive, a condition that has considerably more effect on my work habits than the gender of my bed partner, I would soon be under surveillance for symptoms and signs. I know how a sequence of bad days and sarcastic comments can lead to being fired. And lest you scream "lawsuit," the cause and effect of disability and job loss will be conveniently obscured by the appropriate paperwork.

The diagnostic label for my form of manic depression is "bipolar I," which means that I have experienced psychotic symptoms along with my episodes. But I don't want to give the reader a guided tour of my particular madness. A problem with writing about mania and psychosis is that the narrative can easily become tiresome for both writer and reader. Memories of a manic or psychotic state hold metaphorical clues like the picture cards in a Tarot deck, but they can also keep one mired in the past, spinning out variations on the same tired theme. There is the fear that writing about manic depression will cause the symptoms to return, and the shame of remembering what one would rather forget—the 3 A.M. phone call to loves of the past, the multiple missives to obsessions of the present, the ruined (or potentially ruined) friendships and the beleaguered spouse. Although I could tell one thousand and one nights' worth of tales from the bipolar planet, I'd rather concentrate, for now, on the daily grind. Three solid meals, eight hours of sleep, nine-to-five jobs. Rent, laundry, tax returns. Bills and pills. PMS (it's worse for us; hormones and neurotransmitters are a potent mix). Making do.

I am now fifteen years down the road from my worst and most frightening symptoms. During that time, I suffered a few manic blips and was hospitalized due to a grand mal seizure brought on by a bad mix of medications. I am less afraid than I once was of my manic triggers or stress points—travel, staying out late, attending conferences, drinking a little too much, feeling turned on. I breathe a little more freely now and allow myself on occasion to have fun. One of the worst side effects of manic depression is that happiness itself becomes suspect, so you have to tease yourself into a good time.

In my current nonthreatening, medicated state, I can easily pass as "normal," but there is always a cost. Medication makes me tractable for outward show—what the therapists call "affect." Much of the time, I am on good behavior. I lock my office door to cry, and I walk away from escalating conflict. I try too hard to be the hero of my story, to show strength in adversity, and sometimes the leftover anger and frustration backfires at home, the one place where I don't have to pretend.

In these years, the balance of my writing has gradually shifted. I have become a prose writer and occasional poet rather than a poet who could also, when called upon, write more than serviceable prose. I'm not sure whether this has to do with the dampening effect of lithium (I do believe that it has one) or if it's only a matter of finding my true path. But writing is a romance, and romance can reside in any genre. I am happiest writing about other writers— about the crisis points and identity struggles in their lives and work. Lesbian poets before Stonewall who are not comfortable with this identification, writers who got started late in life or disappeared for long periods, writers from an earlier time who are now being rediscovered. I have a hunch that if there is such a thing as a manic-depressive mindset, it has to do with an encompassing vision of the world, a breaking of the boundaries of body, mind, soul and gender. Think of the shimmering quality of Virginia Woolf's novels, or the intense concentration of Emily Dickinson's poems.

As a reader and writer, I am less interested in "great literature" than I am in the weave of life and work, the missed connections and also-rans, the need to pass or assimilate as it overlaps with the desire for public acclaim. These are my own struggles as well. I will never again be a *wunderkind*, and I'm already a few years past the age limit for the Yale Younger Poets prize. But the great news is that I have found work about which I am passionate and for which I have gained some small recognition, and this after years of just muddling through with a self-image of chronic underachievement. I've realized that I learn the most about myself from looking outward and away, rather than facing the mirror head-on. And I get to fall in love with every new writer or book without risking my cozy relationship. It's a fix I can't live without.

Although in many ways I am doing quite well now, I always want to remember what it feels like to be marginal, to know to what extent, through life's changes, I might have fallen through the cracks, in another era, or even today. I carry these thoughts with me on my trips to the pharmacy, or at the pathology lab when the technician fills five tubes with my blood, checking lithium level, imipramine level, thyroid and liver profiles. The day may come when I can be tapered off lithium—two doctors have offered me the option based on my long period of relative stability on a low dose. Still, I'm not quite ready to test fate.

During the time it's taken to move from draft to final text for this essay, we've gone from the Days of Awe to Chanukah and the miracle of the everlasting light. Tonight I light one candle on the menorah, the *shamas,* and use it to light the rest. This weekend we'll get our tree. It was my idea a few years back, a healing ritual after a grueling November, and Lynne, the Gentile, assented. I look forward to the trimming, to the tinsel and bright red hanging apples, the strings of colored lights and, maybe, to the forbiddenness of it all. I wrote a poem once in which I imagined my cousin Harvey as audience. "Accept all gods," I said, as if he could hear me. And maybe he can.

# PASSING THROUGH SHAME

## Mary Frances Platt

Certified letters never seem to hold good news, at least not the ones addressed to me. The letter I hold today is no different. I scan the two pieces of paper rattling in my hand, "State of Arizona, Department of Law, Civil Rights Division, Mary F. Platt versus Brewster Center for Domestic Violence . . . the Division has determined that there is not reasonable cause to believe discrimination has occurred. The order is hereby entered, dismissing the charge."

It is 1996. I am searching downtown Tucson for a phone I can drive up to. I am not having much luck. I try not to notice how empty the scooterless view from my rearview mirror is. The mountains surround the windows and the saguaro cactus, which the land group I helped create is named after, are beginning to bloom. How I have loved this land, the idea of a disabled women's community in the middle of the desert. Eight years ago we raised the money to buy an acre and a half and put it into a corporation, in the concept of a land trust. The land is owned by no one woman but, rather, available to all women with disabilities; folks contributing what they are able to toward the mortgage, bills and upkeep.

So, I have left this place, Saguaroland, without my broken wheelchair, needing finally to call the number clutched and crumpled in my purse for weeks now. I have no phone in the eight-by-ten-foot environmental illness (EI) safer metal storage shed I call my winter home. The mantra circling my brain offers some strength: It will be okay, it will be okay, it will be okay; please, goddess, let me stay safe. I dial the two numbers and that of an ex back in New England. I leave messages on two beepers and reach the local center for domestic violence. I explain to the advocate that the cop has told me to get an order of protection. I don't have a working chair, my scooter lift is broken, I can't walk into the courthouse. I luck out—she will help me, meet her in half an hour, she'll be wearing red.

The just-hung-up phone rings, it's the counselor from the battered lesbian hotline. I try to explain all the trouble I am in at the moment. She says this is the third call in a short time she has gotten from a woman being abused on rural women's land. I feel less crazy. Do I use the words "attendant abuse"? I am so very scared. Will they hurt the animals I left behind, burn down my shed, destroy the respirator that supports my nighttime breath, cut the electric lines that create the oxygen and purify the air to breathe?

I am lucky; my initial calls for help have been answered. The advocate obtains an injunction against harassment for me, tells me what to expect if I have to call the police, helps me create safety plans and makes me feel less insane. I can't help thinking, *What if I could not move at all without my chair, or could not drive, or could not leave my bed without the attendant who was abusing me?* I manage to feel grateful for what is left working, mechanical and human; try not to remember four years earlier, after a pulmonary embolism, lying in bed, not enough breath to speak or move more than my head, fearing my stressed-out lover, who was tired of caring for me after all friends had fled from fear of my seemingly impending death.

We are so afraid of being locked up that we acquiesce to lesser forms of violence. Attendant abuse can manifest in countless ways: humiliation, sexual abuse, withholding of life-sustaining acts such as feeding, toileting, dressing, transferring, bathing. Manipulation and control can be as subtle as putting red socks on your feet when you've requested the blue ones, or as blatant as "No, I don't approve of Suzy and will not drive you in your van to her house."

Many disabled people receive their assistance from visiting-nurse and home-health-care agencies, which, being based in medical as opposed to independent living ideology, do not provide their services with crip-empowerment in mind. If you're lucky, you get a nurse, health aide or homemaker who allows you control and bends the rules to accommodate your needs and personality. Most likely, you will end up with someone who feels she is better suited to running your life than you are. We take what we can get, for at least we are in our own homes and *can* get out of bed—even if we get put back into bed at 4:30 P.M. because the agency closes at 5 P.M. We learn real good to make do because not making do will surely lead to sitting in what doo-doo we've made for hours or days in some nursing hole.

Often people who grow up disabled have no other reality than that of constant control and disempowerment. They learn at an early age to keep their choices and opinions to themselves, and somehow manage to create a space amid oppression and abuse. Even if the violence is recognized for what it is, what choice exists? How can you leave a situation when the person abusing you is the one who gets you dressed and washed for the day? Too many people with disabilities have spent years in back bedrooms, bound to beds for lack of a wheelchair or trapped in their inaccessible homes. Escape is not even remotely possible. For some of us, our only freedom may be in our silent thoughts that defy control.

Attendant abuse is power and control over a person with disabilities by a person who provides paid or unpaid assistance to that person. Lesbian crips face their own brand of hell in this violence because of homophobia and cultural expectations and norms within the queer community. Disabled lesbians often seek out and hire lesbian attendants so that they do not have to fear reprisal because of their sexual preference. Those same attendants, savvy to their employers' ways of living on the edge with the disability pittance they are allowed, may control that crip by threatening to expose their edge-living ways to the authorities. Some disabled women have been outed by their queer sisters, causing great harm to their survival. I recently was denied access to controlling the fiscal aspect of my personal assistance program because a lesbian assistant whom I had fired reported me for misuse of my funds. She stated I was using some of my hours for assistance for my disabled father. Even though that was seven years ago and there was no proof of her allegations, I suffer the consequences of her retaliation today. How many of us don't fire attendants who are abusing us for fear of losing the services we do have?

At the moment I am safe. My primary assistant is a dyke without a violent or abusive bone in her body. When she becomes too controlling, mostly from familiarity with me, I can voice how I feel, tell her to stop. Upset, we both try to set better limits, boundaries between us that will help each to be in her safe self.

It took me five years to get safe from the one who abused me when I was at my sickest. I lost most of my friends defending her bad behavior because no matter how much she humiliated me, she was still my driver to the doctor's office. I had no help to get free. I made a long-range plan—train a service dog, adapt the cottage, fight for new, reliable equipment, apply for more in-home-assistance monies, learn new ways to protect myself, try and make some new friends. Ultimately, the violence was subdued when I moved out of my own home. Now I am faced again with leaving a good chunk of what I have acquired as well as the dream of a warm wintertime women's land community. But, as I write this, I am safe, even if my pants are shitty, my food fast frozen and my floors filthy. I make no mistake here. I know I am one of the few crips who lives with many hours of no fear.

The price I have paid for less fear is increased isolation. I say increased, for abandonment, exclusion, isolation and loneliness are realities running through the lives of many ill and disabled folk. I was homebound and had disconnected from my fat- and crip-phobic cousins and aunt, as well as my actively alcoholic brother. Both of my parents had recently died, and most of my dyke friends had left shortly after the blood clot almost killed me. As "disenfranchised" and "disabled" seem to go hand in hand, I was looking for a family of friends in a supportive, wheelchair-accessible, EI safer community. I thought I had found it in Saguaroland. Instead, I got battered and lost a best friend and the relationship with a child I had parented. I mourn the winter home that brought me back to life, as well as the $25,000 I invested in the land and living structures.

Loneliness has settled into my cells, and like many of my disabled sisters and brothers, I have learned to live with it permeating every moment of my life. Lesbians with disabilities do not find community easily. If we live with personal assistance and assistive technology, our lives become more complicated. Is the dyke dance wheelchair-accessible? Will I have the personal assistance I need to attend the support group? Whose home besides my own is welcoming to wheels?

What dykes, if any, have worked through their own ableism and can relate to a crip without shame, fear or disgust? And what happens if my clunker of a wheelchair poops out on my date? Or, more likely, who in this community of amazons and fitness freaks will find the beauty that exists in my fat, disabled body?

No person who is experiencing domestic abuse has an easy time of it. The steps to escape can be many and difficult. Over the past twenty years legislation has become more supportive of the battered spouse; in some states, arrest upon violation of a restraining order is mandatory. The battered woman still has to come to terms with her often decreased self-esteem enough to make moves to resist and escape the violence. Although still difficult, a nondisabled woman can usually find support in a center for domestic violence. Shelter doors are not closed to walking and well women, and funding for services for victims has increased.

Attendant abuse is not considered domestic violence under most state laws unless the person abusing you is a partner or relative. Many states have a disabled persons protection agency that takes reports of abuse committed against a person with disabilities. They will investigate the abuse if there is imminent danger. My own experiences with reporting abuse inflicted on my developmentally disabled neighbors in Massachusetts is that the agency is useless and will investigate only if there is severe, documentable physical abuse. The other option battered crips have is to file criminal assault charges. In my own town, the police station has steps at all entrances, and many courthouses across the country are still not wheelchair-accessible. Mental abuse and manipulation as well as woman-on-woman violence are seldom addressed, and there are few avenues for complaint and confrontation.

I was lucky that initially I was able to obtain some services under the domestic violence grant monies; fortunate to have queer volunteer lawyers for whom it was not a big jump from lesbian lover battering to queer attendant abuse. I am forever grateful to the cigarette-smoking, overworked straight lawyer who wrapped her head around just how two women were controlling my movements on the land. She knew that changing the lock on the main gates meant no exit for me or entry for oxygen, police or emergency vehicles. She understood that harassing my service dog with an aggressive Chow-Chow or threatening to cut my electric line when I relied on a respirator, oxygen machine and power wheelchair meant imminent harm. In court she saw my ex-attendant's irrational, violent behavior and contemplated how she would use her intimate knowledge of me to cause harm. When this same attendant put a lock on the community washing machine after dumping all my clothes in the cactus, she joked amid inhaled smoke about how long it must have taken Lucy, my service dog, to pick it all up. It was good to laugh in all that terror.

In court my abusers brought lesbian friends who even after hearing the violence read in statements by the judge continued to support the perpetrators in their control and abuse tactics. Do these perpetrators' supporters really believe the web of lies these women wove about me? Many years ago one of these abusers had her house burned down. Now I understand why. Some woman, finding no way to confront this perpetrator's sinister ways, found her own brand of justice.

After the blood clot traveled to my lung and almost close enough to my heart to kill me, I was unable to do anything, including breathe, on my own. There was nothing I could do but endure the abuse amid the assistance. I did not have the energy to even tell anyone about it. My abuser did not hit me, and I was able to survive the name-calling, humiliation and psychological abuse. At Saguaroland I was well enough and had the physical ability to remove myself from the situation and seek legal and other supports.

As I progressed from victim to survivor, I encountered physical-access barriers and other forms of discrimination from the domestic violence agency from which I was receiving services. When my complaints of discrimination were voiced, I was informed that I really did not fall under the domestic violence act of that state as it was attendant and not spousal abuse, and I was therefore not eligible for services. I managed to swallow my feelings, fear and humiliation and fight them to stay in the program as an ex-battered lesbian. I stayed because I desperately needed my weekly dose of support and encouragement from other battered women. Before I left Tucson I filed a complaint with the civil rights division regarding discrimination based on disability. They won, I lost.

How do I pass through this shame to describe my experiences with the two battered lesbian support groups I tried to participate in? The group in Tucson had to change its location because it was revealed and made unsafe. We moved temporarily to a private home that had a level entry, but was also extremely scented and offered no bathroom big enough for me to enter in my wheelchair. As the group became larger, the rules increased. No this, no that, all for good reasons, but for a crip whose abuse had been a reflection of ableism and feminist process, the rules themselves were reminiscent of that abuse. I recently watched a movie about the one-legged gimp who climbed Mt. Everest. His nondisabled climbing mate, after they were instructed to return to base camp against their wishes, said, "Now I know what it is like to be disabled; everyone else makes decisions about your life for you." The group became the embodiment of that reality for me: no intimate relationships among group members, speak only in the first person, spend only *x* amount of time talking and so forth. When I voiced my concerns as a battered crip who was trying to escape the control of others and gain some independence in my own life, they didn't get it and targeted me, the only crip in the group, as the problem. The leader said that if I couldn't abide by the rules the group set (note how I got excluded as a group member here), then I shouldn't be in the group. I left.

When I arrived back in New England, once again I reached out to battered queers. Again, the rules were set up for those involved in the group, none of them disabled to the point of depending on human or machine assistance to survive. Through those two experiences, and by listening to other battered crips, I came to understand that like everything else within lesbian culture, the battered lesbian survivor network is built on the ideas, values and needs of nondisabled dykes. The shame I felt should have fallen on the shoulders of those lesbians who blatantly excluded and refused to listen to the reality of a crip with significant disabilities. The very places I went to seek a way out of my isolation served only to further my isolation.

Dykes with disabilities are not unfamiliar with oppression and discrimination. Every day of our lives is overwhelming, exhausting, debilitating. And yet many of us rejoice at our daily presence on this planet. We are strong, resilient women who can adapt to most anything. We support each other over computer and phone lines, and pick ourselves up over and over again, for the opportunity to share a meal, read a book, feel the sun on our faces, commit an act of defiance, make love or make a mess. As a group we are poorer, less educated and more vulnerable than our nondisabled sisters, and yet we still manage to give voice to our experiences.

Lesbians with disabilities are being abused by their attendants—some queer, some not—every minute of every day. A recently conducted Connecticut survey revealed that upward of seventy percent of women in that state are currently experiencing violence in their lives. Believe it. Don't be silent when you suspect it. Be that crip's friend. Help her with the physical aspects of getting free. Be her assistant if she needs that. Help her get rid of her abusive attendant and find new ones. Listen to her, break the silence when you know she is being abused. Testify to the abuse you have seen if she asks that of you.

Disabled lesbians are just beginning to identify and speak out about attendant abuse. We're beginning to find our way, to identify the barriers to resisting the abuse and finding our ways to freedom. Most shelters are still not wheelchair-accessible, and a lot of us have no assistance or transportation to get to those shelters. Battered lesbian groups are often hostile and unwelcoming of crips experiencing attendant abuse. We don't even know how to define the parameters of this violence, let alone begin to talk about it. But one by one, and crip to crip, we are telling our stories, doing consciousness-raising about appropriate and inappropriate ways for attendants to treat us. Recently, I attended a women's studies conference that focused on disabled women. I met and talked with other women who had experienced attendant abuse and added my story to theirs. I felt the walls of shame begin to crumble and the mantra circling my brain began a new rhythm: I survived, I give voice, I resist.

# PERSONAL ASSISTANCE
## A Job, a Politic

### Mary Frances Platt

In dominant, white, middle-class, eurocentric* cultures, people with disabilities are seen first as folks who have medical problems or special needs. Disabled folks have something wrong with them that needs to be fixed, and if it can't be fixed, it should be overcome or, at the very least, hidden. "Disabled" is a dirty word, and if you can't pass as nondisabled you should at least try.

If you strive to become "normal" and can't, then you win the pity prize from nondisabled folks. If you accept, love, honor and are proud of your disabled self, you win the bravery prize. And if you actively fight the oppression of people with disabilities and see disability as a cultural issue and not just a medical one, you win the "My, aren't you hostile" and "If you'd only get that chip off your shoulder, your life would be much easier" awards.

No, our lives are made "easier" by barrier-free environments, civil rights laws that ensure equal access, and a health care system that does not institutionalize, infantilize or routinely commit genocide against us.

Part of equal access for some of us involves the use of personal assistants. A personal assistant, or P.A., is someone hired by a disabled person to assist that person in her day-to-day living according to her direction. A personal assistant is not a home health aide, a nurse, a caretaker or a guardian. The sole responsibility of the personal assistant is to carry out the directions of the disabled

---

* Eurocentric: Centered or based on European culture.

person. That may involve shopping, brushing the dog, cooking, feeding, dressing or bathing the person with disabilities. The key phrase here is self-determination. It is the disabled person who orchestrates how, when, where and in what manner she will be assisted.

A good personal assistant is a vehicle for self-determination. That means listening well, following directions exactly and not asking for reasons or offering your opinions or your own experiences. It is the job of the personal assistant to do exactly what he or she is asked or directed to do. Personal assistance is a job, not an act of charity.

First, learn about the basic tenets of the disability rights movement: 1) equal access rather than meeting "special needs"; 2) integration, not segregation; and 3) self-directed living, not medical models of caretaking or institutionalization.

Although disabled folks are glad to have self-directed assistance, most of us hate spending tons of time, energy and so forth hiring, educating and being in day-to-day situations with assistants. Do not take personally our lack of enthusiasm at needing another human being around us so much. The reality is that most of us would really rather have the ability to do the task on our own, by ourselves and in exactly the manner we want it done—whether that manner be very precise or very general. If the person you assist has a day where we would really rather be alone, and can't be, try to detach yourself from her disgruntlement and focus on the task at hand.

A personal assistant becomes very intimately involved in a disabled person's life. It is usually not a chosen intimacy. By intimacy, I mean you may be getting acquainted with poopy pants or a disabled person's favorite dessert and most despised professor. Basically, being around us means being knowledgeable about our lives. Respect and honor that knowledge, and do not use it against us. Unless directed otherwise, assume that everything you hear, see and do is confidential. Don't let it be a big deal that you know what kind of vibrator someone uses or what her daily medications are. Forced intimacy is a fact of life that must be acknowledged between disabled employer and personal assistant employee.

Listening skills are paramount to your effectiveness as a P.A. You must be able to focus intently on what your employer is saying and follow through on the directions you are given. If you don't understand what you are to do or are uncertain, ask for clarification. Don't question your employer as to why she wants something done, or offer how you think it could be done better. There will be times you will be asked to do a task that you do in your own life, but not in the manner to which you are accustomed to doing it. Remember the whole purpose of self-directed personal assistance is to support the ability of the person with the disabilities to maintain decision-making power and implementation in her life, even if she is not the one doing the actual physical task.

If you've always had a great memory and an eye for detail, then this is the time to reawaken those skills or sharpen them. If you are forgetful and spend lots of time looking for your keys, now is a good time to track down and start using all those memory tricks and aids that people always seem to be coming up with. Disabled people who use assistance need to know where everything is at any given time so that they can tell any assistant where something is located. Make sure that everything goes back exactly where it was. An object moved two inches to the right may no longer be accessible, reachable or usable by your employer—and it may be hours or days before the next assistant arrives to correct the error.

Being late, changing your schedule at the last minute or cutting out of work earlier than you are supposed to is a serious lapse of responsibility. Some of us wait in bed for you to arrive, or need your assistance to take time-sensitive medication, or cannot get into bed for the night if you don't show up. Make sure you and your employer have worked out a system for dealing with your not being able to come to work. And please don't come to work sick: You might make us extremely ill, so don't play martyr or ignore your own symptoms and endanger us.

Basically, the most important skill to have is the ability to put your ego aside and get on with what you are being directed to do. You may not agree with the way your employer lives her life or like the hours she chooses to be awake or asleep. You may not get along with her partner or friends, and you may find the cat quite spoiled. As with any other job, you will have feelings that are evoked about the work you are doing, your employer, the salary and so forth. If your feelings are negative, it is important to find a place to vent those feelings and get support. Other than concerns about the actual working conditions, you should be taking your attitudes, ideas, personal thoughts, conclusions and judgments somewhere else. If you dislike the work, you will find a way to move out of the situation. If you like the work, let us know!

Being a personal assistant is not an easy job. It is exacting and at times exasperating. You are required to be a Jack or Jill of all trades, an expert listener, a proficient cook and capable of just about every life task imaginable. There is little room for error; perfection is almost always required. The flip side is that you will probably never be bored and may find that, as you do the work, you begin to move through your own life in a different, sometimes more efficient, sometimes more relaxed manner.

Being a personal assistant automatically means you are participating in the liberation of people with disabilities. It's up to you how much more of a partnership, if any, you will have with the disability rights and anti-ableist movements.

# BODIES IN TROUBLE

Ellen Samuels

On those occasions when I go to political marches or demonstrations—which has been much less frequently in the last four years as chronic fatigue and immune dysfunction syndrome (CFIDS) and environmental illness have gobbled up more and more of my life—I am the kind who wears buttons. My button collection now lives in a ceramic bowl on my bookshelf, silently exhorting passersby to fight AIDS, hunger, homelessness, racism and various other social ills.

When writing this essay, I set two of those buttons next to my computer: One, black with bright pink lettering, declares, "Nobody Knows I'm a Lesbian"; the other commands firmly in red, white and black: "See the Person, Not the Disability." I selected these buttons because they represent two of my identities, the two I'm writing about here, and also because they voice, in their guileless, colorful way, the theme of my essay: the issue of visibility, of being seen—or not seen—for who you really are.

What does it mean to be visible? In the literal sense, it means "able to be seen," and thus carries the limitation of assuming that everyone is *able* to see. Acknowledging that limitation, I believe "visibility," in its political context, is still a powerful and important metaphor, one that has come to mean a kind of active presence, a conscious declaration or performance of identity.

As a feminine-looking lesbian, I am visible when I wear an earring, button, T-shirt or other marker of queer identity; when I take part in a queer event or space, such as a march, gay bar or academic panel; when I hold hands with

192

my girlfriend in the street. I also become visible when I speak or write as a queer person. As a person with a hidden disability, I become visible only when I speak of my disability or when I experience specific symptoms that require assistive devices: hand splints, a wheelchair, a portable air filter. Through these personal experiences, I have come to distinguish in my mind between declarative and implicit forms of visibility. In the examples of visibility I just mentioned, the implicit forms of showing my sexual identity seem to me to be markers of pride, while the implicit forms of showing my disability are markers of illness. In my experience, there is little or no social context for a purely political statement of disability—a button or a T-shirt; if anything, these would be seen as self-pitying, since nondisabled society assumes that one would choose to hide one's disability if at all possible. I am still wondering how to frame a declarative form of visibility for people with hidden disabilities that can be as assertive, proud and powerful as a T-shirt reading: "We're here! We're queer! Get used to it!"

I am speaking from a position of some privilege: the privilege of being able to "pass." Unlike many of my peers, I am not automatically presumed to be a dyke based on my looks. And while it can be painful and frustrating to live with a hidden disability, knowing most people see me as young, healthy and strong, I have the privilege of *that* perception—unlike those people who "look" disabled. In *Feminism and Disability,* Barbara Hillyer writes that, for both lesbians and people with disabilities, "Some of the reasons we pass are survival reasons: for safety, for security, for comfort. But there are political reasons as well: passing increases the possibility of being accepted as an individual." This reasoning brings us back to the message of my second button—"See the Person, Not the Disability"—and suggests that, by passing, one essentially covers the second half of the button's wording, at least until first impressions have been made.

But passing also has its costs. As Hillyer discusses at some length, passing is demoralizing and isolating and usually has strong emotional and social consequences for the passing individual, while coming out, either as gay or disabled, is often empowering and leads to both greater self-acceptance and increased societal awareness. I have certainly noticed that when I am wearing a visible token of disability or queerness, most people treat me very differently.

When their reactions take the form of prying curiosity or outright hostility, I usually have to fight the urge to scurry back to the closet. On the other hand, nondisabled people tend to be much more helpful and understanding when they can see some visible proof of my disability, and when queer strangers acknowledge me in public, I feel that glow of affirmation and strength that can only come from stepping outside the isolation of the closet.

I am sitting in my office at a small northeastern women's college, meeting with each of my Freshman Composition students individually. My first conference of the day is with Rosa, a Filipina woman with cropped hair who dresses in canvas work pants and a T-shirt. ("Baby dyke" I called her to my friends after the first day of class, but later challenged myself not to make such facile assumptions based on appearance. How could I be sure? . . . though my gaydar is seldom wrong.) When Rosa walks into our conference carrying a bookbag festooned with rainbow flags, I feel justified and a little smug. Then a new dilemma hits me: Do I come out to her?

With my shoulder-length hair and red lipstick, I know I do not fit the usual idea of how lesbians look. And this is not only a matter of annoying cultural stereotypes, but a real issue in the lesbian community, and in my life. Ever since I let my hair grow long again, I've been getting far less attention from women—and far more from men. So I know Rosa will not assume I am "in the family." And do I want to come out to her now, in the second week of classes, at a new college where I have only just been hired? I decide not. I feel too vulnerable, too afraid of being labeled the "gay professor" at this tiny, fairly conservative school. Instead, I gush with enthusiasm over our conversation and ask pointedly which of Jeanette Winterson's novels she's read. Rosa leaves smiling, perhaps having picked up on the subtext of our meeting, perhaps not.

Later in the day, I meet with another student, Joann, who has a visual impairment. She is short, with curly red hair, one blue eye zigzagging wildly behind her thick glasses. We talk about problems she is having getting some professors to accommodate her needs. I haven't thought about whether I am going to come out to her as disabled, but suddenly I am leaning forward and blurting out: "I have a hidden disability and I've had to ask for a lot of accommodations—I know how people can be."

For the first time, she looks me in the face and seems to relax in her chair. "Oh! So you know how it is! I'm so glad someone understands!"

Afterward, I wonder why it felt so urgent to tell her I was disabled, why that closet suddenly felt unbearably confining. Was it because I had less fear of repercussion, the threat of homophobia seeming more dangerous and immediate than the threat of ableism? Or was it my perception of her need, her discomfort at having to explain herself to another in a long parade of "normals" who openly or implicitly doubted both her impairment and her ability to transcend it? Or, and this seems closest to the truth, was it my need that drove me to speak, my own feeling of isolation in a new workplace, where I had had to ask for a handicapped parking place to be created in the lot near my building—the school had never had a professor with a disability before. I have been out as a gay person for a lot longer than I have been out as disabled: I have a close circle of gay and supportive straight friends; I have written about being lesbian, spoken about it, marched in countless gay pride marches. But I am relatively new to the world of disability, and I see that I am grasping eagerly for connections with its other inhabitants.

One of my most useful and challenging guides in this ongoing process has been essayist Nancy Mairs, who, in her book *Waist-High in the World: A Life Among the Nondisabled,* writes that "Maps render a foreign territory, however dark and wide, fathomable. I mean to make a map." While Mairs, who has multiple sclerosis, has frequently written about her experiences with illness and disability, this book is her first that consciously and continually devotes itself to the topic of "bodies in trouble," both in individual terms and in terms of the social body that is unable or unwilling to fully accept its disabled citizens.

Reading Mairs's book, I identified strongly with her eloquently described struggle to create and sustain a selfhood that embraced both her progressively disabled body and her passionate vocation as a writer. Like Mairs, I have found that writing has been my lifeline through illness and loss to a renewed sense of self-worth and wholeness. As Mairs writes:

> I am somebody. A body. A difficult body, to be sure, almost too weak to
> stand, increasingly deformed, wracked still by gut spasms and headaches
> and menstrual miseries. But some body. Mine. Me. In establishing myself
> as a writer, however modest my success, I have ceased to be nobody. I have
> written my way into my embodiment and here I am at home.

By writing her way into embodiment, Mairs suggests the tremendous power
of writing as a form of active visibility, one that offers as rich a field to a writer
with disabilities as it does to gay and lesbian writers. Indeed, she explicitly con-
nects her decision to write *Waist-High in the World* with the increased visibility
of disabled people in American society, since "increasingly sophisticated medical technology ensures that more of us who are born with or develop some sort
of impairment will survive, living longer and more publicly than ever before."

Yet when Mairs subscribes to the belief that living "more publicly"—that
is, more visibly—must necessarily lead to greater cultural regard and understanding, I think she (as well as many gay and lesbian activists) misses the
underlying assumptions of privilege that accompany any isolated use of "visibility" as a political strategy. Certainly she rarely questions the class-based
availability of those "sophisticated medical technologies" that have made all the
difference in her life but which are still difficult to obtain and almost never covered by health insurance or Medicaid.

In general, Mairs's book is indelibly colored, and sometimes limited, by
her experience as an upper-middle-class, heterosexual, married and professional
woman. One striking example of how that experience limits Mairs's insight takes
place in an entertaining chapter describing her visits to England with her husband and the various obstacles she has encountered, including absurdly narrow
airplane aisles, the breakdown of her rented electric wheelchair, and English
manor houses with lofty and impregnable flights of stairs. Often these anecdotes involve incredibly helpful and sensitive British people who either conquer
the obstacles or can't stop apologizing for them. Mairs contrasts this experience
with the less enlightened attitudes of Americans: "For some reason, at any rate,

the English attitude seems to be that infirmity in and of itself deserves compensation and solicitude. In the States . . . on the contrary, it is deemed shameful and at least a little suspect."

Mairs has some evidence to support this supposition, as she lists a number of financial breaks given to the disabled in England, including free theater tickets and discounted admission to various tourist sites. Mairs supposes that the English attitude toward disability is affected by their experience with two world wars that left large numbers of the population "maimed." I have heard the same opinion from my support group leader, who is French, and who also has multiple sclerosis. However, after reading Lois Keith's impressive anthology of writing by English women with disabilities, *What Happened to You?*, which includes numerous stories of shame, struggle and poverty related to living with disability in the United Kingdom, I had to question Mairs's overambitious extrapolation from her own experience as a well-off American tourist. After all, free theater tickets aren't much good when your child's school refuses to put in a ramp so that you can enter the building, or when you are a disabled child placed in an institution and no one believes your stories of abuse. As so often in Mairs's work, while she acknowledges her financial privilege to a certain extent, her deeper class-based assumptions and ignorance remain intact.

And perhaps I, with my educated, middle-class, white Jewish background, share some of those assumptions. It's true that I am struggling just to get through each day, while my nondisabled peers are building careers, long-term relationships and families. However, I'm still able, with help from my family, to pay rent on my own apartment, to buy the expensive supplements my doctor recommends, to cover private insurance premiums, to treat myself to a movie now and then. I feel the same joy that Mairs relates in small and simple things, even in such ridiculous contexts as being able to do my own laundry and plunge my own toilet—and when joy has shrunk to such a small thing, it can be hard to see that it is still a privilege. I know that if I had Mairs's level of physical incapacity I would also want the expensive wheelchair, the voice-controlled computer, the chance to go to England. However, both Mairs and I would be wrong if we stopped with satisfying our own needs, procuring our own comfort. Mairs's project, as she explains it, is to let the nondisabled world know that the disability experience is not only tragic at times, but also rewarding, productive and just plain ordinary.

But Mairs's laudable goal may obscure the real need for change in how our society treats the disabled. Mairs is careful not to claim to speak for anyone's experience but her own—which seems, at first, like the right choice. But this choice also allows her to evade the responsibility—as one who has the privilege of writing and being published, of speaking and being heard—to speak for those who do not have that privilege. There is a chapter missing in this book, a chapter in which Mairs goes out into the world and meets disabled people living on the street, in public housing, in institutions and in other settings that she (and I) might find foreign, frightening or morally offensive—but that are a necessary part of any real conversation about disability.

Mairs's politics are her own, and I don't claim the right to impose mine on her. As an admirer of hers, though, I wish she had taken her work further, dared to think about lives unlike her own. At no time did I feel this longing more vividly than when reading her chapter "Young and Disabled," which is based on an essay Mairs wrote for *Glamour* magazine. Mairs advertised in the magazine for women with disabilities to write in and tell their own stories; she then skillfully wove a large number of these stories into an interesting but profoundly inadequate essay. The women quoted represent a wide range of disabilities and a fair assortment of racial and class backgrounds, but mysteriously and infuriatingly, all of them are heterosexual. Now even if we are to believe—since, after all, these are *Glamour* readers—that not a single lesbian or bisexual or transgendered woman wrote to the magazine, why didn't Mairs note this absence and make it her responsibility to find and record our experiences as well? I was excited when I first saw this chapter; I thought it would speak directly to my experience as a young disabled woman dealing with many of the issues of body image, dating and family which Mairs claims to address. But instead, the chapter's apparently untroubled heterosexist bias left me feeling more invisible than ever.

This feeling led me to question Mairs's attitude toward gay and lesbian people, and I could not recollect a sentence in any of her books that indicated either a familiarity and friendliness toward gay people, or the opposite. Instead, as is so often true in the mainstream straight world, we just simply aren't in the picture. Yet, ironically, I can't help but think that in choosing to write *Waist-High in the World*, Mairs drew, at least subconsciously, on the coming-out precedent established through the work of gay and lesbian literature and politics. In the first chapter of *Waist-High*, Mairs explains, "I might have chosen to write in such a way as to disregard or deny or disguise the fact that I have MS. . . . I could have . . . I could have . . . but I didn't." This statement rang strangely familiar when I first read it, echoing so many similar statements by queer authors who have chosen, at various historical times, to allow the truth of their lives to penetrate the veil of language that might be easily—and yet not so easily—drawn to hide it.

Despite the shortcomings I've noted, I admire Mairs's integrity and courage—even as I recognize that she is not writing to earn my admiration, but out of a deeper, more profound need. In many ways, this volume is a form of testimony, an affidavit of the realities of Mairs's life. And again, that burning need to assert, to witness against the half-truths and ignorance of the so-called normal world is familiar from the canon of gay literature.

It's important to remember that the gay canon includes much more than straightforward acts of coming out. Certainly many wonderful queer authors have chosen to be assertively out, yet many others have felt constrained, by circumstance and art, to represent themselves in less explicit ways to the world—through coding, elision, self-censorship. These necessary strategies have at times been stifling to the point of suffocation, but at other times—as in the work of some of my favorite authors: Elizabeth Bishop, W.H. Auden, Virginia Woolf—this strategy has produced works of stunning subtlety and grace. This example highlights one limitation of visibility: It may serve politically, and, on the individual level, psychologically, but it does not always serve artistically.

Another limitation of visibility was illuminated for me when a black lesbian friend of mine said skeptically, "Black people are visible—we're on TV and all that, and it hasn't made all of our problems go away." The circumstances of racism versus homophobia are, of course, quite different and hard to compare; in reasoning out these differences, I realized the extent to which "visibility" is based upon a certain assumption of already existing privilege. That is, the most compelling examples of visibility helping to reduce homophobia involve closeted gay people who already have a certain amount of social currency—the politician, the celebrity, the family next door—coming out of the closet and thus lending a greater legitimacy to gayness through their already acquired mantle of privilege. I think it is difficult to argue that today's society would be at all transformed by learning that homeless people, women on welfare, people with disabilities or any other socially disadvantaged group had also come out of the closet as gay.

I have still not answered the question of how, as lesbians with disabilities, we can adapt the metaphor and strategy of visibility to serve people with disabilities, while acknowledging its reliance on social and economic privilege. Mairs's work offers a rich ground for discussion, both in its achievements and in its failures, and I plan to keep reading and thinking about her work, as well as discussing it with others.

Meanwhile, I pause to pick up my buttons and pin them onto my sweat-shirt—even though I'm home alone and no one will see them. They remind me that witnessing begins in privacy, when we first have the courage to look at ourselves, to see our own truth. But that is the beginning, not the end, of revolution.

Maybe I won't put these buttons back into the ceramic bowl on my dresser; maybe I will keep wearing them, in and out of my house, to keep me thinking beyond the limited metaphors of sight and sightlessness, to think about ways of becoming present: as the writer's voice becomes present in the reader's mind, whether the words are printed black on a page, or in lines of Braille under her fingers, or being spoken on tape. In this way, I believe each of us has the ability to make ourselves visible in the very act of creating ourselves anew.

# HIDDEN DISABILITY
## A Coming Out Story

### Carolyn Gage

I have lived with chronic fatigue and immune dysfunction syndrome (CFIDS) for eleven years, the first seven of which I spent in the closet. This is the story of how I came out about my disability—first to myself, and then to my friends.

I became sick in 1988, after a series of crises in my personal life, systemic reactions to the norepinephrine that is in novocaine, and exposure to pesticides in my apartment. That fall, I contracted the flu and I noticed an unusual pain in my lower back and my upper arms. My recovery took several months, and then, at Solstice, I experienced for the first time the debilitating fatigue that would come to characterize my life during the next seven years. I was at a party, and I became too weak to even sit in a chair. With great embarrassment, I asked my host, whom I didn't know, if I could lie down in her bedroom.

Over the next four years, I would experience this kind of fatigue periodically. More noticeable were my allergic reactions to a growing number of toxins in the environment. I began to experience skin lesions, mental confusion, panic attacks, irregular heartbeats, visual problems, breathing difficulties, sleep disorders and violent mood swings. Gradually, I abandoned bicycling, hiking, backpacking, dancing. I pretended that my focus was shifting away from these activities toward my theatre work.

It did not occur to me that my panic attacks were being generated from internal crises, like malnutrition and a deficient supply of oxygen to the brain. I was convinced that I was experiencing some kind of nervous breakdown, and I became hypervigilant toward the people in my environment, overlooking the toxins that were the real culprits.

For four years, I continued to characterize my extreme symptoms of mounting physical and mental debilitation as the result of "stress." Using this analysis, I was convinced that relief would have to take the form of a change in my material circumstances: I had to become a success, and I had to do it as quickly as possible. Instead of going home to bed, I produced nineteen plays in two years, writing most and directing all of them myself. I also began to accept bookings of my one-woman show at various venues around the country. I was playing a teenage lesbian Joan of Arc suffering from post-traumatic stress disorder. Like the heroine I was playing, I was getting seriously burnt.

My theatre company collapsed at the same time I did, and I spent nearly a year in my room, surveying the wreckage. It still did not occur to me that I was sick, although now I was allergic to fleas, laundry detergent, cars, soap, shampoo, most cleaning products, petroleum-based substances, glue, perfumes, paints, incense and wood smoke. It never occurred to me that I had food allergies, and I continued to eat a diet high in dairy, wheat and sugar.

Because of my physical collapse, I abandoned the plan to produce a record number of plays until someone recognized my achievements. I decided to move to an area where people would acknowledge and reward my work without my needing to prove myself. The area I chose was Northern California, where a successful lesbian theatre company was already in operation. The theatre company had even produced my work, and they invited me to work with them.

When my panic attacks and cognitive disorders followed me to California, I reacted to my new friends with the same hypervigilance and reactive behaviors that had characterized my relations with people in Oregon. Needless to say, the offer to work was retracted, and I found myself starting yet another theatre company—something I had sworn I would never do again.

In the fall of 1993, I was initiated into a coven of witches by Z Budapest in a private ceremony after one of my performances of *Joan of Arc*. Z pronounced a final blessing on me: "No more enemies!" And then she turned as an afterthought and said, "Just the usual ones." The next morning I awoke with the realization that I was sick. Not only did I realize I was sick, but I even knew the name of my condition: chronic fatigue and immune dysfunction syndrome. Furthermore, I knew that I had been sick for almost four years. Hallowmass 1993 marked the end of my denial.

Those four years of ignorance and denial had cost me dearly in terms of lost healing time. They had also cost me dearly in terms of my self-esteem, as I had watched myself become irrational, incompetent, scared of people and increasingly isolated.

Did I come out? Not at first. I told my friends that I was sick with CFIDS, but I did not really tell them what that meant. They watched me give away half the food in my refrigerator, as I began a series of radical experiments with diet. I bought a juicer and began juicing three times a day. At this time, only two or three books on CFIDS were available, and most of what I got from reading them was that I was on my own in terms of finding out what would make me better. I did not have the financial resources to treat the condition medically; my only hope was to affect it through diet. I dropped dairy and sugar. Later, I would drop wheat and soy. I stopped being vegetarian and began to eat liver. I learned to cook chicken, turkey, fish. I ate a dozen eggs a week for the first few months. Slowly, the mood swings began to stabilize.

Knowing I was sick, I gave myself permission to retire from doing theatre. I moved to a cabin in the country and gave up almost all of my social activities. When I did go places with friends, I passed for able-bodied as much as I could. That meant staying in toxic environments, pushing myself past comfortable limits physically and eating the wrong foods. New in town, I was afraid of compromising what little support I had.

Then, in the seventh year of my disability, I seriously overextended myself in an effort to pass. One thing I did was invite a friend to accompany me on a trip to Oregon. She knew I was sick, but she had never really understood what that meant in terms of practical adjustments because our visits together had been brief and I had always passed for able-bodied. After I had invited her for this week-long trip, I realized that I would not be able to protect her from the inconveniences of my disability: We would need to leave in the middle of the night because that was the only time I was well enough, biorhythmically, to cope with the long drive. It was also the only time when the traffic was light enough that I would not need to pull over every ten minutes to distance myself from a polluting vehicle. She would also need to know that I could not eat in restaurants and that motels were too toxic for me—even with the windows open. She would need to accommodate the frequent naps that punctuated my day. She would need to get me home by nine for bed. Our social interactions would need to be brief, and any kind of activity requiring physical exertion would be out. My friend was a young and exceptionally athletic dyke, and I knew that she would chafe under these restrictions. I also knew that I was not willing to pass for a week with this condition. And so I uninvited her. Not surprisingly, she was enraged at me. Her anger made me confront the fact that I was not the only one paying for my passing.

I sat down and wrote "So You Know a Dyke with CFIDS." I mailed it to all of my friends. About half of them quietly dropped out of my life. The rest of them began to respond to my needs. They began to remember the substances that made me sick. They began to ask me questions about my limits, my needs. They began to share with me in screening environments for toxins. And a few—very few—began to ask me if I needed anything. This was seven long years after I got sick. Seven years of struggling against myself, alone and in silence. Seven interminable years of ongoing suicidality.

In my eighth year, against the odds, I began to heal.

This is the letter that marked my official coming out about CFIDS to my friends. I think it is important that we have examples of what this coming out sounds like. Perhaps if letters like this had been in circulation when I first got sick, I would not have spent almost a decade trying to invent one.

*So You Know a Dyke with CFIDS*

This is my personal list of "dos" and "don'ts" for my friends who might find some guidance helpful in relating to my chronic fatigue and immune dysfunction syndrome:

DON'T expose me to your company if you believe that CFIDS is psychosomatic, "yuppie flu" or anything less than one of the most frightening, tragic and debilitating diseases of the twentieth century. Because it is.

DON'T think you're being supportive by telling me how you get tired too sometimes after a hard day at work or a long bike ride. The fatigue (read "debilitation") experienced by people with CFIDS is unlike any kind of physical or emotional state experienced by able-bodied people, even after they've run a marathon. This kind of comparison is as offensive as talking about your experiences with dieting to someone with a wasting disease. Just don't. If you are able-bodied, you have no physical context for understanding my experience, so don't think you do.

DON'T suggest that my symptoms might not be so severe if I didn't dwell on them, cater to them, give them so much attention, let them run my life. In fact, that is the very philosophy that led to the collapse of my health in the first place. I maintain what vitality I do have by careful attention to even small changes in my body.

DON'T try to be helpful by suggesting other "normal" factors that might be causing my symptoms. Yes, no doubt there are other factors—there always are—but I am an expert on my disease and I am on intimate terms with my symptoms. It is arrogant for you to try to interpret them for me.

DON'T spend time with me unless you are grown-up enough to understand that the desires of an able-bodied person should not be weighed in the same balance with the needs of a disabled person. Forget your assertiveness training, your skills at compromise or your "getting to yes" negotiating expertise. If I need to leave an environment because it is toxic to me and you want to stay, it is *not* a solution for us to stay fifteen more minutes. Those fifteen minutes may result in my spending the next two days in bed. I get my way, because the stakes are infinitely higher for me. If you think this is about my control issues or power tripping, get some help with your ableism.

DON'T say things to me like, "God, I don't know how you can stand to live without [your career, your home, swimming, running, eating favorite foods, being able to travel, being financially independent, etc.]." Don't say, "Boy, I could never give up [my career, my home, swimming, running, eating my favorite foods, being able to travel, being financially independent, etc.]." Our losses are our losses. They don't signal fortitude, sacrifice or strength of character. We deal with them in healthy or unhealthy ways, and sometimes that changes every hour. They are our losses, and the only appropriate response is heartfelt sympathy and sincere offers of assistance. A little political activism would not be out of place either.

DON'T punish me with your frustrations at the inconveniences I cause you with my illness. Yes, in the short term, you may get me to "pass" as able-bodied or even take care of your bad mood, but in the long run, I will decide you are an ableist asshole. I have no choice but to live with these inconveniences and disruptions twenty-four hours a day. If you choose to be in my company, you can assume responsibility for temporarily accommodating my disability.

DON'T date me if you want to think of my illness as some footnote to my personhood. It is a central part of my identity now, just as being lesbian is. We all know how icky it is to be around straight people who tolerate our lesbianism, but who flinch every time we bring up the subject of our lover. It feels just as bad to be with friends who know I have CFIDS, but who become stiff and uncomfortable whenever I incorporate my experiences or needs into our interactions. If you can't take the heat, get out of my kitchen.

DON'T *ever* use the word "crazy" in relation to the confusion, seizures, extreme irritability, panic attacks or periods of being emotionally overwhelmed that are part of the cognitive losses and neurological disturbances of this illness. I can identify and name these states and take responsibility for them. I have a whole battery of information and arsenal of strategies for coping with them. In fact, I see dykes acting out all the time from food allergies, blood sugar reactions and the effects of alcohol and caffeine in their systems—and in my experience, those of us with CFIDS are far more aware, more accountable and more forthcoming about mood swings and emotional states than so-called able-bodied dykes who have the dubious privilege of still abusing their bodies.

DON'T persist in pressuring me about an activity once I have identified it as something I have reservations about because of my illness. We folks with CFIDS often question our reality because of the elusive, "moving target" nature of our symptoms. Because most of us are experiencing some degree of social isolation, we are especially vulnerable to pressure accompanied by even a subtle threat of further marginalization. And it's always tempting to see if we can pull off a "normal" activity. But the price of being mistaken can be months of relapse. It's not worth it. "No" means "no." Don't presume to know my limits. They change every day, anyway.

DON'T attribute your lack of sympathy to my attitude. This is a standard defense of bigots. Racists are always sure that there are right ways and wrong ways to be African American, Latina, Asian, Native American. Sexists believe that harassment and discrimination happen only to women with bad attitudes. Ableists are always convinced that there is something in the attitude or the behavior of the disabled person that is causing their irritation or aversion toward us. Nothing unmasks your ableism more than this point of view toward me. I have to fight my way through a toxic, apathetic and even sadistic world every day. I am assertive to militant about my needs, and I haven't got the energy to coddle ableist people. You will not see me looking helpless, tearful or pathetic. Someone suffering for a few weeks with a flu virus may be able to indulge or even luxuriate in their temporary helplessness, but those of us who are sentenced to chronic illness for the rest of our lives must make other adjustments— ones that should be valorized, not excoriated. I need an ally, not a rescuer. If you can't feel empathy for an embattled warrior, it's your ableism and not my attitude. Period.

DON'T think I'm being manipulative when I have to excuse myself from a stressful dynamic. Most people will check out of an argument when it reaches the level of screaming and throwing objects. Because of this disease, I experience much lower grades of conflict as being that stressful and life-threatening, and I have to check out. I am accountable in my relationships to people, but sometimes it takes me longer, with more periods of time-out, to work through a difficult issue. Don't make me hang up on you.

DON'T suggest new supplements or treatments unless I have asked. Like most single dykes with the disease, I have experienced a drastic and terrifying reduction of resources. And like most women living on a very low fixed income, I have had to evolve a highly refined and customized process for cost-benefit analysis. It has taken me years to fine-tune my regimen of supplements and foods. Yes, I am sure I would benefit from massage, blood tests, medical care, organic food, acupuncture and Chinese herbs, but I can't afford them. Unless, of course, you want to buy them for me. Classism and ableism go hand-in-glove, and in case you don't know, health care in this country is a privilege, not a right.

DON'T mistake my periods between relapses for recovery. I have plenty to deal with regarding my own ups and downs. Don't make me have to cope with your hopes and expectations for me. What I most need from you is the reassurance that I am a perfectly wonderful friend even at the lowest point in my health, and even if I never get any better.

DON'T accuse me of being jealous of your health when I confront your ableism. I wish that my able-bodied friends were more aware of how their able-bodied privilege translates into ignorance, arrogance and bland sadism. The issue is not my envy of your privilege, but your abuse of it.

DON'T make me take care of you around canceled plans. Yes, I'm sorry whenever that happens. I do try to know what my limitations are, and frequently I err on the side of conservatism just so that I won't have to change my plans or cancel later. But every now and then I will say I can do something that I can't. Too bad. But the whole life I had planned for myself—my career, home, family, social life, sports, hobbies, standard of living, quality of life—has been permanently canceled. I just can't get too into your pain about a picnic or a camping trip. And you know what? I'm not even going to try.

DON'T think I'm kidding when I talk about suicide. The depression that accompanies CFIDS has been likened to the depression that AIDS patients experience in the last few weeks of their lives. With CFIDS, it goes on for years. Ask me. I may have actually scavenged a piece of garden hose for the exhaust pipe. I may have stockpiled barbiturates. I will probably tell you, because I am hoping someone will help me. If you care about me and I am talking about suicide, consider stepping up your support. I'm not kidding. CFIDS patients do take our own lives, and we do it a lot. And part of it is because nobody seems to give a damn that we are losing or have already lost what we used to consider our lives. Give a damn.

DO make an effort to learn something about the disease on your own. There is a ton of information about CFIDS in libraries and bookstores—

first-person narratives, medical and alternative healing manuals, cookbooks. There are all kinds of Web sites on the Internet. There is a CFIDS Foundation and a CFIDS Institute, and they will send you free pamphlets.

DO acknowledge frequently that I am disabled. I have to run as fast as I can to stay in place, or even just to fall back at a manageable rate. I like to have that acknowledged. Whenever I do participate at a "normal" level in an able-bodied event, it has probably taken a lot of advance planning. Acknowledge that. Appreciate it. I pay higher dues, and I like to be credited for it. Even though I may look like a slacker to the able-bodied world, remember this: I am operating at the absolute top of my physical bent *all the time*. I am probably working harder than any able-bodied person you know. Just because I don't mention it doesn't mean I'm not struggling.

DO ask me how I am when we get together for an activity. That lets me know that you are willing to be my ally in confronting the challenges I am meeting during the time we are together. I have come to learn that when you don't ask, it means you don't want to know. It means that your plan is to grant me the "privilege" of being considered your able-bodied peer for the duration of our activity. In other words, my illness will only be real for you if I bring it up. Experience has taught me that this attitude results in your equating my mentioning of symptoms with my causing those symptoms. And you will oppress me accordingly.

DO adopt a CFIDS awareness when you are in my company. No, it's not codependent. It's supportive. And courteous. Why should the member of an ethnic minority be the one to confront racism all the time? Well, it's her survival issue, but frankly, that's no excuse for her white friends to let her do all the work. A racist world hurts us all. And so does an ableist one. And a toxic one. I love it when my companions allow me to shift some of the burden of my chemical sensitivity vigilance onto their shoulders, even for just an hour or two. The analogy I use is that of traveling with a disabled child: If you want to make it clear that the child is *my* child and therefore *my* problem, because you're interested only in *my* company . . . well, it makes me choose between my allegiance to my child (myself) or you. Guess who's going to win.

DO confront your superstitions about denial and immunity. If you are afraid to imagine yourself in my shoes, to really hear my experience or to adopt a CFIDS consciousness about toxins and stress levels when you are in my company—look at why. Are you afraid that you might become vulnerable to the illness if you let too much of its reality into your consciousness? That is a very human response, but also a very ableist one. If this is your truth, then stick to the company of other able-bodied people. Don't make me deal with it.

DO make it easy for me to say, "I need to leave" or "I need to lie down" or "I need to pull off the road/trail and take a nap." When the plan changes abruptly like that, see how fast you can get behind it, instead of seeing how guilty or ashamed you can make me feel or how difficult you can make it for me. These disruptions are normal for me, and I love it when my companions work together to minimize the social stigmatization that results from my meeting my needs.

DO offer support. Offer whatever you can. The gesture is often the most therapeutic part. I don't have a bathtub, but I experience chronic muscle pain and I love it when friends invite me to come over and take a bath. Can you cook a meal on a really bad night? Can you be there for twenty-minute support phone calls? Ask me what kind of support I would like. I understand that doesn't mean you can give it. I'll just be stunned that you asked. In seven years, no one ever has, but I do keep hoping.

DO clean up your car/apartment/clothing. Remember what I have told you about my allergies: fabric softener, essential oils, perfumes, bleach, *any and all pesticides.* When you keep "forgetting," I get one of two messages: Either you don't believe I'm really sick or you don't care. I *never* get the message you just forgot. That's your fantasy . . . and a function of your able-bodied privilege.

DO tell me how amazing I am. Tell me a lot. Praise my coping skills, my achievements, whatever I am proud of. Praise my ingenuity, my resourcefulness, my optimism (I'm still alive, aren't I?), my courage. Believe me, people with CFIDS hear "slacker," "whiner," "nutcase," "drama queen," "control freak" a dozen times a day in a dozen subtle and not-so-subtle ways. No matter how much you praise me, it can *never* be too much.

DO stand up for me when I'm not around. You will probably have more credibility than I do. Spread the word about CFIDS. Confront others on their ableism. *Talk about the crying need for support services similar to those offered by the AIDS networks in our communities.* Stop others from blaming the victims. When you hear charges that I am exaggerating my symptoms, set the record straight. The symptoms that show, the ones that I talk about, are just the tip of the iceberg.

DO copy this essay and pass it around your workplace.

And if all of this seems too overwhelming to remember, then try this simple formula:

*Pretend it's happened to you.*

# HERITAGE OF HEALING

## Huhanna

$A$h, but where to begin, where to start, I will do my best but remember since the head injuries I have struggled with comprehension, although orally I can still manage to sentence construct quite well.

*Kia ora* (hello). My name is Huhanna, and I am a New Zealand Maori womyn of Waikato descent (Waikato is the name of my *iwi,* or tribe). I am writing about my experiences (and there are many) of being an indigenous (first nations) womyn who lives with disabilities and who also identifies as a lesbian—what happens in my community generally, what actually happened to me, and the many discriminations that have occurred in this journey along the way.

I have other experiences I will relate which include adopting my eldest son, conceiving my youngest son from a rape, entering a psychiatric institution as a result of an earlier rape, motherhood, raising a disabled son as well as living with disabilities myself and being in a violent lesbian relationship with the womyn responsible for causing my head and spinal injuries. I will also cover how I met my American lover and where my life is going from here.

My journey begins when I was born in 1962 to a sixteen-year-old girl who, after two days of breast-feeding me, left me to the hospital to give up. My mother was young; she was facing at that same time losing a brother to drowning and my grandmother was grieving so hard that they knew they could not keep me, and so, my mother, believing the doctors' stories, gave me up to them.

The doctors had other motives. They told my mother I had a hole in my heart and that they would find a family who would care for me for the time I had left. My mother, consumed with grief and possibly postnatal depression, allowed me to be adopted. Because my skin was pale, the doctors falsified my documents, claiming I was of *Päkehä* (European/white) descent, and therefore placed those facts onto my birth certificate. I was adopted by a white Catholic couple who at that time could not have children. This action was typical of policy in place at the time, which was geared toward the genocide of the Maori.

My upbringing was, I guess, typical of many children and therefore not very profound, except that from a young age I suffered physical pain that everyone said I was making up or was in my mind. I felt different; I always knew I was adopted out, but I was told that my parents were European. This never sat right with me; from a young age I saw spirits and spoke to the spirits, although until I discovered my Maori heritage I thought I was maybe mad in some way. Since then, I have come to peace in growing and understanding these spirits who are part of my life in a very large sense.

I was abused from a very young age. I recall being very sexually aware and curious, but it was more than mere curiosity. Most of my cousins had interfered with me by the time I was eleven years old. I also remember dreaming about someday being a nun and a missionary but that was soon laughed out by the nuns teaching me, who told me I would be no better than a housewife with lots of kids. I drew into my shell after that time. I also wanted my birthmother; I often dreamt she would save me from all of this.

At fourteen, a turning point occurred in my life. My father had become very disabled and my own personal journey became one of struggle. I was raped by a stranger the day my father was due to return from the hospital after several months there in rehabilitation. It took from me any remnants of innocence that may have remained. I remember the pain as he sexually violated me, I remember the smells, which for years afterward I couldn't tolerate, and I remember very clearly to this day the fear I felt when I tried to form relationships with people, in particular with men.

I was given Valium by the doctors and became addicted to it at fifteen. I used to turn up at the good Catholic girls' school literally ripped out of my skull. One day I took too many and collapsed in front of my class and teacher. I spent two weeks in the psychiatric ward being threatened and beaten by the nurses, who told me it was my fault I had been raped. I recall being held down at one point because I wouldn't eat and they shoved food down into me while I was fainting and vomiting and they shoved more into me, making me sicker. I developed my hatred of authority then.

As a result, once I was released from the hospital (without having the trauma recognized, but instead being called a spoiled brat), I didn't care about myself. I turned to drugs and prostitution. Every time I sold my body, I sold my soul, so to speak, and moved deeper into depression each time I allowed a man to buy me. I hated what I did, but it paid for my and my boyfriends' drugs at the time.

I tried to improve and change; I even began training as a nurse, but even then I spent more time drinking and drugging and waking up in strange beds than I did nursing. Naturally, I lost my chance there. I also became pregnant, by whom I don't know. I was sent away to a home for unmarried mothers, probably the most drug-free time for me at that stage, where the nuns weren't too bad, although very naive about life. We use to tease them and I was, for the first time in years, a teenager. I was eighteen when my son was born. They took him away from me, wouldn't let me even touch him. He had jet-black hair, but I didn't want to think about that. I signed the papers and got drunk.

By Christmas of that year, I didn't recall days, just sadness. I ached for my son; I wanted him, but I was told to forget—to move on and forget. I wanted my real mother—I was told to forget her, too. Christmas Day 1980 is a day I will never remember but never forget either. Apparently, I was found on my bathroom floor by my family, unconscious and barely breathing. My heart stopped and my sister had to revive me. I was taken to the hospital by ambulance and the attendant had to revive me again. I was in a coma, and they told my family and my best friend Erin that it was unlikely I would come to again and if I did, I would be a vegetable.

I came to but had no memory and had to learn how to feed myself again, how to talk and how to walk. I also had parents who became overprotective: They wouldn't let me go anywhere or do anything without someone around. I guess I didn't know who I was, my sexuality was undefined. I didn't even know lesbians existed, although I had extremely erotic thoughts all the time about womyn. I didn't realize why or what to do with those thoughts. I spent that time with my family basically learning how to function again. They say I took an overdose—I don't know what I did—I have no memory. I was on an antimigraine medication that is known to put people into comas, although at that time I was among the first in the world to have that reaction.

Lots happened to me in the months following the coma. I was placed in a psychiatric ward the minute I became conscious, although the nurses admitted they didn't know how to look after me as I was incontinent and unable to do self-care. I was often left in a soiled state with no conscious understanding of what went on. I hallucinated. As I slowly became aware of my surroundings and I realized where I was, I said the right things, did what they wanted and was able to leave quickly and easily, although no one addressed the real issues for my problems, which were my adoption and the sexual abuse—all undealt with for more years to come.

I split home by Christmas 1981 and I hitchhiked to the other end of New Zealand. I picked fruit and met many great womyn on my journey. I lived hand-to-mouth under bridges, on the side of the road, anywhere I could lay my head, and I had the best time of my life. I began to explore my sexuality then; I was curious although I didn't fully understand who I was or why I felt the way I did. I do remember sensing changes. I also searched everywhere for an answer to an ache deep inside of me. I didn't know what it was, but I was willing to try anything to overcome this hunger inside.

It was at this time I answered the call to become a Christian. I was vulnerable and I believed this was the answer to the void within me. How wrong I was, although I wasn't to find that out until 1986. I was enthusiastic, as I am with anything I put my heart into. I put everything into this. I returned home to Taranaki to help care for my dad, who was still very sick, and I became involved in a fundamentalist Christian movement. My family and I became more estranged. I put it down to the fact they were Catholics and didn't know the truth, which was the noncompromising movement I was involved in.

I was involved in this movement to such an extent that I was also denying myself access to past contacts and I became bold. So bold that I even confronted my ex-pimp one night to tell him to leave me alone. As a result I was raped and became pregnant with my other son. I became ostracized by the church and banned from active involvement. They blamed me for the rape; they said I had encouraged the man, that I was at fault and that the truth came from them. I realized they never took me in as a "family" member. They never accepted me; in effect, they did everything opposite to what is taught in the Bible. So I was alone, just me and this baby growing inside me.

I chose not to abort; it was never an option for me. I did not know, though, that I was putting my life and my child's life in danger. I had developed toxemia, which can be fatal if untreated in pregnancy. I made it to seven months, although I was hospitalized for most of it. I went eclampsic and nearly lost my son and myself. After three weeks in intensive care, we left the hospital and began life together.

This was when my disabilities began to emerge. I had asthma already, but it hadn't had a major effect on my life. My son was also struggling with several disabilities; he had mild right hemiplegia, asthma, attention deficit hyperactivity disorder (ADHD) and epilepsy. I was a very uninformed and scared twenty-four-year-old with no support. I wanted my real mother; I figured Christianity wasn't the answer, and maybe meeting my mother would be. I placed an ad in the paper and asked for a womyn matching the information I had. My grandmother answered the ad and I learned my mother lived in Australia. She came over when my son was three months old and I began the journey of finding who I was. The problem was, I believed she was the answer, not me. And I soon found out that finding her wasn't as I had hoped and dreamed.

I was still self-destructive in my behavior and this showed in a lot of things I attempted over the years. Even when I began to search my sexuality, I never stopped being destructive and as a result I began to emulate this in the relationships I was in. I began to get into the lesbian lifestyle and, while searching for myself, I met and slept with many womyn, but I was basically not changing my lifestyle. I also didn't know where I fit in, which was still a big problem for me. Although I was going to the clubs, I failed miserably in socializing effectively.

All this time I wanted someone to love me for myself, so I searched in the dating magazines and began writing to a womyn in another town. My father had died, I failed in my contact with my birthmother, I had a toddler, and I was lonely, achingly lonely. I often cried at night, feeling unloved and unwanted and believing a womyn who wanted to be with me could love me.

I started nursing training again, and this time I was out as a lesbian. Wow, did I ever get hassled. People said I was chasing the young womyn in my class, which was unlike me anyway because I was always afraid of rejection. I tried to continue my studies, but after two years of targeted abuse I gave up. I was also beginning to suffer lots of pain after a laparoscopy; I endured a lot of pain for unknown reasons at that time. I also suffered lots of fatigue that I couldn't rest from.

The doctors were mystified. I moved from Taranaki to Hamilton in the Waikato in New Zealand to go to university and to be with the womyn I had corresponded with. She was charming, appeared to be everything I wanted, and I appeared to be accepted for myself. My son, who was five at this point, also appeared to be accepted. We agreed to move in together. For the first month things were wonderful, I felt loved and I fell in love. Then, her son moved in. He was a teenager and, I was soon to discover, a teen with massive problems. I came home from university one day to find a hole in the wall; when I asked, I was told it was none of my business. Then I began to have their anger turn on me. I tried working with this lad on his anger and tried to support my lover; however, abuse began to happen and beatings began to occur. For lots of minor reasons I would get a beating. I was also getting hospitalized for pain attacks. The doctors gave me a hysterectomy in 1993 after eight hospitalizations and found nothing, so they basically told me I was imagining the pain and they left me to still suffer pain.

The pain and fatigue got worse; I also spasmed in my muscles, suffered irritable bowel, insomnia, esophagitis, gastric reflux disease, chronic fatigue and got beaten for being sick. My self-esteem was so low I thought I couldn't leave this womyn because no one would want me—I was so unlovable. My son's behavior got worse—he was bed-wetting and when he was upset his epilepsy was out of control. Yet I still refused to leave—when I tried she would be charming and entice me back because I loved her and I believed in making it work. Her son also began beating me.

Well I couldn't take it anymore so I took an overdose. I ended up very sick. Thank Goddess, my cousin had gotten in touch with a Maori womyn who was a blood relative of mine. She took my son and me in and helped me to begin to see that this womyn wasn't what I needed. I needed to know my culture, my ethnic identity, my *whakapapa* (genealogy), which is the basis of Maori *tanga*, or being Maori. Maata supported me and my son. During this time I began to get visits from my spirits, my ancestors, who began to help me see that I had a right to live, that I have a gift and a reason for being here and that I had to get away from this abusive lover. It was through Maata that I began to grow spiritually and as a Maori womyn. I learned that our culture is very balanced in that both genders have an equal role in society and equal status, which is opposite to how the white society views its genders. I began to learn that there is a close link to the land and the spirits and all must be in balance to be healthy. I began to move on; I began to grow.

The abusive womyn I loved still tried to come back. This time I refused to move in with her, although I still went out with her. In 1995 I was diagnosed with having severe fibromyalgia and I also got fitted for my wheelchair. Despite this I extended my one university degree to a double degree in law and psychology. Things went well for me and my lover for a year, until one night when I turned up to surprise her and found her with another womyn. A week before that I had opened up to her about my disability and the possible long-term prognosis; she told me it was likely we would be together for life. I believed her—she hadn't been violent for the entire year, her son was going to an anger-management course—why wouldn't I believe her? When I walked in on her, my eyes opened for the first time.

I left and returned later that night and demanded my things back. I was angry. I walked into what was technically our house, as we were co-owners of that property, so I felt I could walk in. I walked in and as I asked for my things back, her son came at me with his fist, punching me twice, knocking me unconscious. My son says I was kicked in my back while I was unconscious. I came to with them holding my wrists down and yelling at me. I wanted to get out of there. I screamed for them to let me go. Just as they were beating me more, the police arrived. Ironically, *I* was told to leave—barely able to move and bleeding from the head, I was ordered to drive home. I was treated as though I was the abuser. I drove home—how, I don't know. That night I went to the emergency room with a friend and was stitched up to stop the scalp lacerations from bleeding. My head was shaved. My back became worse than it had been.

When the case went to court, the house was sold and I lost everything—my half share of the house, the furniture that was mine. Although the court acknowledged that I had been beaten, my lover and her son said they acted in self-defense; the court agreed. I had to go into hiding from my ex and her son, as they stalked me and harassed me. Although I have a protection order in place, I can't risk being on my own and I have to move all the time in order to keep safe. The police will not act on a lesbian relationship that is violent—it doesn't fit their idea of something worth protecting.

These events turned my life around. I managed to start again. I no longer tried to end my life, but fought to live. I suffered seizures then and still do when under stress. I also had to put energy into my son—I had placed him behind my need for love without even considering him. We worked together to heal the damage I caused.

I began to grow once healing took place for my son and myself. I began to have lots of dreams of my ancestors, who began to guide me into the practices of the old precolonization ways and I began to grow spiritually. Physically I had to go into my wheelchair in December 1996, and began to find that the worse I got physically, the stronger I became spiritually.

The friend who helped me after the beating became my lover for a while. She taught me to love myself despite the disabilities. She loved me for me; she also saw changes in me and while we knew our relationship would never be permanent, she was there teaching me how to stand on my own two feet. Today we are the best of friends.

The last two years have been ones of growth. I have found my independence, my son has healed tremendously—he has grown into a wonderful, gentle young man of twelve and is fast developing his own independence. His epilepsy is under control and he is not medicated. He appears to have grown out of his

ADHD and is doing excellently at school and at home.

I first went on the Internet in November 1997, and have met many wonderful womyn on the chat sites. I met a womyn online. After daily online contact for almost a year, we have decided we want to meet. She is a New Yorker with the craziest accent (and they say we Kiwis have accents). She spoils me heaps with letters, cards, photos and phone calls. My spirits tell me this is the relationship I have been meant to have; she accepts me, my disabilities, and my fiery nature, which gets very worked up when people online show no understanding of life, disability, politics or other issues that I believe are important. I am realistic enough to know if it isn't meant to be, well that's okay, too, because my life can work with or without someone in it, as I have my spirits and they have helped to break the loneliness that has been so prevalent in my life.

I graduated from the university with a degree in law and a degree in social sciences majoring in law, psychology, women's studies and Maori. I have a strong relationship now with my ethnic identity, and as I grow into *kuia* (elder womyn) status, I grow stronger in my culture.

I have grown as a womyn, become closer to my culture and spiritually become stronger; I am, most importantly, at peace within myself now. Ironically, I am in a lot of pain—the fibromyalgia is at a point where I am now being considered for an electric wheelchair. My prognosis is one of progressive deterioration. Yet I couldn't be stronger or happier; the pain is annoying and can hurt a lot, but it is nothing compared to the emotional pain I suffered for so long. My girlfriend gives me something I never had before—a sense of self and love. I give myself independence and self-love. This is where I am now. In the future I hope I can work in human rights. That won't be an easy thing to achieve, but never let it be said dreams can't come true. I have learned that despite pain and disability, they can.

# WRITING FROM THE BODY

## Nicola Griffith

In this essay I want to talk about Art, particularly literature, and the Body—about the ways in which we do and do not connect the two. It's a personal essay about how I feel about my body, my writing and the various changes both have undergone over the years. Art and the Body are huge subjects with all kinds of branches and nooks and crannies. In what follows I poke around in those topics that interest me—the philosophy of dualism, cyberspace as nirvana, the concept of genius, the religious right—and see which pieces connect along the way.

*Art, Theology and the Ontological Problem*
Our attitudes toward art stem partially from theories first formulated thousands of years ago. What we think today is a direct result of what some philosophers thought back then. Bear with me while I take a quick historical tour.

Plato was one of the first to talk about dualism, the theory that the world consists of two ultimately different kinds of being: visible, perishable and particular things; and eternal, abstract and universal forms. Particulars are only imperfectly real. Full reality can only be found among universals. The body, Plato said, is particular and therefore imperfect. The soul, on the other hand, is universal; its aim is to separate itself from the body and return to the divine realm of universals from which it came. From Plato's perspective, anything that gets in the way of that goal—the escape of the soul from the prison of the flesh back to the soaring plane of the universal—is counterproductive. As a result, he didn't much care for poetry or plays because much of their beauty is embodied in the senses of the flesh—what we see and feel and hear. As far as Plato was concerned, the literature of his time was a base distraction, the fall of the spirit into the flesh.

Aristotle saw things a bit differently. Every individual substance (except God) is made of both matter *and* form; and form, for example the human soul, cannot exist without matter, for example the body. This fusion of the particular with the universal was in direct contradiction to Plato. However, Aristotle still thought the soul/form was infinitely superior to the body/matter. He viewed labor of the mind as much more worthy than physical labor, which he considered vulgar and fit only for slaves (who were conveniently left out of all these deliberations). So, unlike Plato, Aristotle saw nothing inherently wrong with poetry and plays. Quite the opposite. Living, he said, is only justified because it makes contemplation possible. (Aristotle practiced what he preached. His contemplations on theater led to a definition of tragedy and its purpose—to evoke the emotions of pity and sorrow—and incidentally introduced that knotty little word "catharsis" into our vocabulary.)

The arts of Greece and then Rome flourished while philosophers teetered back and forth between the Platonic and Aristotelian traditions. And then St. Paul arrived.

Paul came from the Judaic tradition of further splitting the spirit into equal and opposing forces of evil and good. He came to Rome newly Christianized and decided his Judaic theology would fit nicely with Plato's ideas of the soul trying to better itself by separating from the body. Evil, Paul declared (and, oh, we are still feeling the consequences of that declaration today), must manifest itself *in* the physical. The body, with its needs and functions, is evil, something from which we should seek to distance ourselves. The more physical and messy the body, it seemed, the more evil the person. Which means, of course, that as women bleed on a regular basis, and give birth, we were seen to be more closely anchored than men to the less desirable physical realm. (Funny how the exudations of men are never seen as unclean.) This, of course, strengthened the already prevalent view that women are lesser beings: less evolved, less close to the divine. Thank you, St. Paul.

In the fourth century A.D., Augustine, an ambitious colonial lad from Tagaste in North Africa, trained as a rhetorician and traveled to the big city to earn fame and fortune. In Carthage and then Rome he tried on a variety of ways to look at the world, from the wild theology of the Manicheans to the rather juiceless philosophy of the Neo-Platonists. Then he became a bishop and got a good dose of St. Paul.

In 410 Augustine witnessed the sack of Rome by Alaric the Goth. Alaric boasted that he had been able to destroy what had once been the mightiest city on earth because the Romans had abandoned their gods for Christianity. No doubt this boosted Augustine's blood pressure. At any rate, it turned his brain into the organic equivalent of a supercollider: All the conflicting theories he had absorbed over the years picked up speed, went whizzing around his neurons, and came smashing together in his head. The product was *De civitate dei*, his most famous work. Rome, Augustine said, fell *because* of its original paganism, *because* of its inherent shortcomings and moral perversions. It was part of the "city of this world," the physical manifestation of pride and corruption. It didn't matter what happened to worldly cities, he said; all that counted was the City of God, the society of mind/soul/spirit of those chosen by God for the future Kingdom of Heaven. What we did, physically, was almost irrelevant.

During the first millennium of Christianity, then, art was dedicated to the glory of God, to the spiritual being, not the physical. At this time, art was produced not by individual "artists" but by artisans, an interchangeable class. The work was what was important, not the creator of that work. In Christian Europe, poems were firmly oral in tradition, anonymous. Visual art and sculpture went largely unsigned.

But these artisans, the people who laid the stones of the vast Gothic cathedrals, who sculpted and painted and carved, were not educated in the finer points of theology and philosophy. When they decorated the cathedrals they carved angels and saints, yes, but they also labored over gargoyles and griffins, sheelanagigs and coiling serpents: pagan symbols. The inevitable backlash came from the Abbey of Cluny (founded in 910). "Paganism!" they cried. "Something must be done!" They reasoned that if monstrous, evil figures were all these artisans could come up with to decorate churches, then that decoration must stop. The church must move away from these manifestations of evil and return to the wholly spiritual, that is, plain, unadorned houses of worship. They said, in effect, that the aesthetic was evil. It was a revolution within the church against art. However, luckily for Western Civilization As We Know It, the Abbey of Cluny was closely allied with several doomed power struggles within the church; when Cluny fell, so did its revolution. At least in that particular manifestation.

In thirteenth-century Italy, Thomas Aquinas reexamined the Augustinian tradition and decided that the Neo-Platonist parts did not make much sense. He recast Augustine's work, slanting it much more toward the Aristotelian bias. (Remember, Aristotle was the one who said that only in contemplation and moral action do people—unless they are slaves doomed to all that nasty, sweaty physical labor—attain true freedom.) Art became good for its own sake again, and flowered into the Italian Renaissance. With the Renaissance came the rise of individualism, and the idea of creative genius: individuals who sometimes transcended tradition to produce new works, and signed them.

The backlash to this was, of course, the Reformation, and the Puritans with their Cluny-like insistence upon a zero aesthetic: black and white clothes, no dancing, no singing, no painting, no beauty. Art as corruption. (Don't smile smugly yet. The Puritans were not the last to think this way.)

Obviously, not everyone saw art as anathema. However, no matter how reworked, recast and revised the philosophy (and Descartes fooled with it after Aquinas), it was still essentially dualism. Art was still linked with religion, still perceived to be the realm of the divine. Great Art, ran the conventional wisdom, is produced by Great Artists, who are great because they transcend the flesh, reach beyond the physical to the spiritual. Except (what a surprise) where women were concerned. "You women," we were told, "are too close to your animal nature. You can't transcend it, so you can't produce art." No matter what else got rewritten, *that* particular legacy was never questioned.

This general mindset, only slightly mutated, is with us today. Our conventional wisdom says that Great Literature is produced by Great Writers. Great Writers are those who transcend the mundane and speak the great universal truth.

❖

*My Truths, or Some of Them*

The conventional wisdom is nonsense. There is no universal truth. There are only many different and individual truths. It's my belief that we write about what interests, fascinates and obsesses us. We hope that by doing so we can show our readers part of our world view, help others to understand our own particular truth. Who we are—what we have done, how we have been treated and how we feel about that—determines our truth and, therefore, what we want to write about.

Let me tell you some of my particular truth.

I have always enjoyed my body. I grew up using and pleasuring it hard. I played tennis, did gymnastics, competed on the track. I worked as a laborer with pickaxe, shovel and wheelbarrow at an archaeological dig. I dug trenches and planted trees for the city council. I studied karate and taught women's self-defense. I had three lovers as well as my live-in partner. Drank whiskey, ate magic mushrooms, took a lot of speed, sang in a band half the night, went home with one woman or another and cycled to work at dawn after no sleep. I was invulnerable, unconquerable (probably insufferable). The fiction I wrote was physical: explosions, travel through space and time, fantasy figures rescuing fairy-tale characters and so on.

But then I became ill. My body became less able, began to change. Eventually, in 1993, I was diagnosed with multiple sclerosis.

We receive information two ways: somatically and extrasomatically. We can find out about the weather by going outside and seeing the bright sun with our eyes, feeling the heat on our skins. Or we can use our modem or newspaper or TV or radio to get the weather report. My personal preference, where possible, is for somatic information. It is what interests me, what I write from. I write from my body, but my body has changed. My writing has changed, too.

I have relapsing-remitting multiple sclerosis. This means that every now and again my immune system goes awry and attacks the myelin sheathing on the neurons of brain and spinal cord, and I wake up with something not working: a leg, or an arm, maybe both. Maybe my balance is so screwed up I can do nothing but hunch over a bowl and vomit. Sometimes my eyes get weird. Or my mind: Once I was in the middle of writing a novelette and I couldn't remember my characters' names. Most of the time, I recover from whatever it is that has gone wrong, but each time I lose a little more. As of this writing, I can walk (I can no longer run, not even to save my life). Sometimes I can walk far and fast; other times it's an effort to walk to the door.

I sit still outside more often than I ever used to. Much of the time, I watch the sky. Jeep, the world of my first novel, *Ammonite,* is full of sky. Busy sky, blank sky, imminent sky. And clouds: clouds like breeching salmon, like the scum that gathers on the surface of boiling lentils; overcasts like polished pewter; thunderheads like lumps of zinc and magnesium. I use the sky to reflect the emotional states of my characters. I sometimes wonder what I would have put in place of those skies if I had not spent so many hours sitting still, learning about what went on over my head.

And sometimes I wonder if I would have written *Ammonite* at all if I had not become ill. Certainly, I would have started the book, and it would have been about a women-only world, but there might not have been a virus, and without the virus everyone and everything in that book would have been different.

When I was first ill in 1989, in the United Kingdom, I was misdiagnosed with myalgic encephalomyelitis (ME), a chronic disease of the immune system. I moved to the United States, where ME is called chronic fatigue and immune dysfunction syndrome (CFIDS). All anyone knew about this condition was that a retrovirus *might* be involved. I started researching viruses and the immune system. I found a book about lupus erythematosus, a terrible and often fatal systemic disease thought by some to be initially triggered by a retrovirus. Women, I learned, were nine times more likely to contract lupus than men. And, oh, I thought, oh: a sex-linked predisposition to deadly infection. Catastrophe on Jeep would come not by fire or flood or alien invasion, but by virus: little packets of alien DNA. And I knew how the men in my book would die, and how the women would change.

Multiple sclerosis changed some things about my life. As I have changed, so has the way in which I draw my fictional characters. Most of them suffer a great deal, emotionally and physically and—compared with my earlier work—solutions to personal and plot problems are no longer wholly physical. In fact, they are rarely so. One criticism of *Ammonite* has been that the confrontation between the Mirrors and Echraidhe was anticlimactic. "There should have been a battle!" But battles, the simple smashing together of armies followed by a body count, no longer interest me that much. What intrigues me now are the minutiae from which such conflicts spring.

On a good day, I can walk briskly. I set off on a walk to the local park. Blood pumps vigorously around my body. Accumulated toxins are washed away, lots of oxygen gets to my cells, to my optic nerve, my eyes. When I'm fit enough to walk swiftly, I actually see more clearly. Things look crisp, bright, dense. Joyous and different. I pay attention to details.

On a bad day, unable to do anything but lie on the couch on the screened porch, or the rug in the living room, or my bed by the window, I look out, and up. Sometimes there isn't much to look at, so I simply watch. I notice changes. The sliding sunlight on the building opposite; the way the shadows gather on sandstone or brick. Sunlight on the rug, how in the afternoon the pattern is a deep and mysterious red, whereas the morning colors are fierce and young-looking, quite different. I'm not sure I could have written *Slow River,* my second novel, without that kind of observation. I'm not sure I would have *wanted* to write that particular book if it hadn't been for certain changes in my life.

In June 1988 I came to the United States for the first time to attend Clarion, the science-fiction writers' workshop at Michigan State University. I had never traveled so far on my own before. The thread that bound me to my English life stretched and stretched as the plane skimmed across the Atlantic. As we headed down through the cumulus clouds of the Midwest, the thread snapped, and it occurred to me that not a single person on the continent knew me. The sudden sense of not being bound by people's expectations, of being somehow outside the rules, was exhilarating. For the next six weeks, if I chose, I could be anyone I liked. But then I realized that this hiatus in my ordinary life gave me the opportunity to play a much more dangerous and high-stakes game: I could find out who I really was. Me. Not me-and-my-family, or me-and-my-background, or even me-and-my-accent, just *me.* I was coming into this country metaphorically naked, without cultural markers. Everyone I met could evaluate me only on the basis of what they saw. Their reaction to and treatment of me—and my work—would form a human mirror. For the first time, I would see my essential self, stripped bare.

That moment of realization, of terror and exhilaration, prompted me six years later to ask the central question of *Slow River:* Who are you when you have nothing left but your inner resources? That question was modified by the fact of my multiple sclerosis and my consequent interest in another question: Once a particular self-image has been shown to be patently untrue, who and what is there to replace it? Writing the book, of course, did not give me the answer. It was not intended to. Personal experience sparked the questions which led to the book, but *Slow River* is a novel, not therapy. It is fiction, not autobiography.

### Fiction and Autobiography

When I read the first lengthy review of *Ammonite* I genuinely did not know whether to laugh or to cry at the reviewer's mistakes. "Autobiography," he said knowledgeably. Bear in mind that this is a novel about a woman who ends up on another planet and encounters half a dozen impossible things: faster-than-light drive, aliens, conception by a modified parthenogenesis, rearrangement of DNA and memory via a deadly virus and so on. I read the review again, trying to follow his reasoning. Light dawned: I am a lesbian and my main character, Marghe, loves another woman; ergo I must, in fact, be writing about myself. Astonishing.

All fiction is to some extent emotionally autobiographical. A writer will take, say, her fear of heights and write a story based around a character who has a morbid fear of spiders. The experience of fear by the writer is a prerequisite for the properly described fictional emotion. It does not follow that the character who is afraid of spiders is a thinly disguised autobiographical rendering of the author. I have noticed a particularly disturbing tendency on the part of critics to assume that any woman who writes about physical or sexual abuse is drawing from her own personal experience.

Why women in particular? Possibly because, thanks to Plato and Paul and all those other dualists, woman are still believed—however unconsciously—to be unable to transcend the physical and actual and soar into the realms of pure imagination. We are perceived as being hampered by our bodies, incapable of seeing beyond personal experience. Autobiography, the canon-makers tell us, is not art. And as women are not considered to be artists, our work is more often labeled autobiography.*

### Thin Violinists and Consumptive Poets

Have you ever noticed how ballerinas and violinists look similar? Necks so thin you can see tendons and muscles slide under the skin; collarbones sticking out like ridge poles; wrists like bundles of sticks. You could argue that dancers have to be thin (I don't really believe it, but you can at least attempt the argument), but why violinists? And why are painters and singers who are gaunt-cheeked considered to look the part more than their beefy counterparts?

Then there are the diseases. In the eighteenth century, consumption was the ultimate poet's disease: The stricken became thin and pale, specter-like. Much closer to the spiritual. Now there is AIDS: all those nice artistic young men wasting away. Illnesses which reduce body size as cleanly as possible (or, just as importantly, are *perceived* to do so)—those with tuberculosis cough into handkerchiefs; people with AIDS generally disguise their Kaposi's sarcomas—are viewed as more aesthetically pleasing, almost romantic.† Gangrene and weeping ulcers are not. Addictions that reduce body size, particularly the opium family, are more glamorous than addiction to food, say, or beer, which simply rots out the liver and turns the skin yellow.

It seems clear that we are looking at an equation that reads Less Body = More Artistic, that is, closer to God/the spiritual/the aesthetic. Women, of course, have to be even thinner than men, because we're already laboring under the handicap of all those nasty monthly gushings, squashy breasts, et cetera. In fact, the closer women force themselves to the ideals of pre-pubescence, that is, pre-womanhood—the more we shave our legs, shave under our arms, pluck our

---

* See Joanna Russ's *How to Suppress Women's Writing* for more on this.

† Multiple sclerosis is a not-quite romantic disease. It's "clean," but if we do lose weight, we often end up putting it back on again.

eyebrows, use cosmetics that increase the size of our eyes, starve away our hips and breasts—the better we are supposed to look.

## The City of Mind

Of course, if we could just shrug off our bodies altogether, we'd be even better off. Or so some would have us believe.

Some characters in cyberpunk fiction espouse the superiority of the noncorporeal world. People are "wetware" or "meat puppets," merely the means by which information uploads and propagates itself. In fact, the meat strives to imitate hardware, sporting brain ports, eye-gem, and various prostheses. The ultimate aim of the human mind, some characters seem to be saying, is to upload, to become one with the machine—the machine being, of course, some kind of artificial intelligence (AI). AIs have become our new ideal: dispassionate, intelligent, all-seeing and all-knowing. Omnipotent and omnipresent, like gods.

Along with the urge to upload comes a certain contempt for the associations of the flesh. Skin-to-skin sex is not as desirable as slipping into a body suit and data glove and jacking into a juicy bit of software. Friends are those you talk to on the Net. Family is not even discussed. Physical communities are no longer relevant.

Whether life is imitating art or vice versa, this kind of attitude is all around us.

In March 1995 I attended OutWrite, the Lesbian and Gay Writers' Conference in Boston. I took part in a panel called Writing from the Body. The idea, I was told, was to discuss how the physical body—size, health, others' perceptions of us and so on—influences art.

The woman on my left talked about writing as and from the perspective of a fat dyke. Interesting and to the point. When she finished, the audience nodded. I talked about multiple sclerosis and how it has affected my work. More nods. The man next to me talked for a bit about getting submissions for the porn zine he edits. (Oh, well, I thought, there's always one.) But then the next guy went off on a huge rant about, well, I'm not sure, but he quoted a lot of mostly dead radicals from obscure parts of the globe and wouldn't meet anyone's eyes. The audience liked that nonpersonal stuff, the abstract, nothing to do with bodies: vigorous nods, one or two calls of "All right!"

The final panelist hijacked the subject completely. "The means by which we can leave the inequities of gender behind is with us," she declared, "and it is cyberspace. In cyberspace, it doesn't matter which bits of your body do or don't dangle, because we can dispense with it altogether. It doesn't matter how well your body works. It doesn't matter how fat or thin you feel. We can form the perfect community of the mind. Everyone will be equal. The body is irrelevant."

The audience went wild, swept away in an ecstatic tide of techno-worship. I said nothing. Talking about the body in this venue had become pointless: Cyberspace, it seemed, was the answer to everything. We were The Chosen—all we had to do was turn on, jack in and check out of the horrid, prejudiced and sordid world of the flesh. Cyberspace was heaven, the City of Mind.

### The New Cluniacs

The religious right does not get along with art. "No nakedness," they say. "No nasty bodily fluids. No lewd and filthy sex where people actually enjoy themselves. That's not a fit subject for art." And they bully parishioners into banning Robert Mapplethorpe's photography, and Congress into debating the defunding of the National Endowment for the Arts.

Why do they not believe in the body as a fit subject for art?

Plato regarded poetry as a step backward. Augustine dismissed anything that did not relate to the City of God. The Cluniacs led a revolt within the church against all art. Puritans forbade art, and joy and beauty. The religious right and their political supporters—Newt Gingrich, Jesse Helms, *et al.*—are just the latest manifestations of Platonic dualism.

But before we sip our martinis and laugh in superior amusement at the clumsy rantings of the closed-minded, we should look more closely at our own attitudes.

Our aesthetic reeks of dualism. The whole idea of female beauty, that less is more, is lifted whole from Aristotle. Through Augustine, Aristotelian tradition informs our burning desire to get into cyberspace and the City of Mind.

The concept of genius relaying the artistic Universal Truth stems from Aristotle's hierarchy of matter and form.

What does it matter? Sometimes, not very much. When I read a wrong-headed review in which the critic declares my work to be autobiographical, I can laugh: only one reader's opinion, after all. I know what I'm trying to write, or at least why I'm trying to write it. But when I listened to that audience at OutWrite, I wanted to weep. Some of these people have internalized the idea that the body—and women's bodies in particular—are so foul, so impure and unworthy, such sad sacks of meat that there is no alternative but to look for ways to get rid of them. Some hate their bodies. They want to shed them like soiled clothing and live in the City of Mind, where all injustice will miraculously be left behind. But cyberspace is not heaven. Cyberspace is not nirvana. It is not even real. It is just a concept and a tool. A tool built for the use and convenience of the body.

I hope that while we all rush headlong down the infobahn we don't forget how to use our legs, our shoulders and arms, our eyes and ears and tongues. I hope we don't forget to communicate what the world feels like on our skin. I hope we don't forget how to build physical communities. The car has destroyed much. The computer has the potential to destroy more: Why bother making friends in person when you can send e-mail? Even our art is becoming less a thing of oil and pigment and more of mouse and pixel—which is not necessarily a bad thing, as long as we don't forget that there is more.

We must not dismiss our physical selves. The body is where we all live. The body—even imperfect, like mine—is all we have. The body from which all good things come, even art.

# PANIC ATTACK
## A Dialogue Between Polly Carl and Raquel (Rocki) Volaco Simões

*This piece was compiled from a discussion facilitated by Susan Raffo. The reader needs to know that sprinkled throughout this conversation was constant laughter and teasing. Some of it has been preserved in the transcription but much of it just can't quite be translated.*

**Polly:** I'm thirty-two and I've had panic attack disorder since I was ten or eleven. The first time I remember having a panic attack was at a slumber party in fifth or sixth grade. I woke up in the middle of the night in total panic, heart pounding, and thought I was going to throw up. I went up and paced in the bathroom all night. I finally calmed down after a couple of hours of this and went back downstairs to bed. I never told anyone about it because I was too embarrassed, but that was the last slumber party I ever went to.

**Rocki:** So we have to have one soon.

**Polly:** Yeah, definitely we have to have a slumber party. The next time I remember a really major panic attack was when I was a sophomore in high school. I was at the mall and thought I was going to die on the spot. I thought I was going to pass out, I couldn't breathe. My mom was with me and I said, "I have to get out of here, I have to get out right now." I went home and lay down. After that, I remember having the attacks pretty much all the time off and on. Some months they would be really debilitating and I wouldn't feel like I could leave the house, then that would go away and I felt okay for a while.

A lot of times I had no warning that a panic attack was coming, especially during the early days. I would be standing there, doing my own thing, and the feeling would just take me over. There was no way to get over it, nothing I could do. After I became an expert panicker, I learned a bunch of different ways to calm down but back then, there was nothing I could do to rein it in.

For example, one of the major places I would panic would be driving. If I knew I had to drive to a major event, and especially drive on the highway, and this event was going to take place two weeks from now, I would spend the next two weeks figuring out how I was going to get there, how I would get there without having to get on the highway and how I would get there on time. This would preoccupy me for hours and hours. With this kind of panic, you feel like you're going to die right there on the highway. Panic attacks change the way you negotiate the world. Your throat closes up, you can't swallow, your extremities are numb, your heart is pounding. There are times where I have literally been lucky I haven't died. The panic has been so severe that I didn't even know where I was and I almost lost consciousness.

**Rocki:** One of the things that helps me get through a panic attack now is that I know they are only an exaggerated response my body is having to something. That helps me calm down. As a kid, I just thought I had quirks, like I didn't want to eat meat because I was afraid of chewing on something that I couldn't swallow and then choking to death.

**Polly:** I know. This cracks me up. Neither of us could eat meat as little kids because of this. It's like, you would put it in your mouth and just chew it and chew it and chew it and then eventually you would have to either spit it out or else get a huge glass of water and then, quick, gulp it down.

**Rocki:** To this day, that fear still comes up sometimes. Like driving in the car on a road trip, I don't like to eat chips unless there's something to drink. If I choke, I'm thinking, what can I wash it down with? The first time I remember having a bad panic attack, I was probably seventeen or eighteen. I was in bed and we (my family) were living in Ecuador. My parents were sleeping and I was alone when all of a sudden, I just thought I was going to die. I thought I wasn't going to be able to breathe even though, physically, I could breathe fine. There was this pressure on my chest and my heart was racing. . . . It's just this fear, I can't describe it, I just really thought I was going to die.

**Polly:** It *is* hard to describe. I mean, if someone were to tell me this kind of stuff, I'd be like okay, take a deep breath, count to ten. But it's a really weird feeling. You're completely disconnected from your body. I mean, it's like being taken over or something.

**Rocki:** My mind literally splits. I have two dialogues going on in my head. I mean, I could be having a panic attack right now. Half of me would be taking part in this discussion, listening to you and responding, and the other half would be saying, "Oh my God, I'm going to die, my throat is closing in and I can't breathe, what am I going to do, which door should I use to get out of here?" I'm not having a panic attack right now but I could be and you wouldn't know. My panic attacks aren't as bad now as they used to be and, Polly, they were never as bad as yours in terms of time and amount. Like you, though, I still sometimes have them. I call them relapses. I can go for years without one and then suddenly I have them for a bunch of months and they control my days again. That is so frustrating. After two years of not having them there they would be again and I would think, Oh my God, I can't deal with this shit. I don't want to go through this again.

My panic attacks are different from yours because they're almost always about me being alone at night. I'm okay driving during the day, but there were times when I had to drive alone at night and that was problematic. It would be easier for me to be on the highway. If something happened, I could stop and there would be people to help me. Side roads made me more frightened because there wouldn't be as many people. When I'm having a lot of panic attacks, I surround myself with people. That's a major difference between us. There was a point when I was younger where I would have a friend stay in my room and just sit there and read while I fell asleep. It was much easier for me to fall asleep with someone there. That doesn't happen much anymore. But even so, about a year ago my partner went away for two weeks. Before she went I was like, Oh my God, I'm going to be alone for two weeks. I hope I don't have an attack. During the day it was fine but at night before going to bed, I would get worried. Am I going to have a panic attack? I never did, but it's the fear that I'm going to have one that can be as bad as having an attack. Like you said, having to organize your life so that you get what you need, like planning to make sure you have someone to come be with you when your partner is gone.

**Polly:** I know that lots of people think that panic attacks are from people's past abuse and that it's some kind of abuse or something they haven't dealt with. I don't think that's the case. When I treated this a year ago after twenty years of living with panic attacks and I took medication, within three weeks, the panic was gone. That told me that whatever else, something was happening chemically. I tried everything humanly possible to control it in other ways. I was very skeptical of medication, didn't want to try it, finally tried it and I was pretty blown away by how effective it was. That told me, Hey, this is not something I made choices about having or something I could have taken care of in other ways. Panic attacks took over my body, like diabetes. I mean, we wouldn't say folks get diabetes because they're stressed out so rather than taking insulin, they should relax.

It's particularly humiliating if you consider yourself to be this tough butchy woman who is really competent and takes care of others and all of a sudden you can't do a simple thing like get in your car and drive across town. This is what I still have to look at, the humiliation factor. Why did I wait until I was thirty-one to even mention the attacks to anyone? Why did I wait for twenty years before I talked about it?

About three years ago I went to see a therapist and talked to her for about an hour before talking about the panic right before I had to leave. This was during a horrible time. I was at the point where I couldn't even get five blocks from my house without feeling like I was going to die. I would walk my dogs around the block again and again because I couldn't get too far from the house.

I went to see this therapist and told her what was going on. She said, "Well, you look fine to me, I don't think there's anything wrong with you." I was very discouraged by that but I found another therapist. *She* said, "Well, I don't know how we can help you in here. I suggest you get a relaxation tape." I walked out and I didn't try to get help again for two years. I knew I had panic attacks but aside from these two times, I didn't do anything about it. The most that I would do would be to go to a mall, pull out a book on panic and start to read about it. But of course, this was happening in a mall so pretty soon, the noise got to me. There were too many people and the lights were too bright. I'd put down the unread book and get out of there as quickly as I could. High stimulus does it for me—fluorescent lights, background noise, anything like that. I would be in this bookstore, read the first sentences of the section, start to panic and run out of the bookstore.

**Rocki:** I found out about the term "panic attack" sometime in my early twenties but I don't remember how. I think I heard about it or someone told me something and I thought, Wow, that sounds like me. But most of the time, I was embarrassed about it. I didn't want to tell anyone about it or talk about it. Even when I asked a friend to stay over with me and hang around until I fell asleep, I never explained why I wanted them to do this. I really just thought this was about me, this thing was about my mind. I thought it was a hundred percent psychological. I didn't think there could be a chemical component to the picture. And unlike you, I don't take medication. I mean, one of my things is that I can't swallow pills. It's like, what should I do as an adult, crush them with a little spoon and add a little bit of water? I don't think so.

In the future if I start to have panic attacks again and if they're really bad, I probably would take meds. But until now, I've found other ways to deal with them. I think you and I have different experiences and I think yours were more intense than mine. Once I started to tell my friends about it and then when I started to tell my lovers, it became a lot easier. I didn't have to have this split dialogue anymore. If I were having an attack I could say, you know, I'm not feeling well. Let's go for a walk or sit quietly or something. This helped a lot.

**Polly:** It was certainly a relief to me that I wasn't verifiably insane. I mean, that's the feeling. Panic attacks are so irrational, there's nothing rational about them. I'm a person who is a totally rational thinker and so it just rocked my world. I could figure out any complicated math problem but I couldn't figure out why I had these reactions that didn't make sense. There's so much denial caught up with panic attacks. I lived with this for twenty years and sometimes I wonder what my life would have been like if I hadn't kept it hidden for so long. I think I would have had a totally different life. I compensated for the panic attacks all the time. I didn't go out on Friday nights during high school and junior high. I couldn't go to basketball games or any of the other events everyone else was attending. Or else I would go to the basketball game but I would sit there and just keep memorizing where the exits were and then still have to leave during the first quarter. I went through high school and college without making friends. I had a lot of acquaintances, people always liked me, but I couldn't socialize with them enough to make any really deep connections. I must be the only person I know who went to college without ever going to a party. I tried it once but there were so many people and so much noise that I couldn't breathe.

I found a lot of relief and solace in books and quiet and learning to be on my own. I went through college and graduate school and got my Ph.D. I made a life with books and study as my primary focus. Now that I don't panic anymore I am much more social than I ever thought humanly possible. I can't imagine what life would have been like if I didn't have panic attacks for so long.

**Rocki:** I had the opposite experience. I made a lot of friends in high school and college and just basically always had people around me. Whenever things were hard, I would surround myself with people. That was strange because before I had panic attacks I used to love my private time, I used to love to spend a lot of time alone. I am an introvert—a social introvert, for sure, but an introvert. When I started to have panic attacks, I lost my independence. I love camping, and that was hard for me to give up [during a period of having panic attacks]. I mean, the thing you were saying, Polly, about going anywhere and always knowing where the exits were, I would think about that when I would go camping. Would it be car camping, could I jump in the car to get to the hospital, was there a hospital nearby? If I were to stop breathing, would there be someone around to give me CPR? I used to know which friends knew the Heimlich maneuver. I would think about shit like that. There was a period where every time I would open a book to study, my chest would get really tight and I would have to close the book. Something that I used to love and that I did during my whole adolescence, reading, I couldn't do anymore. What do you do when you can't be alone and you can't read? You lose your independence. I love that I can do all those things now. I haven't had a panic attack in a long time. It's strange because I always thought of this as something in my head yet the attack is such a physical, visceral event—it rules everything. When I knew one of my relationships was going to end, I really freaked out. I did everything I could to stay in that relationship because I didn't want to deal with moving out, having my own place, and sleeping alone every night. That's hard to admit because I'm not the sort of person who gets into relationships because I have to be with someone. I like being alone.

Part of me has a hard time that we were even asked to talk about this for a book on disability. I've never really considered my panic attacks a disability. I still don't feel that I have a disability even though I can see how much having panic attacks contributed to a loss of my independence and I know that I had to organize my life in such a way that I could take care of the attacks. But I was a very functional, what's the word, panic attackee? I went to school, got my master's, had relationships, all of that. Not that folks who have disabilities can't be functional.

Still, I have a hard time thinking about it as a disability and that's my bias and maybe even my shit. I can see that some people with a disability might be offended by that, thinking that the last thing I want to do is come out as having a disability. That might be part of it, but I think my discomfort is about something else. Can my experiences be even remotely compared to that of someone who always uses a wheelchair and deals with ableism on a daily basis? I don't think so, and maybe this is where my discomfort about this interview comes from.

**Polly:** I'm not very interested in trying to define disability or categorize it and I'm happy for someone to say to me, "No, you don't fit into the category of having a disability." But would I say that having panic attacks disabled me? Absolutely. Did it deny me access to the world? Absolutely. If that's a disability, well fine then yes, absolutely, I have a disability. In the past, I have wished that I had something that would manifest itself in the world so that I could talk about it, have people actually acknowledge it and then give me some kind of assistance to deal with it. There were definitely times I wanted there to be some visible manifestation of the panic attacks.

You know when you talked about your head being split in two with one part having a conversation in the world and looking competent and the other thinking, There's the exit, okay, my keys are in my right hand pocket and all of that? For me, during the worst of my panic attacks, I couldn't even have this other public conversation. The internal discussion was much louder and I couldn't get away from it. Since I've not been panicking, it's an amazing thing to be able to be present with other people in my entirety. It's the best part of not panicking. It's a whole different way of being with people and connecting with people.

**Rocki:** Most of my lovers didn't know about my panic attacks. It's something I felt like I couldn't explain very well. It's always very frustrating to me to try and talk about because I don't have the right words. The piece you touched on about not being able to be fully present? Well, sometimes I might be talking to someone and going Yeah, uh-huh, okay, and I'm talking but I'm not completely there. People would say, you seem distracted and what do I reply? Oh no, I'm just having a panic attack.

**Polly:** Yeah, it's like, No, I'm fine I'm just thinking about where my car is and whether or not I can get out of here in time and how far away is the hospital.

**Rocki:** And what are you going to do when I suddenly choke and pass out at this table in front of you?

**Polly:** How are you going to talk about that to someone? How are you going to go into something like that, especially with someone you don't know very well?

**Rocki:** I prefer not talking about panic attacks, even though I know that I can. Actually, it's more the fact that people know that I have panic attacks that makes me feel better. I don't have to talk about them. Talking about them doesn't make me feel better. When I'm having a panic attack, I just need to get through it. I need to feel that someone is close to me and then get through it. It's most helpful for me to wait until the attack is done and say, "Ten minutes ago when I was really distracted, I was having a panic attack."

**Polly:** I think it's very difficult to talk about panic attacks when you're having a panic attack. All of your energy is focused on controlling and getting rid of it. They say you aren't supposed to control it, you're supposed to relax and let it take over so probably the best thing would be to talk about it. But I know for me, it's not the way I want to react. My response is to try and get on top of it and make it stop. So when I find my body tensing and getting tight, I find it incredibly difficult to have any kind of dialogue about what's going on. In my head I'm just saying, "Get on top of it, get on top of it."

**Rocki:** When I'm home, I do let it go through my body and what helps me now is that I know, know without a doubt, that I'm not going to die. When I was having panic attacks at eighteen, I really thought I was going to die. Now I still think I'm going to die—because that's part of a panic attack—but I know I'm not going to die, if that makes any sense. I'm not as invested as I was at eighteen in getting rid of it and fighting it. I feel the same way about sorrow and grief. I have many of my big emotions on my own and quietly, but I also let them happen and let them go through me.

**Polly:** Part of the humiliation for me is that, even during the times before I identified as butch, I have always identified as a very competent girl and then woman. And as a butch dyke, I think the weakness of panic attacks just seemed so pathetic. For me, panic attacks have always been centered around safety. While I think it's difficult to attribute any single origin to my panic attacks, I do believe that some of my panic grew through a feeling of displacement. I went to a slumber party with girls and I knew I wasn't a girl. They would be in the bathroom, putting on makeup and having fun and I would be pacing upstairs thinking, I don't feel safe. I certainly didn't feel safe enough to wake up one of the girls with all the makeup on her face and say, "I don't feel good, I'm not sure what's wrong with me, would you sit up with me?" I always wanted to be a boy and never, I mean *never*, fit in as a girl, never felt comfortable in social settings as girl. So much of this disorder is about finding a place where you can just sit and feel safe. I think these things must be connected. My panic attacks must have something to do with the fact that, as a butch woman, I live in a culture which demands that girls must be girls. Even if we can be tomboys for a short time, we have to end up as feminine women.

**Rocki:** As a kid I was a tomboy and now I'm a masculine woman but I never felt out of place as a kid or as a teenager. In elementary school and high school I was a jock, I always had friends. I was never teased. During my senior year I was the only girl who had a motorcycle. I rode it to school and mostly gave rides to girls. I didn't quite get the whole boy thing so I knew I was different but I never felt what you're describing. I always felt respected and appreciated for who I was. Nowadays, like when I go to the Mall of America, that's when I feel displaced. People stare at me, they stare at my chin hair or whatever, because I am masculine. As a kid, that wasn't a problem.

In my adolescence I read the whole time. I had a great time doing that. I didn't date, I didn't go to parties that much. I had friends and I could have gone but I didn't want to. I wanted to stay home and read or go for a motorcycle ride. In hindsight, I think I was always butch and then, as an adult, I found out about the word. Like panic attacks, I had them and then when I was nineteen or twenty I heard this expression and thought, Oh, so that's what I have. But that took a while, identifying with the word "butch"—I came out in an environment that tended to frown upon butch-femme stuff. Most of us did andro in those days at Grinnell College. Anyway, I don't know if things would have been different if I weren't butch. My sense of independence would have felt threatened whether I was butch, femme or anything else.

**Polly:** I think this is one of the reasons why I get cautious about definitions, whether it's about what is a disability or which experience is about being butch. Our experiences are so different and yet each are equally valid and intense.

**Rocki:** Yeah, there is so much difference, but I also like the places where we have similar experiences, like not eating meat because you're afraid you're going to choke. I remember as a kid watching that television show *CHiPS,* only in Brazil we pronounced it *sheeps* (and you can interpret that however you want to). I don't remember much about the show except this one episode. There was a man in a restaurant and one of the guys, the Latino guy, Ponch, did the Heimlich maneuver and a piece of whatever it was went flying out of this guy's mouth. It's intense, that scene is still in my head like I watched it yesterday.

One of the things that I'm happy about with being butch, and it certainly relates to my panic attacks, concerns the clothes that I wear. The women I'm attracted to tend to be girly girls, and there are certain clothes that I like on women that if I would wear them, I think I would die. Like tight jeans or tight little shirts. It makes me happy that the clothes I like to wear and the clothes that I think look best on me are not tight clothes. Of course, now I have to contradict myself. Now that I want to get rid of my breasts, or now that I accept that I want to get rid of my breasts, I have a chest binder that I wear sometimes. It's a horrible contraption that just squeezes and squeezes everything flat against your rib cage. It's tight and I hate it and I hate it because it makes my chest feel similar to how I feel when I'm having a panic attack. Though the more I wear it, the less that happens. And I like the way I look when I wear it.

**Polly:** After my therapy nightmares, I waited two years and then trauma brought me back to therapy again. My partner of almost five years and I separated and this terrified me. While I liked being alone, I also needed one other person in my life to negotiate the world, someone who could drive me on the highway, take me places and do the things that I couldn't do. My partner knew a little about my panic attacks during the first phase of therapy, but she wasn't very interested and didn't want to talk about it much. When she moved out, I was terrified that I had lost my link. Who was going to walk the dog or take care of all the little things I couldn't do? So when she moved out, I hooked up with a therapist.

During our first session, we just spent an hour trying to keep me sitting there and calm, that was the goal. It was the worst episode I had ever had. She finally looked at me and said, "I know you don't want to do medication but I think you should give it a try."

**Rocki:** Yeah, and like, Here's the pill. My God, girl, shove it down your throat.

**Polly:** Yeah, take it before you leave the office, okay, please? I trusted her. I'm not like you, Rocki, I don't have a hard time taking pills, but I find taking medication horrifying because I don't know what it will do to my body. So for ten days I was taking these pills and I was completely freaked out. It was ten days of hell. Then within three weeks to a month I was almost panic free. About a month and a half later I drove out on the highway for the first time in a long time, screaming and yelling with excitement. I was like, I can drive! I'm thirty-two and I can drive! Since that time, every once in a while I have a little inkling of a panic and it just immediately dissipates. I go hiking by myself, I go driving by myself, I'm just living a life. I can go anywhere, I can do anything I want, and I love it.

**Rocki:** Yeah, what we need to do, separately of course, is to still go camping alone.

**Polly:** We can go together because I think two of us would equal one panic-free person, so we should just go together.

Being panic-free is an incredible experience. I can go shopping, I can buy my own clothes. Before I couldn't go into a store without panicking. Now, I get to dress myself. Back then, I just wore whatever I had or whatever people gave me. Medication—I take Paxil—has saved my life. I am not at all skeptical about what it has done and I don't even care if it has some long-term effects because I can actually live how I want to live in the short term. The value of that is incomparable. Now that I'm panic-free, I'm the person I always thought I was. In some ways, I don't feel all that different—it's just that I can now enact that person when I want versus only when I can. That's been the biggest change for me.

**Rocki:** The great thing I can say now is that, regardless of whether I ever have another panic attack, I know they will not control my life. That knowledge takes a lot of the power away. Maybe I'm in denial about this, but I don't think so. The one thing I am not in denial about is that I have amazing friends (not to mention the world's best femme lover) to turn to, if need be. I do not take this for granted.

# GIVING BIRTH

## Julia Trahan

"Yeah, but I wanna be the daddy."

That was my teenage response to the question, "Do you want to have children?" My answer was always said with friendliness and flamboyant bravado. It was my to-the-point way of covering up my alienation from and confusion about the traditional world of gender roles and motherhood.

What I also hid was my bewilderment and resentment when the question was phrased slightly differently and asked with an overly caring, slightly desperate tone: "Will you still be able to bear children?"

My answer was the same, regardless of the questioner's tone, and still hasn't changed. Now officially an adult—in my early thirties—however, my understanding and acceptance of categories and classifying questions have grown tremendously. I am out as a disabled person, a crip, a person with disabilities, a limping activist, a writer who flaunts her partially paralyzed pride. I've been blessed and cursed the last decade with increasing comprehension and tolerance of assumptions that my womb is connected to my multicolored crutch by an umbilical cord that resembles an IV tube.

At age eleven, when an eighteen-wheel cargo truck jackknifed across Highway 5 in Southern California, my thoughts were not about the future of my womb. I, in those moments, and in later years, did not have the luxury of dwelling on negative comparisons or bad metaphors, such as *My life juice was drained from me as the wasted oranges from the overturned truck bled, covering the wet highway with sweet fragrance.* The truck's uninjured driver, smelling of alcohol, bent down to cry tears of remorse. He had damaged a young girl, a baby—and murdered future generations.

But these are not the words that pop into my head when I think of raising children. I really don't appreciate others' oversentimentality being placed on my shoulders. I carry my own weight and expect others to carry theirs.

At this point, twenty-two years after the accident that did change my and my family's life, ignorance neither surprises nor baffles me. Ignorance is often a simple lack of social skill mixed with a need to hide one's vulnerability. It can be annoying, frustrating and even somewhat amusing. Experience has taught me that aggressive judgments regarding my childlessness often come from those who cannot physically bear children and want that experience. And women whose self-esteem is dependent on their success in the role of Wife of My Man tend to be combative guardians of the institution of biological motherhood as the only appropriate choice for women.

My bold "I'd rather be the daddy" at age fifteen meant I didn't just want to change diapers or allow my self-esteem to be based solely on the availability of my nurturing breasts. I was using "bisexual" to describe myself, which, in hindsight, had much to do with not knowing a woman could be gentle, want children, appreciate men's aesthetic appearance and be a lesbian. Now that I'm much better informed, I encounter others' false notions: that I cannot have children, that I don't want children or, occasionally, that I don't like children because I am a gay woman, a lesbian, queer, butch, tomboy.

This is, of course, foolishness. My not easily spoken dream is to fall in love forever with the sweetest woman ever born and raise the best children on earth ("best" in their own definition, of course). I tend to hold this dream secret, as it is easier for me to accept the judgment of being a sexless courageous cripple than to care for someone and feel like an amoeba under a microscope whenever in public showing affection. Also, the need to partner-up and raise little ones conflicts with my dislike of being responsible to or for anyone. Until this dilemma works itself out, I struggle to be a nurturing mother to myself.

The past five years my self-mothering focused on healing from childhood sexual abuse and finding a comfortable niche as an intelligent, creative woman with injuries, without basing my life on what others might think of me. My baby, in those years, was *Queen of the Girls,* my solo theatrical production, the text doubling as essay. Before that, my right hip joint was "my baby," with its chronic pain and eventual need for a third artificial replacement.

I was given the title "San Francisco's Postmodern Daddy" by an innovative visual and performing artist at the end of my self-mothering years. (Although I wore a leather jacket and was an active performer in the queer community, I didn't realize that "daddy" was an S/M term. Or maybe I just didn't pay attention; I often found lesbians—particularly as a group—hypocritical in attitude about disabilities. So I tend to ignore what lesbians, as a group, think.)

In the context given me, "daddy" meant a butch lesbian who nurtured other women creatively—helped them artistically find their inner voice. I'm not certain if I did this well, as I tend to want to inspire anyone—regardless of gender or talent or status—who wants to be inspired.

Helping to guide—but not breast-feed—others is vital to me as a butch woman and as a woman with permanent injuries. If others have no context for me, they lock me into the box of "woman with disabilities." This box has a vacuum seal that robs me of my sexuality and power. This box coaxes me to be taken care of, to avoid risk, to stay at home—and explains, for some, why I don't have a man despite being smart and pretty.

The only certain thing in life is that circumstances change. I am now taking a financially mandatory right-turn to learn about real estate in Hawai'i while living near my family. Hawai'i is a place of awe with the full moon over the warm ocean and misty tropical hillsides, but Hawai'i isn't a queer artistic Mecca—my daddyship has to change.

Living semipermanently in Hawai'i with a fairly secure outlook, real children are a possibility, but only if I am in a secure partnership. I don't have the god-given gift of patience and wouldn't want to inflict my surges of urgency on children.

Sabrina, my older sister, is a widowed mother who lives a block away from my apartment. She gave birth to Kalani, my energetic, nondisabled niece, almost three years ago. In Hawai'ian culture, the role of "auntie" carries tremendous responsibility—to give wise guidance and gentle strength. Fortunately for me, my family (except for Kalani) is transplanted from the mainland, because I can't always live up to *kahuna*-like expectations.* But I do try. I visit Kalani daily to play dinosaurs, swim or share cookies.

Kalani has been a tremendous gift of renewal to me and my family. Her birth unified my parents, my brother, my sister and myself. Before Kalani's first breath, she healed much of the fragmentation that often takes place in families after a major trauma (the 1978 highway pileup that bruised my brain stem also involved my brother—thirteen at the time—and my dad's stepfather).

I am enjoying my auntie role. I had never held a baby until I baby-sat one-year-old Kalani. I had been afraid of looking awkward or of not being able to brace the child properly, because my left arm is partially paralyzed. I got over my fears quickly. The first time I baby-sat Kalani she began to howl. The only thing I knew about childcare was from magazines: If a child cries, pick her up and give her comfort. So when Kalani began to howl, I picked her up immediately. She clung to my neck and only screamed louder. I bounced her and sang songs. She cried more. I panicked. My father finally came in and changed her diaper!

After a week in Hawai'i, I returned to my San Francisco home. I didn't understand my value to Kalani. My parents would tell me, "Kalani asks where you are."

When I later moved to Hawai'i, I didn't understand why Kalani wanted nothing to do with me. I had given up my San Francisco apartment and moved near my family in Waikiki. My intention was to leave as soon as I got accepted to a grad school or found a "real" job elsewhere.

I had brought family presents to Hawai'i, but even then Kalani turned her back to me. About a week after my return I was talking to my mother in the kitchen, and Kalani was sitting on the kitchen floor trying to ignore me. Eventually she turned around and asked, "Are you leaving again?" Without pause, I replied, "No," and we've been pals ever since.

* *Kahuna:* Ancient Hawai'ian expert.

❖

It isn't always easy for me to get the opportunity to spend time with Kalani. At first my sister insisted I put her on a leash to walk her to the beach. I was patient with myself and my family as we found out—and I proved—yes, I can push the baby stroller with one hand. Yes, I do give her food or drink when she needs it or asks. No, I don't let her run near traffic. Some of this concern was probably what every worrying mother goes through; some of it was my learning how to care for a young child—the second time I took her out, to sit by the ocean and drink chocolate milk, she peed in her diaper because I didn't get her home in time. Unfortunately, doubt concerning whether I could properly care for Kalani had much to do with disability stereotypes and difficulty communicating about that issue.

I have stopped trying to understand my family; otherwise I would take things personally. Sabrina modulates from overconcern for Kalani to being an appreciative single mom trying to work and finish school and needing a baby sitter. I don't think my family likes my obvious and overt comfort with my sexuality and disability, which I developed in San Francisco (Berkeley, across the bay, is home of the revolution in disability culture and where I was taught to enjoy my body), so I've toned down my daddiness and beefed up my auntieness just to have peace from my parents' complaints about my unfeminine clothes and mannerisms. Still, Kalani asked Sabrina if I was her daddy and sometimes calls me Mr. Aunt Julie, which I thrive on.

I am inspired by Kalani's athleticism and love of using her body. Jumping off the bed or chair, throwing her feet in the air and standing on new, higher places provide hours of entertainment for both of us. Watching her try and retry activities, as well as playing an active role in teaching her how to swim, has helped me accept my physical limitations. Her charming showmanship has also given me permission to let people see me try new things. Even as a nondisabled child, I hid my trials and errors. I liked to be perfect. I stopped talking at age one when someone teased me about a mispronunciation. I resumed at three in full swing, after hours talking in the mirror—or so Mom says. And after the auto accident, this need not to show any mistakes became a full-blown, paralyzing self-consciousness.

I am learning to feel good even when I also feel awkward. I have recently found a calm ocean spot near Waikiki Beach with fairly firm sand where, using my crutch, I can get in and out of the water independently. "My toy," as Kalani calls it, sticks out of ocean rocks about fifty feet offshore, where I store it while swimming. Sitting in the shallow water near the beach, looking at the tiny bluish-green pole against the vastness of the rocks and expanse of the ocean, I see it from a new perspective: "My toy" is barely recognizable as an artificially created object.

Being able to wake up by doing morning somersaults in the warm ocean waves is definitely worth a bit of self-consciousness. I've been visiting my family in Hawai'i for sixteen years and had always succumbed to my fear of the staring eyes of tourists. Fear of others' opinions and possible disapproval made even the warm tropical air a bitter trap.

But I lost my fear after watching Kalani grab a neglected pair of high-heeled shoes and run down the beach, chased by a thirtysomething Japanese couple. The coconut-butter and sand-covered audience laughed with delight. When we finally caught our rascal and returned the pumps, she and I clapped with the delight of adventures—this one and others yet to come.

# AGAINST THE BODY OF MY MOTHER

## Susan Raffo

I was frightened the first time I was allowed to see it.

Before, the nurses would usher me out, telling me, "It's not good for children to see things like this, and you're too young. Just wait until we're finished and then you can come back in." When I tried to stay behind, my grandmother would push me toward the door, her voice tight and quick, and tell me to stay outside. Waiting in the hospital hallway, I would stand up against the crack between door and wall, close enough to feel the breeze of any movement but not close enough to get hit when the door finally swung open.

The day I was allowed to see was not a planned-for day. The pictures I had drawn for my mother the week before carried no clue of the coming event, no air of anticipation in the images I had scrawled with crayon and pencil. But this time, when the nurses came in to change her bandages, my mother said I didn't have to leave.

I wasn't frightened as they unrolled the gauze from the thinness of her leg. Even when the top layers of white gauze became yellowed, the crust of things I couldn't recognize causing gauze to stick to bandage to stick to skin, even then I wasn't frightened, only curious. My mother watched me closely. "Sue," she said, "you know this isn't pretty. You can stop watching if you want to." She must have been worried. Maybe even afraid. She was my mother, big and strong, and I was only a child.

When the final bandage came off, I didn't shudder or pull away out of disgust or revulsion, the very thing my mother was afraid I would do. What was before me had once been a leg but didn't look like a leg anymore. There was no sliding together of the familiar with the changed. What I saw was only different, and I remember thinking this because I wanted so badly to touch what I saw with my finger: What I saw was beautiful. The shape of my mother's leg held hills and valleys where most people had only a smooth landscape. Her leg twisted into itself and then twisted back out again. There were puckers, like lips pressed ready to kiss, and swellings, like the sides of a peach. And like a peach, the skin was fuzzy and moved between colors, from pink to yellow to something close to white. There were patches of skin that were shiny and flat like glass or ice, and I wondered if I could see myself in her skin, if the patches were little mirrors the car accident had given her even as it had taken away other parts of her leg.

Standing as close as I dared and careful not to lean against the bed or shift suddenly and hurt her, I must have made a movement with my hands because my mother whispered to me, "You can touch it, Sue." Then she said, "It's okay."

I didn't look up at her face. I don't know if I remembered she was there. With my finger, I slowly traced the mirrorlike patches, feeling how hard and tight they were, the skin slick, as if it had been spit upon. Around the shine, the skin was harsher, roughened with the stubble of shaved hair and roughened with the earth and gravel still trapped beneath its surface. You could see the shadows made by small pockets of dirt crouched cave-like in muscle. I was afraid to touch her there, afraid that if I pressed down too hard I would release the small rocks, they would tumble out of her through a break in the skin, and this would cause her more pain.

I was also afraid to let my fingers slide down into the valley where once had been bone and muscle and now was something thin and shrunken. At the bottom of the valley, this place upon her calf, I could see a thin fissure. It was reddened and wet, a slight oozing of something, a welling up from within her body. I wanted to touch this place where her leg was crying, but I was afraid. I was afraid that if I put my finger there, I would go right inside, my fingers would slip through the crack and my arms would be able to reach right up from her leg to her heart. I could enter her here, this place that was once a leg but now is a door and the wet of her crying. This is the place where I could crawl inside my

mother, go into places where I wasn't invited or places where I am too frightened to tunnel. Standing there looking at her, at her leg twisted like the knot of
a root, at the colors that slid and crashed against each other, and at the thin
crack that looked as if it could widen with a grasp, I felt protective in the way of
a seven-year-old child. This was my mother, my mother, my mother, and I
climbed on the bed and hugged her, my body small but feeling so big along the
length of her skin.


I grew alongside my mother's body.

As a child, I was told tales by my grandfather and my grandmother about
my mother the athlete, my mother the sleek. My mother who had won medals
in swimming and diving, in track and field. My mother who played softball like
no one else. I imagined her body in a bathing suit, the muscles hard and strong.
In my imagination, I forgot that my mother was shorter than I was and that her
breasts were larger. When I imagined what she was like at eleven, twelve and
thirteen, I gave her the body I wanted to have, straight like an arrow, her hips
only a pause between shoulders and feet. My mother who should have been
born the boy because she was excellent at sports while her brother was only
average. My mother the athlete. My mother the swift. The perfect. The physical.

My mother whose body by the time I noticed it as a body was bent and
twisted. My mother who sometimes needed to lean on me as we walked, whose
leg would swell into an angry red waterskin, who took a razor blade and lanced
the skin, let out the pus, the collected water, until the leg shrunk back down
again. My mother who would not wear shorts because she did not want the
neighbors to see her legs.

When I was seven and our car took flight from the bridge that led to home,
our family flew away with it. My father, brother PJ and cousin Dawn flew the
farthest. They grew wings and flew until they were lost to sight. I barely flew but
landed with a thud on the earth and a splash in the river. My hands reached
questioningly after the flying form of PJ, but the earth held me still and heavy.
My little brother, Jeffrey, landed so hard against the breathing soil that it almost
knocked the life out of him. When my mother crashed to the earth, her body

was indecisive. Half of her clawed at the rocks on the side of the river embankment while the other half struggled to take flight and follow the path of her husband and son. Her bones shattered, shedding themselves in tiny pieces among the weeds and broken bottles of the riverside. Many of the pieces were never found again.

My mother lost one body in the car accident and was given another. This new body was to be a burden. A body, she was told, that would never walk again. Given a body she had to think about, my mother concentrated very hard.


My mother's pain was unreal to us. There was a point at which her pain only existed for us as information. In the 1970s, when marked parking for people with disabilities was becoming more commonplace, my grandmother, brother and I joked with my mother, telling her she should get one of those little blue cards to put in our car window. The twist of her leg and the tilt of her walk meant that, with the blue card, we could all park closer to store entrances and city buildings, a convenience we all craved. We never understood why she wouldn't take advantage of something we all wanted, something a telephone call would give her. For us, the little blue card was like getting a free lunch on your birthday, a little extra bonus because you fit the criteria. My mother refused, saying she was quite able to walk. It was not uncommon to leave a shopping mall, my mother's hands clenched in mine, her eyes focused somewhere inward as, with each step, she pulled me down against her, step and pull, using my body as the base for her movement, our gaits matching and moving us slowly past a row of empty parking spaces with wheelchair symbols spray-painted on the ground.

My mother's leg was the visible symbol of what had happened to our whole family. The car accident had broken my mother's body along with most of her bones. Her spine had splintered in more than one place, the slivers of bones and roughness of cracked rib somehow missing the nerves that kept her upright and moving. For almost a year after the accident she was encased in various casts of gradually diminishing sizes. Her fingers, arms, legs and back were riddled with the faint traces of scarring, thin white webs that covered much of her skin. As the years passed, the scars disappeared, although pain remained. Her leg could not shift back into what it once was, growing new muscles and flesh, new bones and structure to replace what had been lost. After a period of years, this leg was left as the only visible reminder of the car accident that had affected all of our lives.

In the summer heat, my mother worked in her garden, her butt resting on the earth and her leg, encased in denim or polyester pants, stretched out in front of her as she maneuvered her way around. One summer day soon after the accident, a day so hot that wearing even a bathing suit seemed too much, my mother put on a pair of shorts. She wore them in the front yard, a rural expanse of grass and gravel set on the side of a road with very little traffic. She wore them for a few hours before coming back in to change. "People stare at me," she said, and she was fierce when she said it. "I hate having to deal with their looks and their pity." I told her she was fine, her leg was fine, it was too hot to wear trousers. She moved slowly through the house and went into her bedroom to change.

I wavered about my mother, sometimes thinking her frail and sometimes impenetrably strong. I watched her face, the lines around her eyes that would deepen with the ache of her bones. I expected her to die. Within the silence of her pain and the ways in which she was stubborn, I expected her body to explode without warning, her concentration to wrench her away from health. From the age of eight on, I expected her to die suddenly and soon. This didn't frighten me, it was just what seemed true. Out of the blue, my mother would die, and Jeffrey and I would continue to live.

My mother expected this, too. When I was ten or eleven, she said to me, "When I die, I want you to care for your brother." She said, "I will not be here to teach him the things I want him to learn. You will be older and will remember more. When I die, I want you to teach him the kind of grownup he should be." When I told her I would do this, it didn't seem like a burden. I thought that when she died, she would feel relief.

This belief in her imminent death lay alongside the luxury of often forgetting how much she hurt. Because she rarely spoke of the pain, or if she did, spoke of how it would never stop her from doing what she wanted to do, I often forgot what was humming inside of her. When at seventeen I moved away from home, we shared complicitous phone calls in which I would be told about operations or health problems that had occurred months previously. I would lecture her—"You have to tell me these things; you have to let me know." She would laugh and sigh and say she was sorry, but when we both hung up, there was some measure of relief. We both knew she wouldn't tell me the next time; we both knew that nothing would change. My mother protected me from having to really understand what it was like for her to stay alive.

The fierceness of my mother's concentration and her unwillingness to acknowledge any weakness became like a standard with which I've had to compete. Even when I was young, I learned to hide things, deciding what was important information to share and what could be secreted away. I measured my pain against what I understood as the pain of my mother. I measured my own determination against the determination of my mother and decided that pain and struggle were no excuse for not getting things done. Everyone in my family said my mother and I were very much alike. We were so alike, everyone said, it was uncanny. I didn't know I could disagree with this.

Sometimes in the evenings, after Jeffrey had gone to bed, my mother would begin to cry. She did this rarely, and when she cried, I didn't speak of it. When she cried, I held her. Over the years as I grew older, my arms grew to let me hold her more completely. When she cried she said, "No one understands me like you do." I believed this to be true, and I held her more gently.


Mothers are expected to teach girls how to be girls. Through their words, their actions, whether we resist or settle, agree or disagree, we are taught. We leave home wanting to be like our mothers or wanting to be different. It is rare to have no opinion at all.

At some point, we notice our mothers' bodies as something separate from us, something we call pretty or ugly, thin or fat, stylish or old-fashioned. Something we judge and name. My mother's body was my measure, and within her arms, I calculated the length of my own.

A few years after the accident, my mother, Jeffrey and I went shopping for shoes. We were trying to find something attractive that would let my mother walk without her foot slipping to the side, nerve endings grating where her foot fell, bone barely covered by skin, hitting cement. In the early 1970s, the only shoes that would fit her damaged feet were what she called "old-lady shoes." Orthopedic nightmares. Unrelentingly ugly, usually black, sometimes brown, with hard leather and square heels, these were shoes that never changed with the times, ignorant of skirt lengths and the season's colors.

The doctors told her any other shoe would guarantee constant pain. Only in these shoes, they said, would she be able to walk without a limp, to stand tall. We went—just once—to the only shoe store that carried these shoes. With a wall to their own, they crouched in the back, away from the sleek shoes that other women wore. Though they were displayed in a store right in the middle of downtown Cleveland, alongside red satin heels and steel-toed work boots, they carried with them a hint of antiseptic, something that dwelled among the ringing of bedpans.

My mother was angry. The salesman, an older man with hair sculpted in thin strings from one ear to the other, brought the shoes to where my mother sat. He told her they would be good for her; they would let her walk, let her be like everyone else. As she sat looking up, he stood above her, uncomfortably close but refusing to move. When he finally went to check on another customer, my mother stood and walked to the mirror. *No,* she whispered, *no, I won't wear these, I just won't.* She was crying but without showing the tears. She sat back down, tearing the shoes off as quickly as she could.

When the salesman returned he said things like, you will stand straight, no pain, walk well for the children, for the children, for the children. He touched my brother's head when he said this. My brother was only three years old. For the children, you will be able to run for the children. My mother relented and bought the shoes. Bought them but carried them out of the store in a bag, hurrying to the car, her hands tightly holding ours. In the car she cried, the new shoes locked away in the trunk, her feet in the cheap brown leather ones she usually wore.

I don't remember her ever wearing those black shoes that were supposed to let her run. I don't remember her returning them. Maybe she waited for a quiet night and then, under the stars and the eyes of flying things, maybe she burned them. Standing there in the shoes that slid to the side, one pair after another, lasting only a matter of months before the leather softened and broke, letting her foot slip to the ground, maybe she watched the sparks of flaming leather whirl lazily upward. If she did this, I know she would have been alone, at a time when we were in bed and there was no need for running.

Once, at the home of a family friend, my mother grabbed me as I ran past her and pulled me over. "Look at this!" she exclaimed as she laid her hands against my chest. "My daughter is getting breasts. Soon she will be as big as me!" And with her hands, she molded their growing roundness, pressing my shirt smooth against my ribs. Embarrassed, I struggled to pull away from her hands on my breasts, her eyes on mine. I could feel her pride, I could feel that my body pleased her.

My breasts grew. I grew. Not unusually tall or taller than average, but taller than my mother. With long legs like my father's and no desire to be an athlete. I stayed in my room and read.

When I was a small child, I had been skinny in the way of children, bones, muscle and fat changing shape as my body moved from one growth spurt to another. After the car accident, as my mother lay in the hospital, her body struggling to reassert itself into an earth-bound shape, I concentrated on grounding myself in gravity. My mother's mother taught me to grieve. Baking pies and cookies, crafting homemade noodles out of flour and water and then frying them in butter, I learned how to grieve with the taste of ice cream in my mouth and a bag of potato chips by my side. As the years passed, my desire for gravity grew stronger and I waxed heavier and more solid upon the ground, my thighs touching and my stomach rounding to match the curve of the earth.

One summer, as I lay on my stomach on the floor in front of the television, my mother snapped a Polaroid of my fourteen-year-old body. For a long time, she had been asking me to diet. As the photo developed, my mother explained that she wanted me to see what I looked like to other people; perhaps if

I knew what I really looked like when I wasn't posing in front of a mirror, I would finally lose some weight. She told me I didn't have many years left. "It is harder," she explained, "to lose the fat when you are older." As I watched my thighs like two white boats creep into fullness on the white square of paper, she told me I didn't understand how unhappy the fat would make me. I was lucky, she said, I had my father's long legs, legs she had always wanted for herself. Hanging the photo on the refrigerator, she said my legs would look so good if I would just lose some weight. "I had," and she smiled as she said it, "the most beautiful legs."

Losing weight did not feel like a choice. Thinner was better and I was too fat, so I had to diet. When my mother told me this, it was said as fact, and I didn't know I could disagree. When my body did not shrink, I was secretly pleased, hiding my smiles in the pages of a book. *This is my body,* I thought to myself, *it follows its own rules.* Feeling my body as my own happened in brief moments, a sudden dizziness of *mine mine mine,* followed by the desire to do as I should, grow thinner and thinner. I wanted to be attractive, to be beautiful (which meant I had to be thin), and when I had arrived there, my mother would let me know. If I didn't become beautiful, it was my own fault. When I grew thin, it would be because we did it together.

My mother walked without a limp because she willed it so. Her body was always in pain—at times she held it like a basket of eggs, her skin cautious in its cradle around bones and muscle. Through will she walked, one leg after another in measured tread. Through will I learned to hold my stomach at bay like a wild animal, a thing of want and need. I learned to deny it, an apple a day and lies for lunch—*Of course I ate, I'm not hungry, I had a big breakfast*—and my waist slivered away into something that let the bones show through. At night as I readied for bed, I walked into the living room and held my pajamas high in the air, the cotton pulled up and away from my body. "Look, Mom," I said, the cool evening air soft on my skin, "look at how flat my stomach is." I stood there, turning in her gaze. "Look at my thighs, they've gotten so small." I kept turning around, modeling this body for her; we are so proud of our body, the one we both tend.

My mother longed after my body. When my mother dressed my body, bought me the clothes that matched her tastes, ran her eyes along the places that were visible and wondered about what she couldn't see, I could feel her longing. Isn't this what most mothers of adolescent girls feel? My mother did not long after my body with the ways of a lover; she did not want to feel me thrusting against her or to take me in the ways of sex and secrets. Her longing was about desire, but not the desire of orgasm and fire in the skin.

There is so much we are afraid to talk about. As lesbians, many of us are careful about the words we use, about how we talk about desire and longing, how we describe and long for the relationships we have with our mothers and our fathers, our daughters and our sons. Each of us walks in a tangle of what we feel, what we think we should feel and what we are being told to feel by everything around us. My mother struggled with the body she had been given, never quite accepting the new twists her body took as she watched the new curves that grew into mine.

I think mothers often desire the bodies of their daughters: daughters who reach that certain point of ripeness, their skin still like a child's, unlined and warmed by something pushing out from inside, breasts new and still untouched by the pull of an infant. No matter how powerful our mothers are as women, no matter how wise or aware, their bodies are moving away from what is thought beautiful. Their skin either has or is beginning to thicken and stretch, their flesh to drop with weariness from their frame. It doesn't matter how well defended we are against the worldly foolishness that says this young ripeness is the only kind of beauty that is acceptable. It doesn't matter how much we love the many shapes of our bodies and the pull of the years, soft insistent tugs, on the elastic of our skin. There must sometimes be a longing, a hunger, when we look at our daughters and when our mothers look at us. Within her secret yearning sat my mother with the leg like a knot, a body knotted with pain.

Another piece of our story turns the tangle of desire and adolescence, of mothers and daughters, into a knot. As my body became that of a woman, my mother was struggling with her own desire for women. Sometimes I picked up a kind of lightning in the room, a focus of electricity that licked against all of our skins—my mother's, my brother's and mine. It was never scary. It was never loud. It was just there, and sometimes I understood it. The fire was not about sex, but about the want of too many things. Of bodies long scattered into pieces on the ground.

Within this tangle, I developed theories about attractiveness, about what was beautiful and what it felt like to be pretty. I considered the kind of woman I wanted to be. My legs became very important; my legs were what I had, they were my power. My legs were visible symbols of the fact that I could run, that I could wear short skirts in the summer and melt into the background of bare summer skins.

I am my mother's daughter. This sentence carries a wealth of different meanings. From my mother I learned the strength that comes from moving forward with desire despite obstacles. I learned that bodies are fragile things that can break apart just when they are at their strongest. I learned that when a body breaks, life doesn't stop, but keeps pressing forward.

I learned with my mother to be afraid, that those we love are impermanent and that love can feel like risk. I also learned that it is better to take that risk than to be alone. I learned from my mother how to hide, how to pretend that things were all right when they really weren't.

I learned from my mother how to want. I learned to be voracious and not to settle. I learned that desire is a necessary thing.

The car accident gave me a body reborn from the river without a scratch. It delivered me up on the mud and weeds of the embankment, cleansed and new. It has so far given me a life of days to walk and run. It let me keep my body, and it gave me my mother's relentlessness. *No matter what*, whispered the river, *none of you will ever be the same again. There is no going back.*

I remember PJ and my father by closing my eyes and feeling the parts of my body that contain them. I can feel my father's arms around me: I am so small in the circle of his hug. I can hear my brother laughing: We are wrestling, and he accidentally kicks me in the shin; while I scream with tears, I feel his small hand on my arm, his eyes big with sorrow. But my mother is written throughout my body with more than the distinction of separate memories. She is here not just because she gave birth to me, but because our survival was woven directly into hers. My brother Jeffrey and I are here because after the struggle, my mother's body remained on the earth. Had she died, we would have continued, hearts beating and lungs breathing. We would have found lives with ourselves at the center, and we would have found a way to family. But she did not die.

I am of my mother's body, her skin worn and tired in places, stronger in others. Many years have passed since the accident and now, in the summer when the sun is hot and sweat runs in rivers down her back, my mother wears shorts, the kind that end just above the knee and are wide around the legs. After years of being afraid, her body a thing not to be trusted, she rides bikes with a vengeance, clocking up miles on warm days and crowing loudly that her distance is always farther than her friends'. My mother the athlete, the physical, the perfect.

My mother's body is still the sole visible reminder of what happened to our family. Her house carries no photos of my father and brother, and her conversations don't go further back than a decade. She has now lived more years after the accident than she lived before it, and her life is oriented forward, not back. She begrudges too much conversation about what happened on that day and endures the times when my brother and I feel moved to talk about it.

And her leg, the reminder of the event that changed the way all of us walk in the world? There are no longer places for me to enter; the weeping places are long grown over. The hills have softened, and the twists and turns are expected, their shape understood. Her leg is still there, it still hurts every day, and at times, there are whispered conversations: *Will it come off? Will she need to lose this fickle thing of flesh and gravel before she loses her life?*

I'm not afraid anymore that my mother will die, that her life will slip between our fingers. I know that someday she *will* die, and when she does, it will be time. We will grieve her and do what all children do when they lose their mothers, feel a piece of ourselves break off into confusion. When she dies, she will die because death happens and not because she has been marked as unable to live.

# SEEKING COMMUNITY
## Some Lessons from a Catholic Girlhood

Victoria A. Brownworth

*The Collect*

I grew up solitary. My differentness isolated me from my peers. I had been born with a couple of birth defects—problems with a leg and foot—but these had been corrected by the time I was a toddler. A severe but long-undetected vision problem left me only partially sighted for several years; complicated and traumatizing surgery when I was five years old fixed that as well, leaving me with a permanent defect in one eye, but one that was relatively minor compared to what had been. Thus, with the exception of eyeglasses, which many other children wore as well, there was nothing visible—nothing to point to and say, *Aha!*, *that's* the problem.

There was nothing to see—not even a birthmark or scar. Nothing like the disabled girls who went to my school. (Catholic schools, particularly private ones, always had their share of disabled children prior to the enactment of Title VII; more to do with religious fervor and ready money than a strong civic belief in mainstreaming the disabled, however, if the attitude toward these students was any indicator.)

Big, ambling Rose Doyle, with the pale skin, brightly flushed cheeks and unruly tongue indicative of Down syndrome, at twenty was still trying to finish high school, the nuns and her parents convinced that if she just tried—and prayed—hard enough she could be as good a student as the other girls. Everyone, including the nuns, called her "retarded," but never to her face. Nobody used the term Down's syndrome in the sixties.

Claire Phillips walked aided by wooden crutches with leather straps attached to her arms and wore leather-strapped braces on her spindly legs. She was very small and swung one leg around when she walked in a way that seemed to defy gravity. Did she have polio as an infant, or did she have a congenital hip displacement?

Debbie Miller wore glasses with Coke-bottle lenses, two hearing aids and spoke with an odd, barely intelligible thickness. The nuns called her "tongue-tied" and "slow." What was her disability, and why wasn't it called by its accurate name instead of referred to as something vaguely biblical? She was the youngest of a large family whose father was a doctor; perhaps she'd been oxygen-starved at birth or her mother had had German measles during her pregnancy.

Cindy Williams breathed funny, like she was underwater, sweated a lot and had a strange, sweet odor about her that was excessively cloying. It was difficult to sit close to her, and no one wanted to be placed next to her in class. She was absent a lot, and by the time I was in fifth grade she had stopped coming to school altogether, but the nuns asked us to pray for her because she was sick. Did she have cystic fibrosis?

These girls were obviously different from their classmates, their disabilities striking, if mysterious. In the sixties, despite rampant changes wrought by a range of civil rights movements, disability remained utterly stigmatized. My school was small and private, with fewer than three hundred students in the grades from kindergarten through high school. My eighth-grade class had only twelve girls—whose names and faces I still remember thirty years later. Ours was a cloistered school, a kind of matriculating convent where the nuns who taught us were steeped in dogmas that feared difference and shunned the different.

In those years there was still only one Other—Satan, the Devil, Beelzebub—and he stalked one's every unoccupied moment, every wandering thought, every questionable step. If you didn't remember that fact, the nuns were there to remind you: An idle mind is the Devil's playground. Just as Jesus was omnipresent at our school—his face and flaming heart and crucified form on every classroom wall, in every hallway—so too was the Devil. We had no pictorial reminders of him as we did of Jesus or Mary or even our school's patron saint, the young martyred Cecelia, but the Devil was as real to us as the nun at the front of our classroom or the specter of Mother Superior in the principal's office.

Within this semimedieval context of warring Good and Evil, where we girls were in a constant battle for our immortal souls as we marched single-file from classroom to lunchroom to school yard to chapel, disability looked suspiciously like the mark of Cain. Did the nuns believe the disabled girls were beset by demons? Did they think these girls were somehow marked by either God or the Devil to act as a sign to the rest of us, complacent as we were that prayer and Communion were enough to keep God in our hearts and the Devil—with his near occasions of sin—at bay?

It's difficult to judge from the distance of three decades and so much change exactly why disability—and thus, the disabled—remained so furtive, so hidden, so *embarrassing* at a time when other minorities and women were engaged in civil rights movements that rocked the status quo. And yet thirty years ago we seemed so much closer to the Middle Ages; genetics was still considered more a Hitlerian theory than a respectable science. At my school we learned Creationism; Darwin did not exist; the Scopes Trial was anecdote, not history. Within this medieval context disabilities seemed linked to a dark and demonic past where God and the Devil did daily battle, rather than simply another way of being.

Disability marked not just the disabled but their families as well. It hadn't been that long since "defectives" had been sent to the gas chambers in Germany as part of the Third Reich's ordered plan. A disabled child—even if she was the only disabled child among many nondisabled children in the family—was viewed as a sign that something was not right; she was a punishment from God, not a blessing. Still, the handful of disabled girls at my school each year were the lucky exceptions to all those children marking time in institutions whose families couldn't bear the daily association with divine consequence. Though stigmatized by disability, these girls remained within the community—a kind of acceptance, a step toward wholeness, a measure of change that was to come, a sort of belonging. Whether engendered by faith or fear or even love, the presence of these girls was its own testament, a lesson for us all. Community, *real* community, whether evangelical or secular, meant embracing each member—difference and all.

## The Epistle

I'm not sure how children sense a difference that isn't readily visible, and yet they do. Inevitably the child marked as different gets ostracized, marginalized and ultimately penalized by her peers. Marked by this signal difference—invisible though it was—I spent my childhood on the fringes of camaraderie; I was different, I did not belong. No apparent disabling trait to separate me from the other girls—no crutch or hearing aid, no speech defect or mental slowness—but I was marginalized nevertheless and, unlike with my foot or eyes, unable to fix whatever it was that denoted my Otherness.

The lives of the saints are rife with tales from the fringe—as well as tales of disability surmounted or vanquished or accepted. Thus my Catholic girlhood offered me recourse to my pariah status. As confession heals the soul, hagiography heals the heart. Sainthood, I discovered early on—perhaps as young as seven or eight—is often a clear response to being different. The saints were always Other—until sainthood transmogrified them into the *community* of saints, a kind of Cabinet of God. I avidly read the lives of the saints, searching not just for a higher level of faith and a deepening of belief, but for what I desired most fervently, most passionately—community, that elusive sense of belonging.

Punishing the body for the sins of the flesh—because the very existence of the flesh was an affront to God's noncorporeal perfection—is a dominant theme in hagiography. The saints are, for the most part, flagellants and martyrs—masochists who render their pain to God as an offering, not because God is a sadist (though perhaps the Old Testament God—Yahweh—had a sadistic streak, presented as he is as vengeful and retributive; but Jesus embodies the New Testament concept of God as love), but because God's perfection extends far beyond the physical. We offer our physical pain and suffering as sacrifice for the sacrifices Jesus made for us; after all, what human suffering could match Christ's suffering and crucifixion for *our* sins?

Thus as I read I uncovered the subliminal layering of disabling punishments to the body inherent in hagiography. A luminous beauty, St. Rose of Lima feared her looks would occasion sin in others and so rubbed her skin to blistering burns with caustic substances. A child of the streets, St. Bernadette had tuberculosis of the bone—her leg was rotting beneath her—yet she uncomplainingly scrubbed convent floors on her festering knees. St. Rita embedded a crown of thorns like the one the Romans thrust on Jesus into her own head beneath her nun's veil; the gangrenous wounds never healed, but the superations were said to emit the scent of roses. St. Thomas Aquinas was a dull-witted youth—perhaps a dys-lexic—but mortification of the flesh led him to acuity; his writings place him with the intellectual saints like St. Teresa of Avila who heard voices and levitated around the garden of her convent while contemplating Catholic dogma. St. Cecelia, St. Maria Goretti and St. Lucy all suffered bodily mutilation and mar-tyrdom rather than submit to men determined to steal their virtue as well as their faith.

And then there was Jeanne d'Arc, warrior saint and ultimate fringe per-sona, the model for every Catholic girl disabled by difference. An illiterate young lesbian, Jeanne burned at the stake rather than wear female clothes or renounce the female saints she saw and spoke to in visions; she refused to pretend that her differentness and her spirituality were the irreconcilable elements her torturers claimed they were. She knew she could be both butch warrior and true believer in the word of Christ; several centuries after the Church burned her as a witch and heretic, it beatified her as a saint.

These and other tales gave me hope; if the brilliant St. Teresa could float around her garden communing with other saints, praying and writing to St. John of the Cross (between them compiling some of the great theoretical work of Catholic mysticism), then perhaps there *was* community to be had that could be born of difference. One had only to pray, mortify the flesh and search the soul, and it would, eventually—if only as the flames licked around one's feet— be found.

But in the lives of the saints, a decades-long struggle—such as the prayers St. Monica offered up in the hope of converting her son, St. Augustine, from his profligate life—seems fleeting. Time passes quickly in these tales, the gritty dailiness of the struggle glossed over, minimized. To a child, the forty years

St. Monica prayed is as incomprehensible an eternity as the time spent between purgatory and heaven. The lives of the saints held promise, but promise is elusive. Would prayer be enough? Would I be able to visualize that door to community? And if I did, would it open for me, or shimmer away like the mirage it seemed to be?

## The Gospel

Though I spent years struggling with—and toward—the concept of sainthood, the possibility seemed more linked to the simplicity of a medieval past than to a complex modern future. How, I kept asking my priest with a child's earnest intensity, to hold the pressures of modern life—and the seductive quality of sin—at bay? How was the spiritual maintained above all else? The answer to my questions was always "through prayer," but what I saw was community led to community. Religious community could lead one to the community of saints. But how to enter that religious community in the first place? Catholic school should have been a first step, and yet it felt like the very thing that separated me from community, the very root of my marginalized life. Why was I not accepted? Why did I remain on the fringe of what I perceived to be a warm and welcoming world in which we were all equal in God's eyes? Why did I not belong? Did the other children see some demonizing defect in me that was as apparent to them as Claire's crutches or Debbie's thickened speech were to me? Was there a different kind of disability with which I was afflicted that I could not perceive but others could?

The nuns were enveloped in community. It was obvious as they glided along the paths of the school, their long black habits flowing out behind them, veils caught up together in the slightest breeze, their hands tucked deep into their belled sleeves. In compatriot pairs they would walk to vespers as the bells chimed; they appeared to flock, as birds do, at dusk, toward prayer, ensconced in their black garments, white wimples stark against the gathering dark. This physical evocation of community was emblematic of all they shared: a life predicated on faith and good works, a life devoted to God and prayer and sacrifice. Community meant a melding of belief and purpose. As they moved together, their closeness was palpable, especially to the outsider. I yearned early to be part of that world of women, to be embraced by that same aura of community; whether or not it led toward sainthood, I ached for that sense of belonging.

*Communion*

When I first found community it was, as I had always known it would be, with other women, but not as I had expected it to be. I had left the uniformed and cloistered society of Catholic school and my dream of convents and sainthood behind for a new order: lesbian feminism. No doubt my early indoctrination into a woman-only, woman-centered world at my convent school made lesbianism seem somehow part of a continuum rather than the aberration I knew I should feel it to be. But female society was what I had yearned for over many years. Then yet another girls' school brought me closer to community than I had ever expected to come, this side of a burning stake or some other hideous martyrdom. And though martyrdom of a sort would come soon enough when my lesbianism was exposed and I was expelled from school, when I first stumbled into the arms of a nascent, fledgling, covert community of lesbian girls and women, I knew—as St. Monica must have known the day her son began his conversion—that this was what I had been seeking. The *frisson* of belonging had the ecstatic, enrapturing quality I had read about in the lives of the saints. *This* was community; I was finally home.

The depth of community within lesbian society and culture as I discovered it thirty years ago enticed and seduced me. Here I saw an acceptance and a diversity missing at my convent school—at least in practice. Lesbian society seemed intent on embracing the marginalized, the fringe females cast out of straight society; we were the girls and women who didn't fit. The Jeannes who wore men's clothes, the Teresas who lived an ethereal life of the mind, the Roses who undermined their own beauty to escape the brutalizing force of men. But here too were the Claires and Debbies—the imperfect bodies. Within lesbian society there seemed room for disability: women who couldn't walk or see or hear (I had never seen American Sign Language until I began attending lesbian events). Here it seemed I had found that utopian community of women in which difference became—as it was in hagiography—celebrated, rather than reviled. As feminist Mary Daly told me when she explained why she had left Catholicism behind, the "hag" was the essence of hagiography. Women were themselves goddesses; we had only to *dis*-cover that reality ploughed under by Christianity.

And so I rested within the open arms of lesbian society in its various forms for years. Lesbian separatism lured me as the convent once had. Catholicism was superseded, if not wholly replaced, by a spiritual rémoulade of wicca, Mariolotry, voodoo and goddess-worship. My conflicted relationship with Catholicism; my concomitant beliefs in and devotion to Mariolotry, female saints, goddess-worship, wicca and voodoo; and my passionate involvement in lesbianism and queer culture have all made my search for community an ongoing process over the past three decades since I left the simplicity of my Catholic girlhood behind for a more complex and multifaceted adolescence and adulthood—and spirituality. And yet so many of the same questions remain. How do we create community that is inclusive in the way the convents of my girlhood seemed to be, where the elderly and disabled are as much a part of convent life as are the young and fit?

When I wrote about lesbian nuns twenty years ago—the first journalist to do so in a series that helped spark the path-breaking book *Lesbian Nuns: Breaking Silence* (Naiad Press, 1985)—it was in an effort to reconcile this desire for community by asking women who were nuns, as I had always *wanted* to be, as well as lesbians, which I always *had* been, how these two variant—but not necessarily disparate—identities could meld. The convent had always been my prototype for a community of women; my forays into a range of woman-centered pursuits from lesbian-feminist politics to lesbian separatism to wicca were all predicated on replicating this ideal—utopian—female community.

It isn't that lesbian community failed me or even disappointed me so much as it is that the structure of that community has changed in the thirty years since I came out as a very young teenager. What I experienced between the ages of thirteen and thirty was a community in development and, thus, in flux. Politics raged—and rage raged as well. We were angry women who loved each other but hated a great deal, too. And as I got older I realized that what had first seemed utopian—particularly the woman-centered aspect of the lesbian world in which I lived—was fraught with conflict as well.

Community as I first experienced it was in fact far less perfect than it initially appeared. Despite my differentness within straight society, I was still white and nondisabled; because I personally experienced neither racism nor ableism, I was intrinsically less aware of those problems within my newfound community than were disabled lesbians or lesbians of color. Addressing race and class issues within lesbian society became increasingly important to me over the years as a focus of my writing, but I continued to presume an acceptance of disability within lesbian society that I didn't actually experience because I wasn't disabled—then. I saw disabled women at festivals and conferences; ASL signing seemed *de rigueur* at lesbian events. What else was there? Not merely cognizant but deeply engaged in the political turmoil over the presence of transgendered women and male children at women-only spaces, conversely, the debates over accessibility for disabled lesbians at those same events barely registered—even as I repeatedly stayed in chemical-free spaces due to my increasing sensitivity to smoke, perfumes and other scented products.

Then my own disability reconfigured community for me, renewing a search I had once thought complete. Not since childhood, when there seemed nothing visible to signal my difference from other girls, have I felt the intensity of solitariness and marginalization brought on by disability. But this isolation is antithetical to the chosen solitude of a cloistered convent life; imposed, not chosen, it feels more like prison, and that imprisonment has caused me to experience all the rage of someone detained indefinitely for a crime she did not commit. While the lives of the saints thoroughly detailed the variant relationship between the mortification of the flesh and the path to God, there was no simultaneous exploration of the mortification of the *soul* through the psyche and how one handled that. Certainly for many saints leading the marginalized lives of the social outcast, humiliations were suffered that were not of the flesh; Jeanne d'Arc and many other martyrs exemplify this. Hagiography informs us that these martyrs often chose mortification of the psyche as well as the body as a parallel to Christ's suffering. Christ was reviled as he stood before Pontius Pilate and crowned with thorns as King of the Jews. Even as he hung from the cross, the Roman soldiers taunted him and one of the thieves being crucified with him repeatedly demanded that if he were indeed the Son of God, that he get down from the cross and save himself—and the thief as well. But how to separate a saint's psychic pain mimicking Christ's—pain that is a sacrifice to God—from an insufferably human one in which there seems no hope? That is the human struggle as one searches for community.

Simply put, isolation is the obverse of community. But what could engender more desire for community, instill a greater ache for companionate comfort and belonging than illness and disability? When AIDS began to grip the gay male community in its insidious tentacles, the epidemic spurred a dynamic shift in consciousness among gay men toward an empathic embracing of the sick and dying—a decision that action must be taken not just to rescue men from death, but to save them from the isolation and ostracization that so often accompany disease.

I have spent a majority of the years of the AIDS epidemic as a medical reporter writing about the disease to which I have lost a host of friends, including two very close ones. In the midst of my work, my anger and my own activism, I have repeatedly been struck by the groundswell of community, the way in which queer men and women rushed in to protect and care for their sick and dying comrades. From the very early days when AIDS had yet to be termed an epidemic, when the cases were measured in the dozens, not the hundreds of thousands, the movement toward community had already begun. Money was raised, groups were formed, meals were cooked, buddies were created, quilt panels were stitched—all symbolizing as well as evoking and invoking community.

Despite the deep involvement of and commitment by lesbians in the fight against AIDS, I have yet to experience that same gathering of community for the sick and disabled members of lesbian society. Several of my closest lesbian friends have been struck down by cancer in the last few years; I have been terribly debilitated by my own disease. But despite the burgeoning grassroots cancer activism movement in lesbian society, with few exceptions no supports exist for lesbians with disabling illness—even though women represent the overwhelming majority of sufferers of lupus, multiple sclerosis, chronic fatigue and immune dysfunction syndrome (CFIDS), rheumatoid arthritis and a range of other debilitating and life-threatening diseases. Over a decade ago my dear friend, the writer Darrell Yates-Rist, spoke out at a New York event where AIDS was the topic of discussion. Ever one to take the political high ground and walk the cutting edge, he became furious at what he perceived to be the special regard given to AIDS over other diseases within the queer community. "What difference does it make," he demanded, "if someone is dying of AIDS or breast cancer? Dying is dying—it is just as terrible for those whose loved ones are dying of cancer as of AIDS." For queers, Darrell asserted, *all* illness was political—not just AIDS, even though he would, several years later, die of it himself.

A few years ago I wrote a piece on the epidemic of breast cancer among lesbians for *Out,* a national queer magazine. A surprising number of men responded to the article with anger, claiming I was attempting to establish an epidemic for lesbians to garner some kind of community sympathy—and resources. The implication was as clear as it was disturbing: Breast cancer among lesbians would never rank with AIDS among gay men. This alarming response merely solidified a growing belief among lesbians that caretaking within queer community would inevitably be a one-way exchange. Though numerous lesbians have written extensively about AIDS and others have made AIDS activism or health care for people with AIDS the focus of their lives, there is no comparable response by gay men to lesbian illness. In fact, there is no comparable response by *lesbians* to lesbian illness.

As I became increasingly debilitated by the extremity of my disease and searched for help, my doctor, herself a lesbian, suggested I call on the AIDS community to which I had devoted so much time, energy and effort. "If you had AIDS," she said bluntly, "you'd be getting free meals delivered to your house every day and people coming to help you with anything you needed. We just don't have these kinds of services for lesbians who are sick or disabled."

Why is community eluding me again, eluding any of us who are sick or disabled? Where AIDS created a heightened and deeply committed sense of community for gay men as well as for lesbians *toward* gay men, illness among lesbians has polarized lesbians and gay men and ostracized sick and disabled lesbians from their own community. The feeling of connectedness and inclusion

I first experienced when I discovered lesbian society has all but disappeared, replaced by the disquieting unease that shadowed my days in Catholic school. I now understand the anger and frustration other disabled lesbians feel at their exclusion from what they believe should be a right—that keen, almost palpable sense of belonging that comes with being part of a community of women. Thus disabled lesbians must cope not only with their disability, but with the disabling of spirit caused by exclusion from nondisabled lesbian community.

Throughout the AIDS epidemic, martyrdom has been a recurring metaphor—in art, literature and even politics; words like "courage" and "bravery" have been used with a regularity usually reserved for wartime—though, of course, the fight against AIDS has been a war of sorts. AIDS has often been referred to as the first political disease (though tuberculosis holds that title), and unquestionably the public health and media response to AIDS has been dictated from the outset by homophobia and a host of other prejudices. No other illness claims "innocent" victims—implying, if not outright stating, that everyone else with the disease is complicitous in their own sickness. There has been a medieval—and certainly biblical—attitude toward AIDS; in the eyes of many, this is a disease of divine retribution meted out by that vengeful God of the Old Testament against gay men (that the majority of those infected worldwide are heterosexual is dismissed by purveyors of this theory).

Within that context the metaphor of martyrdom is unsurprising. But this tacit acceptance of martyr status naturally diminishes the status of others—if only by default—and in the way of our society, pushes those others—lesbians—to the margins. Thus, ironically, the disease that so ostracized and marginalized gay men also helped redefine gay male community; conversely it has also diminished the impact of serious illness and disability within lesbian community. The monolithic aspect of AIDS overshadows all else; that the number of women who die of breast cancer each year in the United States is more than all the people (gay, straight and other) who have died in the last decade of AIDS in the United States seems beside the point. One disabled friend feels quite bitter over this altered consciousness within queer community. "The sicker I get," she asserts, "the fewer friends I have. No one wants to stick around. When I think about all the hands I held of gay men with AIDS, all the meals I prepared, all the work I have done to fight that disease, I wonder why there is no one to hold *my* hand or bring *me* a meal. Why doesn't my illness rate community outreach?"

*The Peace*

My quest, what I seek—as lesbian, activist, Catholic, devotee of Mary and the female saints, and as cripple—is that elusive community I have glimpsed and even experienced at various points in my life. That community is experienced as both external and internal, one creating the atmosphere for the other; if I *have* community, I *feel* community—for the parameters of community are not defined merely by politics or religion, but by the emotion evoked in each member of that community.

In Catholicism we talk about the community of the Holy Spirit, of being one within God; as lesbians we talk about a community of the spirit as well— the sense of wholeness one gets from being enveloped and held in woman-centered society. As Adrienne Rich writes: "Every woman's death diminishes me." We are an integral part of a greater whole—the lesbian nation. As a disabled lesbian I seek community much as I sought it while a Catholic schoolgirl; I want to feel once more the sense of belonging that so strengthened me as a teenager when I discovered lesbian society. I now feel as I did on those days I watched the nuns going off to vespers; they were a discrete group unto themselves, an unbreachable force, a column of women with a singular focus and purpose. As I watched I yearned to be part of that complete circle, but stood outside, wholly on the margins, lacking whatever it was that would allow me entree into that world.

Which is worse, I wonder: To always have stood on the fringe and never have known the comforting embrace of community or to have felt deeply, ecstatically succored by community and then to be expelled—or if not expelled, then kept at arm's length—like a nun leaving the religious life, but not by her own choosing. In the climactic scene of Katherine Cavarly Hulme's *The Nun's Story*, Gabrielle is leaving the convent. She must travel through a series of doors as she goes. As she nears the final exit, she exchanges the package containing her habit and all the other accoutrements of her religious life for the handful of things with which she entered the cloister. She is dressed simply now, her hair—covered for years by wimple and veil—inexplicably and unfashionably short for the world she is about to re-enter. She hands over her package and her keys to the nun who acts as porteress, then stands before the final door and waits. A buzzer sounds, and the door clicks open. Gabrielle walks out into a long, empty street, awkward in her secular clothing, unsure how to stand or even walk outside the convent walls with their conventions, confines and community. The door shuts behind her with a reverberative echo. She has passed from one world to another merely by crossing a threshold, but her life is utterly changed. We cannot know if she has made the right choice, but whether she has or not, community as she has known it is lost to her forever; she can never reclaim it, only remember it.

Never having made the choice to leave, I want desperately to reclaim community lost to me through the isolation of disability. I search my past for the key to that reclamation, believing it lies somewhere between my spiritual beliefs and political action, but—not unlike Gabrielle—I am stunned that so subtle a shift as a door opening and closing could signal such a radical change in one's world.

I remember standing in the steamy kitchen of the convent. (How many nuns lived there? Twenty? Perhaps thirty?) I was in eighth grade and had been asked to deliver a message to Sister Marie Dolores, the nun who cooked for the convent, who did not teach.

The convent was a big, rambling house, built, as were most of the school's buildings, of gray fieldstone, stucco and wood. What wasn't stone was painted white, and there was a big, glass-paned enclosed porch at the front. The convent was surrounded by ground; in the front a winding driveway led to the porch while on the east side lay a large expanse of shady lawn. Behind the house, outside the kitchen, a long vegetable garden got full sun, especially in high summer.

On this day I was sent with a message for Sister Marie Dolores, whose face had the milky, freckled look of an Irish girl. It was a startlingly bright day in early summer, and the sun beat down on the back of the house in such a way that the kitchen fairly shimmered with heat as I crossed the threshold onto the cool ceramic tile. My school uniform—navy-blue wool serge with the pale-blue long-sleeved blouse of the upper-classwomen—clung to me in the heat, my long hair hot and thick on my neck. The kitchen was surprisingly dark, given the brightness of the day; the light seemed not to reach into that part of the house, though the heat surely did.

Grateful as I was to escape the tedium of classwork to deliver a message into the inner sanctum of the convent, the heat made the errand far less pleasurable. As I waited for a written response, I noticed, seated just outside the kitchen door in a shadowy alcove, one of the high school nuns who no longer taught, Sister Joseph Michael. Like the girls in the school whose disabilities stayed shrouded in the mystery of not being named, whatever was wrong with Sister Joseph Michael had also gone unnamed and was thus equally mysterious—made more so by the fact she was a nun, a mystery in itself. Perhaps the hovering presence of the Devil made disability within the convent walls highly problematic, but whatever the reason, Sister Joseph Michael's disability was never discussed.

I had heard about her disease from another classmate: multiple sclerosis. Sister walked haltingly with a cane, and her head always seemed weighted down by the heaviness of her veil. She had thick, black eyebrows (the rejection of vanity demanded by religious life precluded the plucking secular life would have demanded), and because her head was always tilted to the side, these seemed somehow frightening on her pale face, with her blue eyes like pinwheel marbles. When she spoke her voice was surprisingly soft, but had a strange slurred quality to it that I associated with drunkenness, not nuns. Often we would see her standing, pitched slightly to the side as she always seemed to be, near the side door of the convent, which was just across the driveway from the building that housed the junior high school classrooms. She would stand there, looking off—where? Toward her past, before disability? Toward the high school and the mathematics she had taught with an excitement lacking in many of the other nuns? Toward a future where she would likely be unable to navigate the many steps of the convent? Invariably another nun would appear—sometimes it would be the nun at the front of our classroom who had looked past the blackboard and out the window, seen Sister there and excused herself from the class—and speak softly to her, a hand placed gently on her arm. Sometimes Sister would remain standing there at the convent door; other times she would be guided back inside the convent.

How many times had I witnessed that particular scene before seeing Sister Joseph Michael there in the shaded veranda overlooking the vegetable garden? Proximity demanded acknowledgment, yet I was aware she hadn't noticed me; if I spoke, would I be intruding? If I didn't speak, would I be perceived as disrespectful? And so I clear my throat and softly acknowledge her with a near-whispered "Good morning, Sister."

My voice has startled her, I think, because she shudders perceptibly. She turns slowly toward me, using her cane for support, even though she is sitting. Her voice, when she speaks, is barely intelligible, and her head bobs up and down, seemingly uncontrollably. I realize I haven't heard her speak in a long time, perhaps a year, maybe more. I am unsure what it is she has said to me, so startled am I by the peculiar timbre of her voice and the tremors. And so I talk to her, unstopping, in part to keep her from speaking again, in part to cover my embarrassment at not understanding her. I talk about the brightness of the day, the heat, the thriving vegetable garden already in full flower, despite the earliness of the season. I look just past her as I speak; a trait born of shyness that I have yet to conquer, but I wonder now if she thought I was avoiding looking at her, shaking, with her features seemingly askew, as if I had caught her in some state of *deshabille*.

I pause, and in the short hiatus Sister Marie Dolores appears to save me from this terrible moment, handing me an envelope to take back. The three of us are mired there, unsure how to complete this scene, to break away and return to our individual tasks—I to class, Sister Marie Dolores to preparing lunch and Sister Joseph Michael to whatever contemplative act she was engaged in before I broke her concentration. Sister Marie Dolores leans forward and takes my hand. Would I like to help Sister Joseph Michael inside? she asks me. I am torn between a desire to help, an even deeper desire to enter the mysterious world of the convent and perhaps fear at the thought of touching this nun who seems so ill and fragile.

The trip inside and up to Sister's bedroom is terribly slow and punctuated by occasional bursts of manic talk from me and sounds of exertion from her. This is not a journey either of us wants to make, and yet somehow this is a chance to prove my right to inclusion in this world. For the shy and awkward girl I am, tall and gawky and prone to clumsiness, this is so obviously a test that I sweat well beyond the welter of the heat.

The convent is a beautiful and remarkably silent place. Unlike the kitchen it is cool and far less spare than my ascetic imagination had envisioned. Were I not so nervous I would perhaps be disappointed at how little signals this as a convent instead of the home of any other large family. We must stop as we enter each room so that Sister can sit and rest a few minutes before we continue on our arduous way to the second floor and her room. Athletic and spry, I could have run through this entire house from floor to floor and room to room in the time it has taken us to get from veranda to kitchen to dining room to library to the foot of the winding stairs that lead up to the nuns' individual rooms.

I am unprepared for the stairs and for Sister's reaction as we reach them. I hear her sudden intake of breath, see her shudder quite perceptibly in my peripheral vision. Suddenly Sister Marie Dolores has appeared again. *You will need to lift her a little,* she says, *sotto voce,* and makes a little pushing motion with the dishtowel she is still holding. *The stairs are very difficult.* There is a nuanced intent behind her words that I am perhaps too young to understand, but I realize that I, one of the tallest girls in the school and a full head taller than either nun standing beside me, have been recruited for this task because I am a strong young girl and it is believed I can do it.

And I do. I hook my arm around Sister's waist and half-guide, half-carry her up the seemingly endless staircase. I want to ask her about penance and the mortification of the flesh and how she does this every day, but don't. She is trying not to cry from the effort and embarrassment and I, terribly averse to tears, don't want to see this. Instead I take in everything around me. While the rooms downstairs appeared much like any other family's house, the nun's rooms themselves are spare as cells—bed, bureau, night table, crucifix. All the doors are open; privacy another sacrifice to convent life. In Sister Joseph Michael's room there is also a chair directly inside the door and she nearly falls in her haste to sit.

Exhausted, shaking more than ever, she looks incredibly pale, which only makes the skewed, Frida Kahlo eyebrows more dramatic; she looks a little crazed.

I stand next to her, uncertain what my next move is expected to be. Here I am, in the heart of the convent, layers of secrets peeling away before me. There is so much silence. Even Sister's labored breathing has calmed to match the quiet. Suddenly she touches my hand and speaks. A thank you, I think, and something else I can't discern. *Do I want to be a nun?* That is what she is asking me, I realize after a short space of translation time. *Yes,* I say without reservation. *It's beautiful here.*

Sister Marie Dolores appears again, this time holding a glass of iced tea, a slice of lemon embedded among the ice. She puts the glass on Sister's night table and then helps her over to the bed. As I stand by the doorway she bends down and unlaces the black shoes Sister is wearing and slips them off, placing them just under the bed. Then she lifts Sister's feet onto the bed, steadying her back as she does so. The movements are brisk and efficient, but there is an almost breathtaking tenderness to them. This is what being a nun is, I see in them both. Sister Joseph Michael, disabled as she is, but struggling to maintain herself; Sister Marie Dolores offering the best help she can while also maintaining the distance dignity requires of them both. How each acts is symbol for the other of faith and sacrifice. What holds them together is community.

I slipped out of the room as Sister Marie Dolores held the glass of iced tea to Sister Joseph Michael's lips. In my pocket was the envelope holding the message I had been sent to retrieve. What would I say if I were asked what had taken me so long? I had been gone not the ten minutes expected of me but close to three-quarters of an hour. Such a brief time to see all I had seen.

I haven't thought of that day in thirty years, yet how vivid the memory is, emblematic and evocative as it was of all I understood community to be, of all I saw embedded in female religious life. But now, as I invoke that memory, I think how much sick and disabled lesbians would benefit from the sheltering care of convent life, how we need the same kind of communal ministration within a society of women who believe the same things and share the same faith in a woman-centered world. And so I am left, thirty-odd years after I first began to contemplate the complexities of Otherness versus the inclusivity of community, still searching for what I saw with such clarity that June day between Sister Marie Dolores and Sister Joseph Michael. I have glimpsed it over the intervening years—in the early days of lesbian nation, in the darkest days of the AIDS epidemic—but have no grasp on it now. Yet I can see myself and so many other disabled lesbians in the remembered face of Sister Joseph Michael—except there is no coterie of friends and compatriots to unlace their shoes, help them into bed and hold the glass to their lips because they can no longer hold it themselves. As I spend my days in a solitude more stark than any cloistered order of nuns, I think of Sister Joseph Michael standing outside the side door of the convent, staring off into the distance. What was it she saw?

Perhaps it was all the disabled women who would come after her—a phalanx of women that would one day include the athletic young girl who half-carried her into the secret world of the convent on a hot, sunny day in early summer. I knew then, as I breathed in every nuance of their world, that this was a signal moment that would influence my future. Then I thought the message was in Sister's garbled question: *Do you want to be a nun?* I could not know, chosen as I had been that day for my health and strength to aid this disabled nun, that one day I would *be* her—but without the comforting, enveloping security of community. Since disability and its accompanying isolation have thrust me back onto the fringes, this time not of religious life, but of lesbian society, I see how the bridge that kept Sister Joseph Michael linked to community was that the other nuns never viewed her as different, as Other. Perhaps they would call on a strong athletic young girl to help out on occasion in the care of her, but they did not reject her. In the earlier days of her disability, when the nun at the head of my classroom—or another nun at the head of another classroom—would spy her standing outside the convent door gazing off into the distance, they would rush to her aid. Perhaps she didn't need their ministrations at that time, perhaps she did. But what was certain—and what was clear to any of us students keen enough to notice—was that each member of the convent held a deep regard for every other member and that that regard was as instinctual as prayer.

That regard, predicated as it was on faith, on shared belief, on maintaining the continuity of religious life, was evoked anew every time another nun went out to check on Sister Joseph Michael. Their presence was meant as both protection and strength: *You are one of us; we will not abandon you.* Sister Joseph Michael's disability appeared to have no negative connotations to it—unlike those attendant to the occasional disabled student in the school. Her disease held no taint of sin or Evil; this disability may have been God giving her the opportunity to sacrifice, but it was not, as with the students, a sign of possible Evil, of a biblical retribution—the sins of the parents being visited on the children. Community protected Sister Joseph Michael, who in turn gave back, with her need for care, the opportunity for members of her community to sacrifice on her behalf, in God's name. Sister Joseph Michael's disability provided both her and the other members of her community the opportunity to exercise their beliefs, to sacrifice, to give uncomplainingly, to act as Christ would have acted, to invoke his teachings of acceptance and inclusion and charity.

Perhaps politics can never demand as powerful a commitment as the spiritual, and as a result, sick and disabled lesbians will never garner the same care and attention as Sister Joseph Michael received from her convent community. Conversely, what I have witnessed within the gay male community—and among lesbians toward gay men—in response to AIDS has been a very similar concentration of care and concern, the majority of which has been engendered by a politically inspired anger. So why can't lesbian society open the arms of community to embrace its disabled sisters? Why have we not understood that we are made stronger as a society—in this instance, lesbian society—by inclusivity? We have striven over the last three decades of lesbian nation to understand racism, classism and even complex gender issues—why have we ignored disability?

Thirty years after I watched Sister Marie Dolores unlace the shoes of her disabled sister, gently lift her onto the bed and then hold the icy glass of tea to her lips, I wonder if there will ever be a place within lesbian community for such tender protection and care. For what I saw that day was defining enough to have stayed deep within my consciousness for decades, an evocation of community—simple, uncomplex, not utopian by any means, yet fully, completely responsive. And so I think of it as I once did of the convent itself—as a prototype for what community could and should be. These nuns *were* community for each other. Can lesbians—women whose lives are predicated on loving other women—be anything less?

# BETRAYAL

## Ruthann Robson

First, I loved your hands
for their determined if inaccurate grasp
and your shiny slate eyes
that sucked with as much power as your mouth

Later, I appreciated your legs
strong in their stubbornness
taking me *here*, away from *there*
And yes, I must mention the pleasure of your breasts

If it's true that memories inhabit the cells,
then somewhere on the beach of your DNA
I am soothing your skin with sunscreen
so carefully that not even the folds of your ears will redden

And on the dark porch of your RNA
the stars like impatient spectators
as the moon prepares to be challenged
I am unbraiding the double helix of your waist length hair

But you must have forgotten the good times

—or perhaps they meant nothing?—
otherwise these evil Cartesian doctors
would not be serving me with the papers of their diagnosis

Oh body, how could you divorce me?

# LITERARY AMBITION

## Ruthann Robson

to write a poem
spare, clear, and lyrically
honest
unabashedly autobiographical

to write a poem
that begins: Twenty
No, better, Thirty
years ago, they pronounced me incurable

to write a poem
without closure

# ACKNOWLEDGMENTS

*Restricted Access* required the help, support and effort of many people, but it would not have happened at all without two women—my partner, Judith M. Redding, and my friend, Susan Raffo. Throughout the encroachment of my own disability, Judith has been not only my lover but my literal helpmate. Without her daily care and ministration—in addition to the sharing of a household, work, ideas and, of course, love—it would have been difficult to finish one book, let alone the six we have collaborated on in the past three years. And though she is not an editor of this anthology, she contributed a massive amount of work to the finished product, including the physical things I simply could not do. Computers were essential to the implementation and completion of this project, and Judith's expertise with computer technology has been indispensable, as I remain, even as Y2K approaches, computer-illiterate.

My level of appreciation for all that Judith has done since I became disabled, on this book and in life, is immense. Earlier this year *Inside MS* magazine estimated the "worth" of such spousal help at a few thousand dollars; this seems a gross minimizing of the efforts of spouses aiding their disabled partners, equivalent (and I use that word advisedly) to the way the "worth" of a stay-at-home parent (usually a woman) is calculated. Inevitably the nondisabled partner's life becomes conscripted by her partner's disability as well, because there is so little help for us in the nondisabled world. "Thanks" seems paltry for the help Judith has given me.

As I gradually came to the realization that my disability was not a temporary period in my life, but was *my life,* friends became increasingly more distant—disability and illness, as this book elucidates all too starkly, are often unbearable for the healthy to acknowledge. Friends seemed to presume that somehow I would manage—without help—as I had always done when healthy. Awkward silences would ensue when I talked about how distressing, frustrating, enraging and painful my life had become. Unless my friends became ill themselves, there was little comprehension of how incredibly different and difficult my life had become, how hard it was to accomplish the most basic tasks in life, let alone the seemingly insurmountable task of work—especially on the workaholic, overachieving scale I had always maintained.

Susan Raffo was the one friend who talked to me about what it was to become disabled, to lose autonomy, to be in constant and unrelieved pain, to spend endless amounts of time in doctors' offices, hospitals and emergency rooms, to not know how large a clock ticked over my head or for how long. Sympathetic without being pitying, Susan encouraged me to write about my experience, my thoughts, the evolution of my disability activism. And when I finally realized I wanted to do this book, she offered to help—not as an acknowledged co-editor, but as a friend. That encouragement made this book happen, for which I am tremendously grateful. I am also grateful that Susan allowed me full control over the editorial content of *Restricted Access,* was willing to be a managing editor and took orders from me with grace.

Other influences propelled this book along. I am grateful for the help of those who provided a range of support while I worked on *Restricted Access:* Jennifer Goldenberg, Theodore Brownworth, Meredith Kane, Joan Poole, Carolyn Phillips, Sharon Bender, Mabel Maney, Jennifer Dowdell, Lisa Williamson, Diane DeKelb-Rittenhouse, Meredith Baird, Charlotte Abbott, Roz Warren, Marcia Brown, Kathleen DeBold, Dr. Tish Fabens, Story Clapp, Dr. Jonathan Gomberg and Jan Meiers. I'd like to thank the MS Society for the generous gift of a motorized wheelchair, which has given me moments of much-needed autonomy.

Ruthann Robson and Roberta Hacker provided what I have come to expect from them, but never take for granted—a depth of friendship that consistently sustains me on a multitude of levels, from the literary to the political to the spiritual.

Joshua Goldenberg, Tirzah Goldenberg and Shifra Goldenberg have repeatedly been a source of joy and comfort to me.

Linda Wright, Nicola Griffith, Lizard Jones, Carrie Dearborn and Mary Frances Platt shared their own disability experiences with me in ways that helped me understand my own disability better. Carolyn Gage reminded me that righteous anger is an essential part of any civil rights movement. Beth Brant made me think a great deal more about the role of class, race, gender and illness in a society that devalues all that isn't middle-class, white, male and nondisabled. Sharyn LaBance detailed her own harrowing experience of cancer with me, a story that took us to a place very different from the one we had shared twenty years ago when we lived together. Shelley Tremaine's and Nancy Mairs's work on disability have made me think and think some more. Thanks also to John Catania and all the other persevering folks at *In the Life* TV; to Chris Culwell and Roberto Friedman, who spurred me to write about disability for the popular press and then had the editorial guts to publish what I wrote, and to Michael Pakenham, who has supported—and published—my writing in the mainstream since I was a twenty-year-old college senior with something urgent to say, and who was the first editor in a major daily newspaper to give me space to write about disability in today's literature.

Thanks also to my agent, Laurie Liss, who has always shown a keen interest in my work and ideas, regardless of their marketability.

The team at Seal Press continues to be fabulous. Thanks to Ingrid Emerick, who found the great cover image; Lynn Siniscalchi, who put me in touch with a series of Deaf women after I thought I had exhausted all avenues; Kate Loeb, who worked intensely on publicity; Lee Damsky and Alison Rogalsky, who moved the manuscript smoothly through production; and Faith Conlon, who manages to keep Seal together even as feminist publishing becomes increasingly imperiled. Cathy Johnson provided thorough and often thought-provoking copyediting. Jennie Goode has been, once again, a thoughtful and insightful editor, whose enthusiasm for this project never wavered and whose patience and equanimity were a great gift. I feel blessed to have shared another project with her.

Finally, thanks to the many incredibly courageous disabled women who contacted me over the last few months, some to tell their stories to anyone who would listen, some to encourage this project, some to vent their anger at being marginalized by a straight, nondisabled society. This book is for all of you—all of *us*. —VAB

❖

My relationship to *Restricted Access* and its subject feels intensely personal and woven throughout relationships that cross my life span. As always, I think it is impossible to acknowledge all of the conversations and connections that contributed to my part of this book's life, but I'll try to name some of them: Victoria Brownworth for her constantly gratifying friendship and her excitement at having me work on this book with her; Annalee Stewart for her contacts and interests; Joyce Peltzer and Polly Carl for being willing to share their lives and experiences with me; Judith K. Witherow for the many levels of her care; Jennifer Fennell, Elissa Raffa and Lynette D'Amico for their friendship and editorial support; my mother, Kay Raffo, and brother, Jeffrey Raffo, and Pat Lindsley for reasons too numerous to mention; and my partner, Raquel, because all of the things about her make me that much more excited about life. —SR

# ABOUT THE CONTRIBUTORS

**Polly Carl** currently works as the development and communications director for The Playwrights' Center in Minneapolis. She is finishing her Ph.D. in cultural studies and comparative literature at the University of Minnesota and has taught courses there in queer studies since 1992. She describes herself as a short butch who used to panic a lot but doesn't anymore.

**Eli (Elizabeth) Clare** is a poet, essayist and activist living in Michigan, transplanted from Oregon. Her work has been published in a variety of periodicals and anthologies, including *Queerly Classed* (South End Press), *Staring Back* (Plume), the *Disability Rag* and *Sinister Wisdom*. She is the author of a collection of essays titled *Exile and Pride: Disability, Queerness, and Liberation* (South End).

**Vicky D'aoust** is a Deaf dyke with other disabilities who watches *The X-Files*, lives with a teenage Deaf daughter, writes, researches and laughs while trying to fight violence and poverty (and has sex when she can).

**Carol Anne Douglas** has been on the staff of the feminist newspaper *off our backs* since 1973. Her book *Love and Politics: Radical Feminist and Lesbian Theories* was published by ism press in 1990. She lives happily in Washington, D.C., with her lover and her cat.

**Carolyn Gage** is a lesbian-feminist playwright and performer. She is recovering from CFIDS and currently gives workshops on nontraditional roles for women. She is the author of *Like There's No Tomorrow: Meditations for Women Leaving Patriarchy*, a book that combines recovery tools with radical feminism. She has also written the first book on lesbian theater production, the first collection of radical feminist plays and the first book of scenes and monologues for lesbian actors. She was recently a lecturer at Bates College in Lewiston, Maine.

**Nicola Griffith** was born in Yorkshire, England, but has lived in the United States since 1989. She is the editor of the *Bending the Landscape* series and the author of three novels: *Slow River* (Ballantine), *Ammonite* (Ballantine) and *The Blue Place* (Avon). Her fourth novel, tentatively titled *Red Raw*, is forthcoming. She has won several grants and prizes for her short fiction, and numerous awards for her work as a novelist and editor (including the Nebula, Tiptree and World Fantasy Awards, and five Lambda Literary Awards). Nicola lives in Seattle with her partner, writer Kelley Eskridge. Her homepage can be found at *http://www.sff.net/people/Nicola*.

**Huhanna** is a recent graduate with bachelor's degrees in law and social sciences. She is currently writing a book on sexuality and disability and working on a master's in law. She has a weekly political radio slot, lectures and runs workshops on sexuality and disability and is raising a wonderful teenage son. The disabilities she lives with include fibromyalgia, CFIDS, GFD, IBS, chronic asthma and head and spinal injuries. She lives in New Zealand.

**Lizard Jones** is a writer and artist in Vancouver, British Columbia. She is a member of the lesbian art collective Kiss & Tell, creators of the postcard book *Drawing the Line* and the Lambda Award-winning *Her Tongue on My Theory*, as well as many performances and videos. Her novel *Two Ends of Sleep*, about a lesbian with multiple sclerosis, was recently published by Press Gang Publishers. She was diagnosed with MS in 1994.

**Maura Kelly** was born with arthrogryposis in New Jersey in 1970 into an Irish

Catholic family that already boasted five children. She quickly decided she loved being the center of attention unless, of course, it was due to her using a wheelchair. After receiving a bachelor's degree in psychology from Temple University, Maura stayed in Philadelphia. She works as a technical writer, writing and editing procedure manuals for systems projects. Among her other activities are rowing on the Schuylkill River with the Philadelphia Rowing Program for the Disabled, being an active member of the Philadelphia Dyke March and volunteering for the lesbian radio program Amazon Country on 88.5 WXPN. She is currently single.

**Nomy Lamm** is a freelance writer, lecturer and performance artist who lives in Olympia, Washington. She has been published in *Ms.*, *Seventeen*, *HUES* and *Radiance* magazines, and has essays in *Listen Up: Voices from the Next Feminist Generation* (Seal Press), *Present Tense: Writing and Art by Young Women* (Calyx Journal) and *Adiós, Barbie: Young Women Write About Body Image and Identity* (Seal Press). She has a CD of music and spoken word on Talent Show Records in Olympia. In her free time she performs in drag shows, writes rock operas and is in a gang of big scary queers called The Sleazy Fuckers.

**Erin Lawrence** has a master's degree in education with a minor in health education, and a bachelor's degree in sociology/linguistics, with a minor in gender studies. She enjoys biking, playing and coaching ice hockey and softball, playing with her two cats and being with her significant other. Her biggest challenge was training for the Twin Cities-Wisconsin-Chicago AIDS Ride last July. Her biggest joys are watching the sun rise and set each day and seeing the Northern Lights in Alaska.

**Deborah Peifer** is a lesbian, writer, critic and feminist. She likes being all of them.

**Joyce Peltzer** was born July 21, 1931, in St. Paul, Minnesota, where she grew up. She attended Macalester College in St. Paul, where she earned a B.A., and the University of Minnesota Graduate School of Social Work, where she earned an M.S.W. in 1957. Her employment in social work spanned a thirty-two-year period. Joyce loves to travel, go to the theater, read and be with friends. She is active in her Lutheran church and has worked for the inclusion of gays and lesbians throughout the Lutheran church. Her lesbian "herstory" has been included in the archives of the Minnesota History Center.

**Mary Frances Platt** became involved in radical crip politics when she began using a chair in 1987. She was the first lesbian to conduct anti-ableism workshops both in and out of queer community. As access and needs coordinator for the National Lesbian Conference, she developed and introduced integrative access models and designs that enabled the event to become and remain the most integrated crip and noncrip gathering of lesbians to date. Mary Frances was referred to as an "abusive bullying infiltrator of lesbian culture" in *off our backs* after blocking the entrance to the first East Coast Lesbian Festival with four other queers who were protesting the inaccessibility of the gathering. Mary Frances's writings on disability and class have been published in numerous anthologies, journals and newspapers. She is one of the few gimp writers to have her crip erotica and writings on disabled sexuality published within feminist and mainstream media. Mary Frances is a member of Not Dead Yet, a group fighting the legalization of physician-induced death, and ADAPT (American Disabled for Attendant Programs Today). She documents her defiance as well as her spirit on her GeoCities Web site, *everydaycrippl.*

**Faith Reidenbach** is a senior medical editor for an international newswire service and formerly ran a freelance medical writing business. She was born in 1960 in Columbus, Ohio, came out there in 1974, and has been not-married since 1986. She recently moved with her beloved life partner to coastal Connecticut, where they live by an estuary and feel delighted to be able to watch shorebirds from the breakfast table.

**Ruthann Robson** is the author of a collection of poetry, *Masks* (Leapfrog Press), as well as several books of fiction and nonfiction including the novel *A/K/A* (St. Martin's Press) and a collection of lesbian legal theory, *Sappho Goes to Law School* (Columbia University Press).

**Sue Russell** is a poet, critic and journalist who lives in the Philadelphia area with Lynne Maxwell, her partner of eight years. Her work has appeared in numerous literary journals and magazines, including *Kenyon Review, Lambda Book Report, Poets & Writers* and *Women's Review of Books*, in anthologies such as *My Lover Is a Woman* (Ballantine) and in reference books on literature and popular culture. By day she works as a medical editor.

**Ellen Samuels** holds a B.A. from Oberlin College and an M.F.A. from Cornell University and currently lives and teaches writing in Boston. She has published poetry and essays in numerous journals, including the *American Voice*, the *Lesbian Review of Books*, the *Journal of Lesbian Studies, Sojourner* and *Kalliope* and is the co-editor of the forthcoming anthology *Out of the Ordinary: Reflections on Growing Up with Gay Parents* (St. Martin's Press). She received a 1997 artist's fellowship from the Constance Saltonstall Foundation for the Arts and is currently working on a memoir about her mother's life and death from breast cancer. She has been disabled since 1995 with CFIDS, fibromyalgia and environmental illness.

**Marj Schneider** was cofounder of Womyn's Braille Press, which produced feminist and lesbian literature on tape and in Braille for thirteen years. Her writing on the Karen Thompson–Sharon Kowalski case for WBP's newsletter led her to a part-time career teaching college courses on disability rights issues. After finishing a graduate degree this year, she is wondering what might come next. A native and resident of Minneapolis, she makes her winter home nearer the ocean, on Tybee Island, Georgia.

**Raquel (Rocki) Volaco Simões** is a Brazilian citizen living as a temporary resident in Minneapolis. A social worker by training, she is the coordinator of Project OffStreets' GLBT Host Home Program, a community-based response to queer youth homelessness. Raquel and her partner, Susan Raffo, plan on figuring out how to move back and forth between Brazil and the United States as often as possible.

**Julia Trahan** studies arts management and animateuring at the Victorian College of the Arts in Melbourne, Australia. She might be found writing beat love poetry and drinking cappuccino at an outdoor cafe or buying stone fruit (peaches) at the outdoor Victorian market. A resume of her work and samples of her writing can be found at *http://members.tripod.com/Dolphin_J/oz.html.* Or just look for the curly-headed blonde dressed in black.

**Sharon Wachsler** is a cartoonist, poet and writer living in Ashfield, Massachusetts, with her wonderful cat, Ferdinand, and her adorable dog, Jersey. Her latest essay appears in *Bodies of Knowledge* (Women's Press, Canada).

**Patricia Nell Warren,** in forty-eight years as a published writer, has written on a wide range of subjects, from novels on gay life *(The Front Runner)* to novels on women's history *(One Is the Sun).* She has also written hundreds of magazine articles on diverse themes such as censorship, conservation and the religious right. In 1998 she received the Lambda Literary "Editor's Choice" Award for her novel on gay youth, *Billy's Boy.* Presently she lives in Los Angeles, where she co-owns the publishing company Wildcat Press with Tyler St. Mark. With veteran screenwriter Barry Sandler, she is writing the screenplay for a new film development of *The Front Runner.*

**D.A. Watters** was born on August 31, 1953 in Philadelphia to two preachers. At ten, she was found to have a 212 IQ. She started college at sixteen. She graduated, many different hometowns and arrests later, at thirty-one. Then she worked in her father's ministry office until, at thirty-nine, a car wreck and five-week coma left her paralyzed on the left side with a damaged right brain. Currently she works at home on the Internet for the university she first attended when she was sixteen. She describes herself as "a preacher's kid jail-bird lesbian genius who is brain damaged." She now lives in an apartment within walking distance from her father's house in Springfield, Missouri. Although she and her father were not close when her mother was still alive, D.A. says that her father is "now the best thing in my life." Her homepage can be found at *http://members.wbs.net/homepages/d/a/9/da99900.html.*

# ABOUT THE EDITORS

**Victoria A. Brownworth** is the author of seven books, including the Lambda Award finalist *Too Queer: Essays from a Radical Life* (Firebrand Books). She has edited seven anthologies, including *Night Shade: Gothic Tales by Women* (Seal Press), co-edited with Judith M. Redding. An award-winning and Pulitzer Prize–nominated journalist, her writing has appeared in numerous newspapers and magazines in the queer, feminist and mainstream press, including *Ms.*, the *Nation*, the *Village Voice*, *Out*, the *Philadelphia Inquirer*, *Lesbian Review of Books*, *Lambda Book Report*, *Disability Studies Quarterly* and the *Baltimore Sun*. She has been a columnist for the *Philadelphia Daily News*, the *Advocate*, *POZ* and *Curve*. She also writes weekly columns on television and politics for a variety of national newspapers, and has written screenplays for several award-winning films and videos. She lives in Philadelphia with her partner of twelve years, four cats and a dog.

**Susan Raffo** is a writer and community activist living in Minneapolis. She is the editor of *Queerly Classed: Gay Men and Lesbians Write About Class* (South End Press) and has had her work published in a number of newspapers, magazines and anthologies. She is currently looking for more homes for a column called "Making the Links," which focuses on the connections between GLBT political issues and broad-based social justice issues. She shares her life with her partner, Raquel.

# Selected Titles from Seal Press

*Cunt: A Declaration of Independence* by Inga Muscio. $14.95, 1-58005-015-8. An ancient title of respect for women, "cunt" long ago veered off the path of honor and now careens toward the heart of every woman as an expletive. Muscio traces this winding road, giving women both the motivation and the tools to claim "cunt" as a positive and powerful force in their lives.

*Lesbian Couples: Creating Healthy Relationships for the '90s* by D. Merilee Clunis and G. Dorsey Green. $14.95, 1-878067-37-0. A new edition of the highly acclaimed and popular guide for lesbians in couple relationships.

*The Lesbian Health Book: Caring for Ourselves* edited by Jocelyn White, M.D., and Marissa C. Martínez. $18.95, 1-878067-31-1. This practical and readable book brings together a wide range of voices from the lesbian community, including doctors and other health care providers, women facing illness or life changes, health activists and many others.

*The Lesbian Parenting Book: A Guide to Creating Families and Raising Children* by D. Merilee Clunis and G. Dorsey Green. $16.95, 1-878067-68-0. This comprehensive and helpful book covers a wide range of parenting topics as well as issues specifically relevant to lesbian families. Information on each child development stage is also provided.

*Night Bites: Vampire Stories by Women* edited by Victoria A. Brownworth. $12.95, 1-878067-71-0. Featuring sixteen original works, this subversive collection offers gothic atmosphere with a contemporary twist, scintillating writing and enough blood and lust to satisfy even the most discriminating connoisseurs.

*Night Shade: Gothic Tales by Women* edited by Victoria A. Brownworth and Judith M. Redding. $14.95, 1-58005-024-7. At once erotic and entrancing, this chilling collection of gothic fiction depicts a world where the abnormal is the norm and shapeshifting is an everyday phenomenon.

*Past Due: A Story of Disability, Pregnancy and Birth* by Anne Finger. $10.95, 0-931188-87-3. In this eloquent and deeply moving book, a writer disabled by polio explores the complexities of disability and reproductive rights through a riveting account of her pregnancy and childbirth experience.

Seal Press publishes many books of fiction and nonfiction by women writers. If you are unable to obtain a Seal Press title from a bookstore or would like a free catalog of our books, please order from us directly by calling 800-754-0271. Visit our website at www.sealpress.com.